MAN OF VISION
•
WOMAN OF PRAYER

Marilee Pierce Dunker

THOMAS NELSON PUBLISHERS
Nashville

All Scripture references are from the King James Version of the Bible.

Copyright © 1980 by Marilee Pierce Dunker

Second Printing

All rights reserved. Written permission must be secured from the publisher to use or reproduce any part of this book, except for brief quotations in critical reviews or articles.

Published in Nashville, Tennessee, by Thomas Nelson, Inc., Publishers and distributed in Canada by Lawson Falle, Ltd., Cambridge, Ontario.

Printed in the United States of America.

Library of Congress Cataloging in Publication Data

Dunker, Marilee Pierce.
    Man of vision, woman of prayer.

    1. Pierce, Robert Willard, 1914–1978 2. Pierce, Lorraine. 3. Evangelists—East Asia—Biography. I. Title.
BV3785.P53D86   269'.2'0924 [B]   80-19698
ISBN 0-8407-5220-2

CONTENTS

	Acknowledgments	iii
	Foreword	v
	Introduction	ix
1	Uncommon Man, Uncommon Woman	11
2	The Scarlet Thread	15
3	Cross-Country Romance	20
4	"A Youth Aflame"	31
5	The Center Days	41
6	Seattle	52
7	A Season of Night	56
8	China—One Step at a Time	62
9	God's Time in China	71
10	China Challenge	81
11	The Wrong Direction	89
12	Korea at Last!	98
13	Birth of a Vision	106
14	"Cross the Ocean in a Silver Plane"	109
15	The 38th Parallel	119
16	Home: Coffee, Friends, and Love	124
17	At Home With Daddy	129
18	In the Presence of Royalty	134
19	Elephants, Measles, and Memories	138
20	The Evangelical Syndrome	144
21	Robin	150
22	Korea Welcomes Mrs. Bob Pierce	153
23	Heading Into the Storm	160
24	The Gathering Storm	167

25	Sharing the Spotlight	173
26	End of an Era	176
27	"Who Are We Now, Mama?"	180
28	Sharon	185
29	Through the Looking Glass	195
30	Home Again?	207
31	Separation	216
32	Reality vs. Circumstance	222
33	Leukemia!	233
34	The Miracle	242
35	An Affair of State	251

ACKNOWLEDGMENTS
•

My heartfelt thanks to the wonderful people who supported me with their love and prayers throughout the writing of this book, and a special thank you to those who actively participated in its creation.

Sandy Patterson, for selflessly giving of her time and ability to type and retype this manuscript.

Linda Harfman, for also helping with the enormous job of typing.

My husband, Bob, and daughters, Michelle and Stacey, for so patiently sharing me with my typewriter, for sacrificing the comfort and convenience of a full-time wife and mother for nearly a year.

My sister, Robin, for her unfailing enthusiasm and constant encouragement.

Mama, for the countless hours of remembering even when the memories were painful, and for having the courage to be honest in order to see others healed.

The Holy Spirit, who first spoke to my heart about writing this book and then helped me to write it.

FOREWORD
•

This book is a combination of an incredible novel, a believable biography, a textbook, and an excerpt from the Bible.

As a novel, adventurers and romanticists will revel in it.

As a biography, historians and fact finders will be enlightened by it.

As a textbook, seminarians, pastors, and church leaders need to learn from it.

And as an excerpt from God's Word, which courses through these pages, Christians everywhere will be inspired by it.

But above all, it is a testimony. And like every testimony that glorifies Jesus Christ, there is an overcoming power in it. Wretched times and satanic warfare confront us all, but there are lessons here to teach us God's way to triumph. We see these exemplified in Lorraine Pierce, aptly described by her daughter as a "woman of prayer," and in Bob Pierce—the man known for his extraordinary vision.

My involvement with the Pierces began with the author of this book, their daughter, Marilee Pierce Dunker. The story of my role is not crucial in the grand sweep of Bob Pierce's life and work, but I was involved enough to know the genuineness of his love for everyone he touched. I also know of the pain experienced by his wife and daughters. It is in the honesty with which the whole story is told that I believe there exists a certain genius to this book.

In relating Bob's vision, Marilee has been willing to acknowledge his blindness. In declaring triumph, she has been honest enough to admit trauma.

MAN OF VISION, WOMAN OF PRAYER

But it is all true. For that reason this book has a liberating quality about it. Truth will always make people free.

This book can free the selfish from preoccupation with small concerns as they read of one man whose compassionate heart unselfishly cared for those who hurt and were in such need.

It can free the lethargic from bondage to sloth and an absence of zeal if they will see the passion of a man to reach souls, whose needs went beyond the temporal to the eternal.

It can free visionaries from the starry-eyed idea that a vision can be realized without self-sacrifice, as they read of a man who fulfilled his vision by wading through the muck of human misery, doing something to provide help and healing.

It can free idealists to think realistically while grasping onto the unseen Reality through faith.

This book will smash the idolatry of those who would raise the memory of any man above the sad facts of his human failures, and in this respect it will provide encouragement, for who among us hasn't failed!

My life, like so many others, was touched by Bob Pierce's life long before his was ever touched by mine. Through the 1950s and the 1960s, the dynamism unleashed by God's grace through the yielded life of that one man made waves around the world, which added impetus to thousands of pastors' ministries. Mine was one of those. The stimulus of this saint, whose spirit of sacrificial service burned as a consuming fire, stirred millions with a new breadth of awareness as to the social implications of the gospel. Because of Bob Pierce's evangelistic zeal that left the brand of the Cross on multitudes and due to his clear prioritizing of the Word and the work of the Holy Spirit, cooler hearts began to finally understand: Evangelism and social service are to be companions.

In the last decade of Bob Pierce's life, my life became intertwined amid the tangled threads that constitute God's weaving in the tapestry of Bob's, Lorraine's, and the two young girls' lives. The fact that I was woven into the picture at a time when darker threads were in the pattern has in

FOREWORD

nowise caused me to lose sight of the splendor and magnificence of the bright, blessed, and mightily highlighted years that are framed in the whole of God's masterpiece named Bob Pierce. And always standing in the shadows was another, the beauty of whose life and influence was of no lesser value in God's eyes—Lorraine, the woman of prayer who almost singlehandedly raised their children, who knew deprivation of a different kind than those to whom her husband was ministering, but whose devotion to Christ and the Word could never be challenged.

My life has been enriched by reading this book; I believe yours will be too. This is my prayer.

> Jack Hayford, Pastor
> The Church On The Way
> Van Nuys, California

INTRODUCTION
•
"Marilee's going to write a book."

Those are some of the last words I heard my father speak. For years I had spoken of writing a book on singles' ministries—the area my husband, Bob, and I worked in for over four years—and I think Daddy wanted to see me put a pencil where my mouth was.

It wasn't until several weeks after Daddy went home to be with the Lord that the Holy Spirit spoke to my heart about writing this book. Thus began the most challenging period of my life.

Few people have the opportunity to know their parents as I have come to know mine in the past year—to study an overview of their lives and see them not only in the light of parent-child relationships, but as individuals who loved, hurt, struggled, and even failed. I had no concept of the magnitude of the story when I began researching for this book. Not one area of human experience is left untouched—from the highest possible peaks of joy and accomplishment to the deepest pits of despair and defeat. It has been my prayer throughout this undertaking that my parents' story will encourage and inspire you, challenge and teach you, the reader. I'm sure it will provoke and disturb many.

I found my parents' story one of great adventure and romance. But most of all it is a story of miracles, and there is no point in writing about miracles if one is not willing to expose the dark side of a situation so that the subsequent redemptive work of God can be fully appreciated. Consequently, anyone who reads this account must be prepared to be stirred both emotionally and spiritually. One cannot read the revelation of lives such as my parents'—two very human people called of God *not* to be perfect, but to be used to accomplish His will—and come away unchanged.

Undoubtedly there will be those who will ask if it was necessary or wise to be so honest. Wouldn't it have been better to leave some parts out, or not to write the story at all?

You hold my answer in your hand. Rarely is anything accomplished for the kingdom of God without a very real spiritual battle proportionate to the magnitude of the work being done. God honored my parents with a worldwide ministry. Consequently, the warfare they faced was unusually intense and vicious. To talk about the thrilling, positive things God did through my parents without showing the satanic attacks and wilderness experiences they went through would be a disservice both to them and to the reader. It would also present a distorted picture of how God often works, for nothing of any real value or lasting significance comes without paying a price.

This book is written as an expression of praise to our Lord for His continuing work of grace and mercy in our lives as a family, and as a loving tribute to two people who were willing to pay the price.

Chapter 1

UNCOMMON MAN, UNCOMMON WOMAN
•

"So many suffer so much while so few sacrifice so little." Those words ring as true today as they did when my father first spoke them in 1951, as part of the narration for one of his first films, *New China Challenge*. Only three years before, he had traveled through China as an evangelist, seeing more than twenty thousand people receive Christ as their Savior. But within weeks of his return, China was swallowed whole by the governmental dragon of darkness called communism. Believers were systematically purged in an attempt to snuff out the flame of faith ignited during the greatest spiritual revival in China's history.

Two years later, Daddy witnessed similar tragedy as a war correspondent in Korea. Shaken by the naked, desperate pain and need of the people, he wrote in his Bible, "Let my heart be broken with the things that break the heart of God." Out of that brokenness of heart and his determination to do something about the suffering around him, World Vision was born. Today it is one of the largest, ministry-oriented Christian organizations in the world.

But what does it cost to touch the world for Christ? What does it cost in terms of loneliness, personal tragedy, and tears? How do you put a price on the life of a child or the death of a marriage? How much of the price is the family expected to pay? And more importantly, when all is said and done, *is it worth the price?*

On September 6, 1978, Robert Willard Pierce went to be with his Lord. Nearly one thousand people gathered to pay

MAN OF VISION, WOMAN OF PRAYER

tribute to his memory. The "dignitaries" of the evangelical world came to praise God for this man who had touched so many lives.

Almost everyone there had a story to tell of how "Dr. Bob" had been used by God to meet a desperate need, whether it was $100,000 for a new hospital wing or a simple prayer of faith for the wasted body of a child dying of malnutrition. His work throughout the Orient, especially Korea and later Viet Nam, is legendary.

Bob Pierce was a man who specialized in the impossible. His whole life was an illustration of the saying, "They forgot to tell him it couldn't be done, so he did it anyway."

Missionaries loved him because he truly understood their needs, both physical and emotional. He knew how important it was for a husband to have a few days away with his wife, or for missionary children to have a special Christmas. For these people, his efforts on their behalf sometimes meant the difference between giving up and going on.

To thousands of children orphaned by war or some other tragedy, to countless sick, crippled, and starving people, Bob Pierce came in the name of Jesus, offering both physical and spiritual health. My father often said, "You can't feed a starving man's spirit if you don't first feed his stomach."

A filmmaker who worked with him once said, "If I were in Asia and saw a woman with a baby at her breast, dying beside the road . . . if I really wanted to capture the agony of that woman, I wouldn't watch her; I would watch Bob watching her. He used to say, 'I can't do everything for everybody, but I can do something for somebody. And what I can do, I must do.' And he did."

Yes, my father had an unusual ability to "weep with those who weep," and he was driven relentlessly to do something about the intolerable pain and despair he saw.

But Bob Pierce was a man of flesh and blood, and some of his greatest strengths were related to his greatest weaknesses. His very need to minister to the multitudes often made it hard for him to recognize the desperate needs of those closest

UNCOMMON MAN, UNCOMMON WOMAN

to him, or to allow himself the luxury of expressing his own needs.

Sitting at his memorial service, my heart was flooded with tender memories of my own and the painful realization that my Daddy was really gone. My entire life had been punctuated by trips to the airport to kiss Daddy good-bye before he flew off to some distant land across the ocean. But this good-bye was different; the sense of loss was much deeper.

As one man after another stood to speak of the miracles God had worked through my father's life, I wondered how many people were aware of the miracles we as a family had experienced, as time and again the enemy had sought to destroy us. I looked at my mother, her face composed but pale with grief, and I wondered how many people knew anything of this woman who for forty years had participated in every aspect of Daddy's ministry through her undying love, her unshakable faith, and her continual prayers. Twenty of those years are chronicled by almost three hundred letters, written in my father's backhand scrawl and postmarked from nearly every country on the face of the earth.

Mother's sentimental heart has always found it hard to throw things away. She has boxes full of her children's original poems, crayoned art works, special cards, and little love notes. She also carefully preserved every letter Daddy wrote her through twenty years of travel and separation. Unfortunately, most of *her* letters were lost; some never even reached my dad. But the few that survived the round trip were added to her collection.

The first time I read these letters I was enthralled by the story they told. Here was the account of one of this generation's most phenomenal adventures in faith, recorded as it was happening by the man who was privileged to live it. In this day when the world and even much of the church takes a skeptical attitude toward God's wonder-working power, preferring instead to restrict Him to the comfortable and familiar

MAN OF VISION, WOMAN OF PRAYER

definitions of traditional religiosity, these letters are a testimony to the fact that God has not changed. He is still the all-powerful God of Israel, Creator of heaven and earth, the One through whom "all things are possible" and through whom final victory is assured!

The letters were not written with posterity in mind; rather, they are tender declarations of love, intimate revelations of a man's heart to the one person in the world he could trust with his innermost thoughts and feelings. Daddy's letters beautifully confirm the reality of something I have known for years: God does not single out a person for ministry and then demand that he fulfill that assignment alone. Rather, He wonderfully weaves us together that we might strengthen and encourage one another to accomplish His work.

Some people may have thought my parents were mismatched; Daddy was constantly on the go, and Mother seemed to be a homebody. But God brought Bob Pierce and Lorraine Johnson together, knowing that in them He had a unique and necessary combination—a man of great passion and courage, whose humanity might sometimes cause him to stumble but whose heart always desired the will of God, and a woman whose outward frailties were no indication of her inward strengths. This woman would have the courage to send her man to the ends of the earth and raise her children alone, because she trusted God to be her strength and provider.

This is the remarkable story of two ordinary people who believed that God could do extraordinary things in them and through them . . . a man of vision and a woman of prayer.

Chapter 2

THE SCARLET THREAD
•

My parents' story doesn't begin with the day they met, or even with the day they were born.

My mother's father, Grandpa Johnson, used to preach a sermon entitled "The Scarlet Thread," in which he explained the spiritual heritage that is passed on from one generation of believers to the next. The scarlet thread winds its way from generation to generation, starting from the foot of the cross upon which Jesus died. Of course, the precious gift of Christ's blood is only effective as we personally and individually receive it; we do not inherit our salvation.

But who we are is greatly influenced by those who have come before us—those who have loved, taught, hurt, encouraged, and most importantly, prayed. There are countless generations of men and women who have through the power of effectual prayer touched the lives of those they will never know on this earth, but who are, nevertheless, their offspring.

Such is true of my mother and father. Both Grandpa and Grandma Pierce loved the Lord; on my mother's side that scarlet thread can be traced back as far as my great, great, great grandmother!

I hold in my hand four pieces of yellowing note paper that are precious beyond words. Written upon these pages, in her own flowing handwriting, is the testimony of my mother's great grandmother, Helen Cathrine Palmgren. It is dated April 13, 1909, and it begins, "I was born in Sweden, Christmas Day, 1835."

MAN OF VISION, WOMAN OF PRAYER

Helen goes on to describe her own mother as a Christian "whose consistent life and earnest prayers put a genuine desire in my young heart . . . to become a Christian." She received the Lord at fifteen, but until the age of twenty-six she lived without any assurance that her sins were forgiven, continually confessing her sins and asking God to have mercy on her.

Then a traveling evangelist came to Stockholm from England, preaching "salvation full and free."

"Oh! My poor, stammering tongue cannot begin to express the flood of joy and peace that swept into my soul when I found that I was free. . . ." Kathryn married John Lindgren in July of 1862, and together they immigrated to the United States, settling in Chicago.

The scarlet thread wove its way from Helen down through her only child, Emma, to my grandfather, Floyd Ballington Johnson, who not only was an unshakable source of love and support to my mother, but who had an immeasurable influence on my father's life and ministry.

Papa, as we affectionately called him, grew up with a deep respect for God and authority. He went to church, read the Bible, and prayed to the God his mother knew so well. But it wasn't until he was twenty-three that a visiting evangelist ripped the blinders from his eyes and confronted him with the need for more than a passing acquaintance with God. When the service was over, my grandfather waited in a long line to shake hands with this man whom God had used so powerfully. Paul Rader clasped Papa's hand warmly, sensing something special about this intense young man. In fact, after talking with Papa a while Rader invited him to join his ministry if he ever felt God leading that way.

Several years later, Papa would take Mr. Rader up on his offer, traveling with him as a singer and eventually becoming one of his associate pastors at the Chicago Gospel Tabernacle.

But first, Papa had to go home and try to explain to my grandmother this miracle of rebirth he had just experienced. Ethel Neimeyer Johnson came from a strong German

THE SCARLET THREAD

Methodist background, but as yet she had not come into a personal relationship with Jesus. Thus, the radical changes in her previously easygoing young husband were a bit disconcerting to her. But the love she and Papa shared was strong and deep, and Grammy did her best to adjust.

Into this home of strict religious doctrine and warm human relationships my mother was born, presenting herself as a birthday present to her father. Her memories of early childhood are full of the sweet, simple pleasures that most impress the heart of a child—like warm summer days picnicking beside the Des Planes River and huge chocolate sodas at Walgreens drug store.

Monday was always wash day, and Grammy also would fill her largest kettle with homemade German sauerkraut and large meaty ribs, allowing the mixture to simmer the entire afternoon until the whole house was filled with the pungent odor and the meat separated in tender chunks from the bones. Since sauerkraut was not her favorite thing, Monday was not my mother's favorite day. But Friday was fun, for on that day Grammy would gather up the newspapers from under foot to reveal her spotless kitchen floor. Then, with the determination of a true Swiss housewife, she would scrub every inch, covering the floor with fresh newspapers as soon as it was dry. As a small child Mama frequently felt a flutter of surprise whenever she saw a bare floor without its proper covering of newspaper.

And so Mama's early years are rich in sweet memories, providing a foundation of love upon which she would someday build her own family.

When Mama was nine, my grandfather quit his job with Sunkist and joined Paul Rader's ministry. Life took on a faster, more demanding tempo.

The Chicago Gospel Tabernacle was one of the most influential spiritual forces of its day. Paul Rader's ministry was nationwide, and as one of his right-hand men my grandfather found that his life was no longer his own. The demands of ministry were constant and ever increasing as Papa grew under Mr. Rader's discipleship and began developing his own ministry potential.

Both Papa and Grammy were active in the Tabernacle's music ministry. Papa had one of the country's first Christian radio programs—"The Sunshine Man"—which presented live gospel music over station WHT from the Wrigley Building in Chicago. Papa also began a powerful preaching ministry during this time, and after about four years he decided it was time to step out on his own.

Grammy had loved the excitement of being at the Tabernacle; but she never quite took the step into a more committed walk with Jesus, although she found great satisfaction in seeing others do so. But when Papa began traveling as an evangelist, life took another sharp turn and Grammy found herself an "evangelical widow," a role she was unprepared to accept. (Years later, Mother would be thrown into an exaggerated version of this same situation.)

My grandparents were married for nearly twenty years, and for Mama their divorce was like the end of the world. As a teen-ager, she wasn't concerned with the spiritual implications or the psychological explanations. She just wanted her parents to love each other and to be together always.

But they didn't and they weren't, and there was nothing she could do about it. So Mama learned to cope, respecting God too much to get angry with Him, and sympathizing with her dad too much to blame him. It was Grammy who finally left, and that made her the perfect candidate for all of Mother's repressed feelings. For several years, a serious emotional gulf existed between them. It wasn't until years after Mother was married that their relationship was fully restored.

In the spring of 1936, Papa was invited by a group of Nazarene churches to hold a series of evangelistic meetings in the Los Angeles area.

Mama was a typical eighteen-year-old—pretty, perky, and caught up in her own world. At the time, she was informally engaged to Bill, a nice, responsible Christian boy with no unsettling plans to save the world or travel more than once a

THE SCARLET THREAD

year. Going to California would mean leaving her friends, quitting her job, and most unbearable of all, saying good-bye to Bill for two whole months. (It was painful enough just saying "good night" at the end of a date!)

But Mama loved her father dearly, and she couldn't bear the thought of sending him on the long trip all alone. So Mama settled herself in Papa's new Buick for the long drive from Chicago to Los Angeles.

Bemoaning her fate with every passing mile, she fervently prayed, "You know I love you, Lord. But don't ever ask me to marry a traveling evangelist!"

Chapter 3

CROSS-COUNTRY ROMANCE
•
"Lorraine, you've just got to meet Bob Pierce. He's studying for the ministry at Pasadena Nazarene College, and he's darling!"

Mama just smiled at her friend Virginia Wallin, daughter of the pastor of the First Church of the Nazarene in Los Angeles. Virginia was doing her best to make Mama feel welcome in this strange new land where palm trees stood like giant sentries along the streets and orange groves ran in symmetrical rows as far as the eye could see.

In those first few weeks Daddy's name came up more than once, and every time it did Mother felt an inexplicable little flutter inside. She was still in love with Bill, she told herself, but there would be no harm in just meeting this young man Virginia kept talking about.

One night Papa Johnson was speaking in the Long Beach Church of the Nazarene, and many of the Nazarene College students were in attendance. This particular night Mama was surprised to hear Pastor Williams ask one of these students to lead in prayer. Even before she heard his name, Mama found her eyes fixed on the slender, curly haired figure as he worked his way to the front, took the steps to the platform two at a time, and presented himself with unusual assurance before the large crowd.

So this is the one I've heard so much about, Mama thought. Her heart began to beat a little faster as she studied his deep-set blue eyes and his warm, spontaneous smile. He certainly

CROSS-COUNTRY ROMANCE

seemed to be an unusual young man, and Mama looked forward to meeting him.

Seated on the platform that night, Bob Pierce had a bird's-eye view of the audience. More than one person had told him he should meet Floyd Johnson's pretty daughter, and he found himself trying to pick her out of the crowd. Being careful to appear properly attentive to the speaker, his eyes returned several times to a lovely, fresh-faced girl with soft, brown hair and gentle, green eyes. Somehow he knew she was the girl he'd been hearing about. And, extraordinary as it sounds, he also knew he would marry her.

After the service, Mama made her way to the front of the auditorium, confident that she would be introduced. But Daddy had immediately involved himself with the many who had come forward to receive Jesus.

Papa was scheduled to do a radio program immediately after the service, so he needed to leave. With one last, hopeful look, Mama was propelled out the door and rushed to the KPOX radio station across town.

By the time Papa, Mama, Pastor and Mrs. Williams, and the quartet had squeezed into the tiny recording booth, the fellowship was definitely close. Mama sat in the corner, lost in thoughts of a young man, Bob Pierce, weeping unashamedly as he knelt in prayer beside a new child of God. Her thoughts were interrupted by someone quietly kneeling at her side. Turning her head, all she could see was the back of a head of curly hair. Mama practically held her breath until the end of the program. Surely someone would introduce them then!

As Daddy knelt by Mama's chair, he rehearsed what he would say when they finally met. It had been no easy trick to talk his friend Hal into driving him to the radio station, but he wasn't going to let this opportunity slip by.

Suddenly the program was over, and everyone was leaving. Before Mama had a chance to think, she was out the door and on her way with Papa and the Williamses for a hot fudge sundae. Sick with frustration, she silently watched her ice cream melt while the others talked excitedly about the wonderful things God had done that night.

Suddenly the conversation stopped and Mama looked up to see two young men standing hesitantly at the door, waving at Mrs. Williams. She excused herself, talked to them a minute, and then invited them to the table.

"Lorraine, I'd like you to meet Bob Pierce. Bob, Lorraine Johnson."

It isn't uncommon for two people whom God has brought together to sense something special right from the start. Daddy wasted no time and asked Mama out, and she eagerly accepted.

On one of their first few dates Mama went to hear Daddy speak at the Brea Nazarene Church. The church was small and only partially full—nothing like the large, jam-packed churches Papa spoke in.

The young man in the pulpit was unpolished and somewhat less profound in his theology than the speakers Mama was accustomed to hearing. Yet, she sat that night with tears streaming down her cheeks, her heart deeply stirred by his impassioned words. God had obviously gifted him with an unusual ability to translate the Word into the common language of his listeners. He didn't preach at them; he talked to them, painting verbal images that allowed them to see the message as well as hear it.

"Aw no, Ma! Not hamburgers and potatoes again! We always have hamburgers and potatoes. Couldn't we have steak once in a while?" The young man in the pulpit spoke as the prodigal son, expressing the restlessness and discontent we all battle from day to day.

Hamburgers and potatoes! Mother had to laugh at this down-to-earth illustration. She had never heard anyone dare to be so natural when preaching the Word of God, and she was understandably curious. Who was this forthright young man who presented the gospel the same way he lived his life . . . without pretense or affectation?

CROSS-COUNTRY ROMANCE

The Pierces' family roots lie deep in the soil of western Vermont in one of those small country villages of clapboard houses and white steepled churches that nestle in the green, stony hills of New England. The community remains much the same as it was in 1800, the year my great grandfather, Asa Pierce, was born. At least that's how it appeared in the late fifties when my dad went there in search of his heritage. His quest ended in a small, tree-shaded church graveyard, its weather-beaten stones noting the birth and death of several generations of Pierces like roadsigns to the past. Asa and Mary Pierce had two sons, Ephraim and my paternal grandfather, Fred Asa Pierce.

Grandpa Pierce was a widower with three daughters—Ethel, Blanche, and Lulu—when he met Flora Belle Harlow Evison, a widow with two sons, Don and Alton. The two decided to join forces. Times were hard; Grandpa worked primarily as a carpenter, but he did other jobs when his carpentry skills were not in demand. It was no easy task to feed five hungry mouths, and the number grew with the arrival of Fred, Jr., and finally little Bobby.

Daddy made his debut on October 8, 1914, in Fort Dodge, Iowa. He announced his arrival with shrill, staccato wails that seemed to convey his impatience to get on with life. He learned early the need to assert himself in a home where everyone was at least a head taller and twenty pounds heavier than he was. And I'm sure he got his share of spoiling; I know Grandma always took a special joy and pride in her youngest boy.

I know little of my father's early childhood, except that the family moved to Greeley, Colorado, in an attempt to find some relief from the financial stranglehold of the depression. Even there it was a hand-to-mouth existence, but the more rural life-style made what they didn't have seem less obvious. It might have been a happy time if it hadn't been for a tragic turn of events.

Sometime before my dad was born, Grandma fell and injured her hip. It was a painful and disabling injury that stubbornly refused to heal and was a constant source of concern. After they'd been in Greeley a couple of years, it was discovered that the hip was tubercular. For one whole year my grandmother was forced to lie on her back, unable to turn or sit up, while weights affixed to her leg kept her hip separated from its socket. It was a tedious, grueling ordeal that tested both her physical and emotional endurance, and developed within her an unusual amount of patience.

During this time it was my father's job to care for Grandma after school and on weekends. It was a heavy responsibility for such a young boy, and many times his feet would make a dash in the other direction before slowly turning to trudge back home. But Grandma's years of suffering never diminished her faith, and her prayers supported Daddy as long as she lived.

When my father was twelve, Grandpa gave up on Greeley and moved the family to Redondo Beach, California, where he had a steady job with the Safeway market chain. By this time only Freddie and my dad remained at home, and the little family joined the Grace Church of the Nazarene.

The pastor of Grace Church was Earle Mack, a deeply spiritual young man who immediately took a liking to my dad and went out of his way to encourage his involvement. It was under his ministry that Daddy made his own personal commitment to Jesus, a decision that not only secured his salvation but also proved to be a source of strength for days ahead. Shortly thereafter, Grandpa died of a strange, undetermined ailment.

Losing his father was a terrible blow for my dad at his tender age, but the loss was at least partially cushioned by his newfound relationship with his heavenly Father and by the wonderful people God brought into his life. You've heard about a family adopting a child? Well, Daddy adopted a church. His life became inseparably linked with that of Grace Church and its people.

On Saturdays the church would load up the "Gospel Car," an old Ford truck they had converted to a bus, and rumble

CROSS-COUNTRY ROMANCE

down to the corner of Manchester and Broadway. On most of those Saturdays an earnest-faced boy of thirteen or fourteen could be seen standing on a soapbox and preaching his heart out to a good-sized crowd of passersby.

But the greatest contribution these years made to my father's life was the cementing of a relationship that would last his whole life. Earle and Ruth Mack took Daddy into their hearts—loving him, encouraging him, and even digging into their pockets for him when necessary. When the Lord moved them on to pastorates in Monrovia and Pasadena, Daddy became a frequent customer of the "P.E. red car" (southern California's Pacific Electric mode of transportation in those days), dropping in unannounced to spend the day or the weekend, whenever he could get the fare.

In college, I'm afraid my father was far better known for his outrageous pranks than for any great spiritual or intellectual gifts. But while the faculty might have found my dad quite a handful, the other students loved him. In his junior year he ran as a "dark horse" for student body president and won. It was the most important and thrilling surprise of his life, until the night he met a brown-haired girl with gentle green eyes.

When Papa returned home, Mama stayed to finish the school year as a special student at Pasadena Nazarene College. Papa was well aware of the reason for Mother's sudden interest in a college education, but he wasn't hard to convince. He had dedicated Mama to the Lord while she was still in Grammy's womb, and he didn't believe the fulfillment of God's purpose for her life was waiting back in Chicago. Too, he was greatly impressed with my father, and he decided that if God wanted to do something with the relationship he would do what he could to cooperate.

Mother's arrival on campus created quite a stir. Not only was she a rather glamorous addition to the conservative student body, but it quickly became apparent that she had taken one of the most popular men on campus out of circulation.

Daddy courted her with all the style his 1927 Model-A Ford

and her seven-dollar-a-week allowance would allow. Frequently, Daddy would find himself temporarily financially embarrassed. But the school was on the side of a hill, and by coasting the old Model-A down the hill Daddy would be able to afford a ten-cent cheeseburger and still have enough gas to drive Mother back up to the dorm. Mama always knew what to expect when Daddy asked her out for a "coast" instead of a drive.

In the tradition of all great loves, Mom and Dad had their share of obstacles to overcome. At the time, Pasadena Nazarene expressed an extremely conservative attitude toward male-female relationships. Any public display of affection was prohibited.

I'm sure Mother and Dad weren't deliberately rebellious, but the attraction they had felt for one another at the beginning was rapidly ripening into a deep and undeniable love that neither could help but express. At the time, Daddy was president of the student body and a highly visible figure on campus. So when he and Mama boldly continued to hold hands and even kiss good-night on the dormitory steps, they soon received an invitation to the dean's office.

My father, who was not exactly famous for his mild temper or diplomacy during moments of great stress, let it be known in no uncertain terms that he didn't think Mother and he had done anything wrong. "If you think it is sinful for two people in love to hold hands, the problem is in your own minds, not ours!"

I can just see Daddy's blue eyes flashing, his voice trembling with righteous indignation. The poor dean of men and dean of women left with tears in their eyes at being talked to in such a manner. Mother was restricted to campus and forbidden to see Daddy again during the remainder of the semester.

That might have been the end of the story if it hadn't been for Papa's timely intervention. In response to Mother's plea for help, he wrote the president of the board of directors, and it was arranged for the couple to meet once a week at the

CROSS-COUNTRY ROMANCE

parsonage for a closely supervised "date." After a few weeks of tea and cookies with the pastor and his wife, the restrictions were mercifully dropped, and Mom and Dad gratefully did their best to demonstrate true repentance. Still, I'm sure the entire faculty breathed a sigh of relief when the school year ended.

The end of the semester meant a return to Chicago for Mother and an uncertain future for the young lovers. It was 1936, and the country was still struggling to recover from the depression. Jobs were scarce, and Daddy had no recourse but to send Mama home.

Unwilling to say good-bye until the last possible moment, Daddy rode the old Union Pacific *Challenger* with her to San Bernardino, as far as his limited funds would allow. Those last few hours he held Mother's hand and talked confidently about the future. They had committed their relationship to the Lord, and surely He would bring them together again. And yet, Chicago was so far away . . .

As Daddy waited by the roadside to hitch a ride back to Pasadena, he earnestly poured his heart out to the Lord. Only moments before he had kissed Mama good-bye, and already he was aching to be with her.

His "conversation" was interrupted by the sound of a car coming down the road. With the casual expertise of an experienced hitchhiker, Daddy stuck out his thumb. Watching the car roll to a stop, Daddy had an idea. . .

Back in Chicago, Mama moved in with her brother, Floyd, and his wife, Marge. While Papa continued his evangelistic meetings, Mama found herself selling jewelry at Wiebolt's department store and living for the letters that arrived from California every day or so. The pain of separation grew more unbearable every day as the seeming hopelessness of the situation became more evident.

About the time she thought she couldn't stand it any longer, Mama received a letter instructing her to be home at nine on a certain Friday morning. Apparently Daddy missed her as much as she missed him, and he had decided to splurge and call her on the telephone.

The night before the expected call Mama couldn't sleep a wink, and the morning sun found her wrapped in an old terry robe, her hair in curlers, her face dotted with cold cream, nervously pacing the apartment.

At nine sharp, there was a knock at the door. You guessed it. Daddy's old thumb had carried him clear across the country!

He stayed about a month, and he and Mother felt the bond between them deepen and solidify. But Daddy was only twenty-two, with no job, no money, and no apparent future. He couldn't stay indefinitely with Mother's friends, who had kindly given him a place to sleep. Soon it was time for him to make his way back home.

Mother said good-bye, not knowing when she would see Daddy again or even where he was going. He might hitchhike home, he said, or to his sister's in Santa Fe, or stop somewhere along the way if he found a job.

This uncertain state of affairs caused a major problem when Papa called a few days later to invite Mama and Daddy to join him for two weeks of camp meetings he would be conducting in Grand Rapids, Minnesota, a beautiful resort town. If Daddy would meet them in front of the YMCA in Minneapolis at six on a certain afternoon, he could be the songleader for the meetings. This would give the young couple precious time together.

It was a perfect answer to Mother's prayers, but how could she reach Daddy, who was floating around somewhere between Chicago and Los Angeles?

On a "heavenly hunch," Mother felt led to write Daddy in Santa Fe. She didn't know his sister's address or even her married name, so the letter was simply addressed:

> Bob Pierce
> Care of General Delivery
> Santa Fe, New Mexico

CROSS-COUNTRY ROMANCE

A few days later, Daddy was aimlessly walking the streets of Santa Fe praying and asking God to give him some clear direction for his life and for his relationship with Mama. As he walked, he noticed the post office across the street. No one knew he was in Santa Fe, and it was not his habit to walk into strange post offices to inquire if he had any mail. But the impulse was so strong that he found himself across the street and inside the door before he had time to think about how silly he was.

The look on Daddy's face must have been something to see as he incredulously took the envelope and checked to make sure it was really for him. The post office clerk probably talked for days about the strange young man who ripped open his letter, laughed out loud, and danced out the door shouting "Hallelujah" and "Praise the Lord" all the way down the street.

Daddy left Santa Fe with fifty cents in his pocket and only a few days to make it to Minneapolis. When Papa and Mama pulled up in front of the YMCA on the appointed day, they were astounded but delighted to find him waiting out front, freshly showered and shaved, a big smile on his face and two dollars in his pocket.

Safely settled in Papa's car on the way to Grand Rapids, Daddy described how he had prayed his way across country, trusting God to send him motorists who would pay him for driving while they slept. He never even missed a meal. It was this kind of impetuous spirit and unhesitating faith that would one day qualify Daddy for one of the most unique and effective ministries of his generation. Mama just shook her head in wonder and thanked God for taking good care of her unpredictable young sweetheart.

More months of painful separation followed Daddy's return to California. He worked at anything he could find—one month he killed rattlesnakes in the Chevy Chase hills between Pasadena and Glendale; the next, he sold musical instruments up through central California.

By November he had saved enough money to travel back to

MAN OF VISION, WOMAN OF PRAYER

Chicago one more time. Mother was thrilled to see him and so was my Uncle Floyd. For months he had nursed his little sister through the emotional roller coaster she had been on ever since she met Daddy. In his opinion, enough was enough!

"For Pete's sake, why don't you two get married?" he asked one evening. That was all the encouragement the young lovers needed. That very night the evangelist's daughter married the carpenter's son in the Methodist parsonage in Crown Point, Indiana.

Chapter 4

"A YOUTH AFLAME"
•

It would be nice to say that Mom and Dad hitchhiked off into the sunset and lived happily ever after. But even the movies don't try to sell that kind of fantasy anymore.

I strongly believe that the foundations of hell tremble every time a man and woman of God commit themselves to one another. The ministry potential of a couple yielded to the will of God is a threat Satan can't afford to ignore. In my parents' case, he was determined to defeat the troops before they had a chance to get on the battlefield. And he almost succeeded.

After a one-week honeymoon, Daddy decided he'd better return home to California and find a job to support his new bride. It was early December, and there was little hope that he could send for her soon.

Christmas morning found Mama still in Chicago, half-heartedly entering into the family festivities. As everyone opened their presents, she saved Daddy's until last. Under the tree, the little box was almost lost among all the big, brightly colored packages. It certainly couldn't compare to the large, well-packed box she had sent off to him a week or so before.

As she tore off the brown paper and opened the small white box, Mother stared disbelievingly at the velvet jeweler's box inside. Daddy still had no job, and surely there was no money for this!

Her thoughts drifted back to a clear day the previous spring. She and Daddy had been strolling down Pasadena's Colorado Boulevard looking at the window displays and dreaming about the future.

MAN OF VISION, WOMAN OF PRAYER

This particular day they had stopped to look at wedding rings in a jewelry store window. One set caught Mama's eye—a sparkling diamond solitaire coupled with a delicate gold wedding band, encrusted with seven small diamonds. She had commented on how lovely they were, the way we all admire things we'd like to have and know we never will.

Now, fingers trembling, Mama slipped off the dime store ring she wore on her left hand and slipped on the simple gold band with seven small diamonds.

It was February before Daddy was finally able to send for Mother. Through Ruth Mack's father he had gotten a job laying hardwood floors. It was exhausting, difficult work. Daddy had to bend over at the waist for hours at a time, hammering nails down the length of one board and back the next. But the job was a real answer to prayer, and he was grateful.

If she could have, Mama would have run all the way to California. Instead, her father offered to make the lengthy drive once again. This time, far from silently sulking her way across the country, Mama rejoiced in every passing mile.

Finally she and Papa arrived in Glendale and checked into the hotel where Daddy was to meet them. Stationed at the window, Mama's eyes were glued to the street below, where any minute her Prince Charming would appear. Up chugged the old Model-A. The door opened and out stepped Prince Charming, still in his work clothes, his hair escaping wildly in all directions from under his white painter's cap.

Mama felt a strange sinking sensation in the pit of her stomach as she recognized the young man she had married—a poor substitute for the romantic figure she had pictured the last few months. But as soon as he burst through the door and swept her into his arms, all her fears and reservations disappeared.

But hugs and kisses are not enough to sustain a lasting relationship. Until this time, Mom and Dad had lived in the fantasy world of lovers, their relationship spiced with constant uncertainty. Now they were husband and wife, and the realities of married life came crashing down upon them.

Soon after Mother arrived, Daddy's job ended abruptly, and he began drifting from job to job. None of them lasted very long, and Daddy's discontent grew greater with every new venture. He knew he had been called to the ministry, not to sell cars or insurance, or to work in a bank. But since he hadn't returned for his final year of school he could not be licensed by the Nazarene Church, so all the obvious doors of ministry were closed tight. For the first time Daddy felt no definite leading or direction. Instead of flowing with the stream, he found himself fighting the tide, struggling to keep his head above water.

At the same time, Mama struggled to adjust to her new life and to the unpredictable young man she had married. She had fallen in love with a promising young preacher, president of the student body. He had seemed so sure of himself, so confident about the future. Now she found herself married to a young man who was seemingly going nowhere and who was obliged to take her with him.

With romantic impracticality, neither Mother nor Daddy had considered the extreme differences in their personalities. Daddy's naturally impetuous spirit seemed in direct opposition to the stable and orderly life-style to which Mother was accustomed, and she often found herself battling feelings of insecurity and doubt.

With few friends, no transportation (the old Ford had finally died), and only enough money each month to squeak by, there was little for the newlyweds to do but worry and argue. Finally, defeated and frustrated, Mother went back to Chicago for a visit. As she waved good-bye from the train window she wondered if she would ever see Daddy again.

The next weeks were agonizing for the young couple, as they each tried to work through the tangled web of emotions in which they were caught. The last months had given them a frightening taste of the vicious warfare they would have to be prepared for if they were to continue on together.

The weeks turned into months, and except for a few

guarded letters, there was little communication between the two. Then one day Mama received a letter.

"My Darling Wife," it began. Mama's heart leaped at these words of endearment. The letter continued, and for the first time Daddy honestly shared his fears and frustrations. The last year had raised so many unanswered questions. Had he and Mother made a mistake? Why were things so difficult if God had ordained their marriage? Was he out of divine order? If God really had a sovereign plan for his life, where and how had he missed the boat? Surely God was not the author of confusion, and Daddy was one confused young man!

One afternoon Daddy found himself standing on a street corner, unable to decide which way to go or what to do. Unwilling to return to the empty apartment, he stood for a long time watching the cars stop and go. The street light changed from green to yellow to red and back to green again. The unending progression seemed an appropriate parallel to his life at the moment—endless striving, going nowhere.

"Bob! Bob Pierce. Over here." He was startled from his thoughts by several old friends from school who were beckoning him to their car.

"We're on our way to camp meeting. Want to come?"

The Nazarene denomination was holding its annual convention on the Pasadena Nazarene campus that year. Pastors and ministers from all over the country would be there, as well as many of his old friends. Daddy wasn't sure he wanted to face the old crowd just now. Many considered his sudden disappearance from school an indication of spiritual backsliding, and at the moment he thought they might be right. But it beat standing on the corner all night. So with a casual "Sounds great!" he jumped in the car and off they went.

It didn't take Daddy long to recognize that it was no accident he was in the meeting that day. Everything that was said seemed directed right at him, and the Holy Spirit dealt powerfully with his heart. Broken, rejoicing, and renewed, Daddy stood before the entire assembly and confessed with tears of

"A YOUTH AFLAME"

repentance his difficulties of the past year, proclaiming with fresh conviction his determination to serve God.

His testimony had such an impact that after the meeting several pastors sought him out and invited him to hold revival meetings in their churches. Doors of ministry flew open, and once again his direction was clear.

Daddy ended his letter, "I love you and want you with me. But whether you come or not, I'm going on with God."

It was the summons for which her spirit had been waiting, the reassurance for which her heart longed. Mama's answer was short and to the point.

"Yes! I'm coming!"

And so Mother and Daddy entered into their second year of marriage and their first year of evangelism.

Their first meeting was in San Diego at the University Avenue Church of the Nazarene, a large, prosperous congregation that welcomed them with expectancy and enthusiasm.

> Revival Services
> Nightly, 7:30
> October 3rd–17th, 1937
> "The flaming truths of salvation,
> In burning words from the
> Anointed lips of youth!"
> This is your personal invitation
> To attend revival services and
> hear "Bob" Pierce—a lad aflame!

Pastor and Mrs. South went out of their way to make the young couple feel appreciated and loved, placing them in someone's lovely home, graciously providing all transportation (Mom and Dad still had no car), and generally treating them like the biggest names on the evangelistic circuit.

God greatly blessed those first meetings. Every night the church was packed with people eager to hear the dynamic young preacher, and Daddy spoke with greater power and authority than ever before.

As on the first night she had heard him speak, Mother was again impressed by God's obvious anointing of Daddy's ministry. Night after night she watched as people crowded forward to respond to the invitation to receive Christ or rededicate their lives to Him. Convinced that God was going to do a powerful work through her husband, Mama was overwhelmed by feelings of her own inadequacy.

She had always been prepared to accept God's calling for Daddy's life. Part of the reason she loved him so much was because of his all-out commitment and desire to serve the Lord. But never before had she been so aware of what God was requiring from her, and suddenly she became conscious of weak areas in her own life—feelings of hurt and bitterness left over from her parents' separation, and fears that had unconsciously put conditions on what she would allow God to do. Now He was challenging those conditions, and Mother's spirit was stirred and discomforted.

One afternoon Mama knelt beside her bed, determined not to rise until she knew that all the questions were settled and she had total peace and confidence. Trusting the Holy Spirit to bring significant things to mind, she went through her entire life, confessing areas of sin and confusion. What Daddy had done publicly Mother now did privately. This was her Gethsemane, her place of dying to self. Unconditionally, she prayed, "Not my will, but Thine be done." The years would prove that God took her at her word.

Mother and Daddy left San Diego charged up and raring to go. If this was what they could expect in the ministry, they were going to enjoy every minute of it!

The following are excerpts from newspaper clippings that show God's mighty hand on my father's ministry even at the tender age of twenty-three. The churches were filled with people eager to hear the "flaming truths of salvation, in burning words from the anointed lips of youth." God gave him favor with young people, for whom he had a special burden.

"A YOUTH AFLAME"

Escondido, California, November, 1937
Nazarene Evangelist Draws Large Crowds
　　Bob Pierce . . . is drawing increasingly larger audiences since his first lecture Sunday evening. One of the largest Monday night congregations in the history of the Church was present Monday.

Glendora, California, December, 1937
Nazarene Young People's Revival
Hear Bob Pierce—A Youth Aflame!
　　Rev. Pierce is a youthful, dynamic speaker. He is also a splendid singer and has brought messages from night to night in *sermon and song* with telling results.

Santa Ana, California, February, 1938
Revival Fires Are Burning!
Come Hear This Young Man!
Bob Pierce (A Son of Thunder)

Pomona, California, March, 1938
Pomona Hears for the First Time
BOB PIERCE, "Youth Aflame"
　　This young man is one of the most unique and colorful men in the pulpit today. Hear him.

Ojai, California, April, 1938
Ojai Hears BOB PIERCE, "A Youth Aflame"
　　The evening services which the Reverend Bob Pierce of Pasadena is conducting . . . [were] to have ended this Sunday, but [are] being continued for another week by popular demand.

Wilmington, California, May, 1938
　　By popular demand, it has been decided to continue the revival services at the Church of the Nazarene. . . . Attendance and interest are increasing nightly and all ages are enjoying the preaching of Rev. Bob Pierce, Young Evangelist.

In the year that followed, God continued to bless. But He also continued to teach, and nothing leaves a deeper impression than the lessons we learn through experience.

As traveling evangelists, Mom and Dad were totally reliant upon the host church to supply them with food and lodging. Occasionally they would be treated with the same hospitality and thoughtfulness they had received in San Diego, but those times were the exception, not the rule.

In one town they stayed in a barn loft that had been crudely converted into a room with no bath. Another church provided them with a room and a bath, but no running water.

In yet another town they were informed that accommodations had been rented within walking distance of the church. They were greeted at the door by a walleyed old lady dressed entirely in black, her unkempt hair stuffed haphazardly under a wide-brimmed black hat, which she never removed.

Each night Mom and Dad would come home to find the house dark and their landlady in the kitchen, surrounded by her five cats, rocking in front of the pot-bellied stove and strumming on an old guitar.

Needless to say, they stayed only until a place a little less bizarre could be found.

These are the experiences that are fun to remember, the kind you look back on and laugh at. But there were also genuinely painful experiences. Mother and Dad were young and fresh, with an enthusiasm undampened by years of struggle and disappointment. They were talented, attractive, and obviously very much in love. This was usually a big plus in their favor, but occasionally it caused resentment in some who were older and less satisfied with their lives.

Disdain for Daddy's youth was expressed in discouraging ways. My parents' only income was from the love offerings taken during the meetings. It was never very much. In fact, at the end of the year Daddy figured they had averaged five dollars a week. But occasionally the Lord would touch people's hearts and they would give generously.

On one such occasion, the youth pastor in the church was so blessed by the congregation's response that he enthusiastically confided to Daddy the amount of the offering. Mother and Dad were thrilled. But after the closing meeting the

"A YOUTH AFLAME"

pastor handed them a check for fifteen dollars. Dumbfounded, Daddy told the man that he knew the offering had been several times that amount.

Caught in an extremely uncomfortable position, the pastor exploded, "Why, you young whippersnapper (or something to that effect), you don't need any more money than that. Why, when I was your age, I would have been thrilled to have received that amount!"

Daddy firmly slapped the check back into the pastor's hand. "Here, you obviously need this more than I do!"

At times like that Mama couldn't help but wish Daddy were a little less impetuous and a bit more practical, but for Daddy the satisfaction was well worth the cost.

Someone once said, "You don't fall in love; you grow into it." As difficult and unpredictable as this period was financially, it was a very precious time of growth for Mother and Daddy. To quote Mama, "I began to truly love your father during that year. We may have had nothing, but we had it together."

Laughing together, crying together, encouraging one another, learning to trust God together, seeing one another in the reality of the present and in the potential of what God would someday make them to be—all these priceless things established a root system, like that of a fine old oak, which was to sustain the relationship despite the raging storms and blistering droughts through which it would pass.

Thanksgiving was rapidly approaching, and Mother and Daddy returned to Los Angeles for the holidays. My grandfather had come out from Chicago several months before at Aimee Semple McPherson's invitation. God's blessing had attended his ministry so powerfully that Mrs. McPherson had extended her invitation from two weeks to thirteen months.

Unable to afford a place of their own, Mama and Daddy would stay with Papa between speaking engagements, and it was to his apartment that they now returned.

One afternoon Mama went shopping for Christmas cards. While she was out it started to rain, and her feet were soaked through her open-toed shoes. Later that evening she was dismayed to feel her throat getting scratchy and raw. By the next day her throat was so sore she could hardly swallow. Usually a sore throat was no cause for alarm, but for some reason Papa felt prompted to send for a doctor that very night. It took Dr. Matousek only five minutes to examine Mother's throat and diagnose her sickness as diphtheria.

At that particular time there had been only a few cases of diphtheria recorded in California; probably only one doctor in a hundred would have recognized the symptoms. But this doctor had just come from North Dakota, and he had seen it before. He immediately sent Daddy to buy some antitoxin, and within the hour Mama had received a massive dose of the life-saving medication.

Diphtheria can be deadly and is easily transmitted. Normally, Mother would have been taken immediately to the county hospital, where she would have been carefully isolated for two or three weeks of treatment and observation. But not wanting to relinquish his daughter to the care of an institution, Papa imposed upon Mrs. McPherson to use her considerable influence. Within the hour, the gracious lady had made the necessary calls and arranged for Mother to remain at home.

Each day Dr. Matousek would stop by to check on the patient, and Papa would stand at the door to reassure Mama of his love and prayers. But it was my father who tenderly nursed her, hardly leaving her side for the weeks it took the disease to run its course. It was Daddy who took her in his arms to comfort her when she cried out in delirium, who fed her, bathed her, changed her sheets, and emptied her bedpan.

Finally the crisis passed, and Mama began the long process of recovery. It would be a year before her full strength returned.

Chapter 5

THE CENTER DAYS
•

Mother's illness put an end to that first year of travel and marked the beginning of the "Center" days.

"The church that radio built" was the way the July, 1944, issue of *Radio Life* described the Los Angeles Evangelistic Center on the corner of Eleventh and Hope. Born of Papa Johnson's highly successful radio ministry, the Center sprang into existence almost fully grown. God richly blessed my grandfather's ministry, and soon he gained a reputation as one of the greatest Bible expositors of his day.

Every Wednesday and Friday night and three times on Sunday, the Center's lovely sanctuary was filled to capacity with people hungry to hear the Word of God taught with great simplicity, irresistible compassion, and unquestionable authority. At times, the power of the Holy Spirit charged the air like electricity, working physical healing. At other times the sweetness of His presence fell like thick honey, quietly restoring emotional health and drawing people to Jesus.

Mother once eloquently expressed the indelible impression those years made on her and Daddy's lives: "Bob and I were absolutely submerged through those years in the message of the Cross. Papa loved the Word of God and made it come alive for us both. In the years that followed, I would find it necessary for my survival, for getting through the dark seasons of night as well as the day times—the assurance that the Word of God is true.

"The Word of God became a life-style: believing it, knowing it, watching it become the reality of living. God said it, and we believed it, and it was that simple. Bob and I met life-and-death issues, and we survived the way we did and came through as *long* as we did and through *what* we did because God's Word was believed. It had been tried in our lives and it hooked in and found its way into our very core, becoming life. It could not be denied."

Mother remembers the four and a half years Daddy was a youth pastor at the Center as some of the happier and personally more gratifying of her life. It was during these years that they had their first real home, a little apartment in Glendale. Here they went through the typical "learning-to-make-do-with-little-or-nothing" stage, furnishing their home in "early orange crate" and "classic thrift shop." But Mama loved every minute, and the two of them discovered many hidden talents. For instance, when she was pregnant with Sharon she wanted a rocking chair, but every extra penny was needed to pay for the baby.

One night Daddy burst through the door, grinning boyishly from ear to ear. He proudly presented Mother with something that resembled a rocker. He was obviously pleased with his offering, explaining he had rescued it from the back of one of the Center's huge storage closets. Mother hadn't the heart to point out that it had no seat and that one of the "rockers" had been practically rocked off. It wasn't exactly what she had pictured.

For the next few days, Daddy devoted every spare minute to refurbishing the old chair, using his carpentry skills to make a new seat and securing the wobbly arms and legs. By the time it was ready for sanding, Mother was caught up in the project. She tried her hand at sewing a seat cushion and a matching skirt. In its fresh paint and custom-designed dressing, the old chair was a natural scene stealer, and it became one of Mother's prized possessions.

These years at the Center gave my folks their first real opportunity to enjoy a normal social life. Until then, their gypsy-like existence had allowed them to stay in one place only long enough to regret having to leave when it was time

THE CENTER DAYS

to move on. Now they had a chance to cultivate close friendships with several of the young couples in the church.

Of course, much of the joy of those years was centered in the ministry. Mother and Dad worked together to build and sustain an effective youth program and evangelistic outreach, organizing mass rallies with music and special attractions designed to reach young men and women for Christ.

As an associate pastor, Daddy also had other responsibilities—such as leading the singing in the main services and doing his own radio broadcast every Monday night over station KMTR, Hollywood.

Music played a big part in my parents' life during this time. Mama always loved to sing and play the piano, and in his earliest years my dad was billed as an evangelist/singer.

Now they joined their best friends Riley and Flossie Kaufman to form a mixed quartet. Mama also sang in the choir and ladies' trio, while Dad sang with the "King's Ambassadors." This was Papa's radio quartet, and it included Riley, Dean Nauman, Wilbur Nelson, and my father. (Today Riley is associated with the *P.T.L. Club*, Dean works with "Food for the Hungry," and Wilbur has long been known for *The Morning Chapel Hour*.)

I often heard Daddy call Papa Johnson his "seminary," for it was from Papa that Daddy learned many practical aspects of ministry. But far more important than learning the "how to" of ministry, God used Papa to open and expand my father's vision for ministry. Until this time, Daddy had never ventured outside the confines of the Nazarene denomination. But at the Center, men of many denominational backgrounds came to exalt Jesus and proclaim the gospel, loving and accepting one another despite doctrinal differences.

"Preach the Word, not the manual," my grandfather often said. It was a concept that released Daddy to feel comfortable in any church and with any group of people who honored Jesus Christ as Lord.

It was during these years that Mom and Dad first became acquainted with many people who would have a profound influence on them—men like Percy Crawford, Billy Graham, Hubert Mitchell, David Morken, Raymond Richey, Peter Deyneka . . . all came to the Center at one time or another. It was through Papa that Daddy met Dr. Charles Fuller (of *The Old-Fashioned Revival Hour*) and Paul Meyers, better known as First Mate Bob (from the *Haven of Rest* broadcast).

The Meyers took a special liking to my dad and were a great encouragement to him in his early years of ministry. Even during the Center days finances were tight, and occasionally, when a replacement was needed for the *Haven of Rest* radio quartet, Daddy would join the "Crew of the Good Ship Grace" to earn a little extra money.

Another man who had a profound influence on my father was the great missionary statesman Dr. Oswald J. Smith. It was he who brought the first real missionary challenge Daddy ever heard, depicting with heart-wrenching clarity the hopeless, aching need of a world without God. In those moments of revelation the soil was broken and the first seeds of missionary ministry were planted within my father's spirit.

With the hindsight of many years it is easy to see the spiritual significance of Dr. Smith's message. But for years Mother remembered that evening for quite another reason.

At the end of the service a missionary offering was taken. Daddy, his eyes burning with visions of naked, starving people dying without ever hearing of Jesus, dug into his pocket, pulled out a small wad of bills, and dropped the entire lot into the plate as it passed. Speechless, Mother watched as their thirty-five dollars of rent money disappeared down the aisles and out the door.

This was the first of many times when Mother questioned whether Daddy's irrepressible giving bordered on irresponsibility. She was torn between her conviction that paying the bills on time was pleasing and honorable in the Lord's eyes and her own desire to see the money used to ease suffering and spread the gospel. After several years of seeing God always provide abundantly, Mother learned to rest in the assurance of God's faithfulness and the promise of Philip-

THE CENTER DAYS

pians 4:19: "But my God shall supply all your need according to his riches in glory by Christ Jesus."

So the first years at the Center were busy and productive. God blessed, Mother and Daddy grew, and Satan raged.

I suppose if she had been more discerning, Mother would have seen the warning signals in Daddy's growing restlessness and discontent. Daddy battled feelings of dissatisfaction over his position at the church. He felt in competition with the other young men on the staff, and it began to annoy him that Papa didn't give him a position of greater authority.

Another point of irritation was Mother's unusually close relationship with her father. In most marriages, time and separation naturally "cut the umbilical cord," but the close association at the Center seemed to give Papa all the advantages, leaving Daddy feeling like a poor second. It was a difficult situation, for Daddy deeply loved and respected my grandfather. But at the same time he was being eaten up inside by the need to prove his worth to Mother and to himself. Of course, Daddy's feelings were only symptomatic of a deeper, more disturbing battle within his spirit.

It was April, 1941. Mother was in her last month of pregnancy, looking forward to the arrival of her first child. She and Daddy had been arguing quite a bit lately, suffering through the last few weeks of pregnancy, which can be as hard on the prospective father as they are on the mother.

Sharon surprised everyone by coming nearly two weeks early. Mother and Dad were both thrilled with the beautiful little girl God had given them. Daddy came to the hospital every day after work to look at her and spend a few minutes with Mama. Then he would rush off to an evening service or to sing with the quartet on Papa's radio program.

One night Mother tuned in the broadcast to discover someone else singing Daddy's part. Confused and concerned, she tried to reach him. Failing that, she called Papa.

"Dad, I just finished listening to the broadcast. Bob wasn't singing. Is anything wrong?"

"I'm sorry, Dear, we didn't want you to worry while you

were in the hospital. Bob and I had an argument. He quit over a week ago."

Entering Mother's hospital room the next day, Daddy felt desperate and torn inside. The look on Mama's face said what words couldn't express. Hurt, anger, confusion, fear, and that great, overpowering "Why?"

How could he explain to her what he was helpless to understand himself? All he knew was that he was angry and frustrated and felt like punching somebody! But who and why?

Papa—because his success and years of experience constantly made Daddy feel like a rowboat racing a windjammer?

Himself—for expecting so much?

God—for not making things happen faster?

The man next door—for just being there?

Never before had Daddy felt such waves of discontentment and rebellion. Like a swimmer floundering in the surf, Daddy seemed unable to get his footing or do anything to resist the tide of emotions that threatened to carry him away.

The following weeks were strange and unreal. Daddy was moody and uncommunicative, vacillating between guilt and anger. Only Sharon seemed to penetrate the shell into which he had withdrawn. Holding her close, he would bury his face in her little neck, inhaling her sweet baby fragrance. Other times Mama would discover him staring at Sharon as she slept. Mama couldn't be sure he was even aware of her presence until he would finally slip his arm around her waist and whisper, "Thank you, Sweetheart."

Sharon was two months old when Daddy announced he was leaving. He had been invited to speak at a series of meetings up north, and he felt it would be a good time to think things through.

As Mama watched him walk out the door, she tried to convince herself that he would find the answers he was seeking and be back to his old self again in a week or two. But deep inside, she knew it wouldn't be that easy. As the days became weeks and Daddy sent no word, Mother was forced

THE CENTER DAYS

to acknowledge the truth. He was gone. He had walked out on her, on Sharon, and on his ministry. And most frightening of all, he was walking away from God's direction for his life.

When the meetings ended, Daddy headed for San Diego. His brother Fred lived there, and it was the only place he could think of to go. With World War II in full swing the shipyards were constantly in need of more workers, and it would not be hard to get a job. He would be one man in a city of thousands. It would be a good place to lose himself . . . or maybe find himself.

After the first week or so of Daddy's absence, Mother and Sharon moved in with Papa and his wife, Opal. With every passing day the uneasiness in Mama's spirit grew, twisting into an aching agony.

During the weeks that followed, the only place she could find any comfort or peace was in her prayer closet. Unwilling to simply wait, she grabbed up the only weapon she had—kneeling in prayer for hours at a time. That was the only time she felt safe, the only time hopelessness and helplessness did not prevail.

With childlike simplicity, Mama claimed the most basic promises of God: "And whatsoever ye shall ask in my name, that will I do, that the Father may be glorified in the Son" (John 14:13). "If ye abide in me, and my words abide in you, ye shall ask what ye will, and it shall be done unto you" (John 15:7). Taking God at His Word, she claimed the restoration of her home and family.

Unable to eat, Mama lost forty pounds in a few weeks. She refused to leave the house or receive visitors. It was as if all her strength and energy were directly channeled into a spiritual battle.

Genesis 32 tells about Jacob, who wrestled all night with a man and refused to release him until he received a blessing. It was with this kind of tenacity that Mother laid hold of heaven on behalf of her husband, refusing to let go until she saw some kind of breakthrough.

On a Wednesday night about six weeks after Daddy had

left, Mama stood in the living room, staring out the window into the distance of her own thoughts. She felt totally drained beyond tears or words.

In the quiet of that moment a voice spoke, saying simply, "I have heard. It is done."

Now Mama was not accustomed to having God speak so distinctly to her, and it took a moment to fully comprehend what she had heard. But the comfort and joy that flooded her soul convinced her of the reality of what had just happened.

Laughing and crying, she rushed to call Papa who was at Wednesday night prayer meeting, insisting they call him from the platform. "Daddy, Bob's coming home!"

For the next few days Mama's feet hardly touched the ground. She lived in a constant state of expectancy, believing that at any minute the phone would ring or the door would open, and it would be Daddy. And so it was with a light step and a slightly pounding heart that she answered the door bell the next Saturday afternoon.

"Are you Lorraine Pierce?" a strange, little man asked.

"Yes."

"This is for you." Without another word, he handed her a white envelope and walked away.

Papa heard the cry all the way in the kitchen. He found Mama collapsed on the floor, holding her stomach as if she had just been kicked, and hysterically crying "No, no!" over and over again.

Picking up the crumpled piece of paper, Papa read the court summons. Daddy was suing for divorce.

As he gently carried Mama to the couch, Papa helplessly grasped for words of comfort. As hard as it was to understand, perhaps this was God's answer, he thought.

The court date neared, and Mother and Daddy still had not seen or talked to one another. All communication had been between their lawyers. Both attorneys were highly sympathetic and truly desired to see the young couple reconciled. And so, when Mama requested to see Daddy just one time before going into court, it was arranged.

THE CENTER DAYS

The first few minutes of the meeting understandably were stiff and uncomfortable. After a few awkward attempts at discussion, the lawyers gave my folks some time alone.

Kneeling in front of Daddy's chair, Mama took his hand and looked him straight in the eye.

"Just tell me one thing. Do you love me?"

Daddy's answer was unhesitating. "Yes."

"That's all I need to know. We'll make it."

"You don't understand. I've changed. I don't believe the way you do any more," Daddy said in anguish. His words revealed the devastation of soul the enemy had wrought in the last months.

Taking his hands in hers, Mama said, "Then I'll just have to have enough faith for both of us."

Mother and Daddy walked out of that office arm in arm, but the next year and a half continued to be a time of incredible testing. While Mama fought her battle in prayer and tried to be encouraging without appearing judgmental, Daddy continued his lonely warfare, seemingly unable to find the key that would release him from his spiritual torment.

He worked in the Los Angeles shipyards, scrupulously avoiding the church and all his old friends. Like the prodigal son about whom he had once preached, he had left his Father's house to taste of the world and had found it bitter and unsatisfying. Now he belonged nowhere. Thoughts of "going home" popped into his head, but they were quickly dismissed. "Home" seemed so far away. Once he had had it all—God's promises, a vision, a future. Now it was gone; he'd thrown it away. He'd hit the bottom, and the climb back up was too overwhelming to contemplate.

During this time Mother continued singing in the choir. Each Wednesday and Sunday night Daddy would pick her up, waiting outside in an inconspicuous spot until the service was over.

One Sunday evening in December, 1942, Dr. Paul Rood, president of the World Christian Fundamentals Association, was speaking. From her place in the choir loft Mama had a clear view of the sanctuary. Dr. Rood was well into his message when one of the side doors slowly opened and a lean young man slipped into the back row.

One by one the choir members recognized their former youth pastor. Many began weeping and praying as Dr. Rood ended his sermon and gave the altar call. Her heart bursting, Mama silently begged Daddy to respond. But as the service ended and the choir filed out, he was still sitting in the back of the sanctuary, apparently unmoved.

As Mother mechanically removed her robe, she tried not to let disappointment overwhelm her. God was still in control. She would just have to wait a little longer.

She looked up to see Ruth Buck standing at the door, her face aglow and tears streaming down her face. The Bucks were two of Mother and Dad's closest friends, and they had been faithfully praying through these difficult months.

"Lorraine, come quick. Bob's at the altar!"

Daddy knew even before he entered the building that night that God was bringing him to an unavoidable point of decision. Sitting in the back of the church he felt totally exposed, as if a spotlight were directed at him and everyone was watching to see what he would do.

"The sacrifices of God are a broken spirit: a broken and a contrite heart, O God, thou wilt not despise" (Ps. 51:17). The first move was the most difficult: stepping out into the aisle and making the long walk down to the altar to humble himself before the Lord in the presence of those he had worked with and ministered to. His feet itched to run the other direction, but his heart cried to go home.

To this day, Mama still weeps with joy at the memory of that night. Rushing into the auditorium she was stunned to find Daddy not kneeling but lying across the altar, his body racked by the gut-wrenching sobs of deep repentance.

It had been a year and a half since Mother had received the Lord's reassurance that He had heard her prayers and the work was done—a year and a half of waiting and believing and holding on. Now the promise was reality. God had

THE CENTER DAYS

proved not only His faithfulness but also His omnipotence in a seemingly hopeless situation. It was a lesson Mother would remember and draw strength from many times throughout her life.

The very next Sunday Daddy stood before the congregation to testify of God's mercy and redeeming grace, contritely asking to be received back as "a doorkeeper in the house of the Lord."

Papa stood and, embracing him, said, "Son, we have no need for a doorkeeper, but we sure need a youth pastor. Welcome home!"

> Humble yourselves therefore under the mighty hand of God, that he may exalt you in due time (1 Pet. 5:6).

Chapter 6

SEATTLE
•

Nearly two years of effective ministry followed my father's return to the Center, as God solidified and reinforced the deep work He had done within Daddy's spirit.

It was during this time that Daddy first tried his hand at filmmaking. Borrowing a friend's movie camera, he and Mother set off to interview on film thirty of the world's best-loved hymn writers. They traveled as far as Catskill, New York, to interview George Stebbins, who at ninety-nine was to die only a few weeks later. People like George Bennard and Virgil Brock were included in this little film that presented the inspiring stories behind such hymns as "The Old Rugged Cross" and "Beyond the Sunset."

The film was received so well that Daddy followed it up with one about successful Christian businessmen. From then on, his camera equipment was second in importance only to his Bible. In later years it would be an indispensable ally in depicting the great suffering and need of a world without hope.

The films completed, Daddy began to feel a new restlessness, and it soon became evident that it was God's time for Mother and Dad to move on.

They became youth evangelists for the World Christian Fundamentals Association, and they hit the evangelistic circuit once again. Newspaper ads brought out the crowds.

> "Geared to the times, but anchored to the Rock!" Hear Bob Pierce and the Sally Martin Singers at the San Bernardino Evangelistic Center, December 3–10, 1944

SEATTLE

Here tonight! One service only. Bob Pierce and Al Zahlout and his Singing Violin. . . . the Chicago Gospel Tabernacle. February 25, 1945

Great Youth Crusade! Bob Pierce and the Eureka Jubilee Singers. Over 1700 people attended the closing service of our Youth Crusade, forcing us to move to the Benson High School Auditorium to accommodate the crowd. The Youth Evangelist, Bob Pierce, and the Eureka Jubilee Singers make a great team. . . . They radiate the Spirit of Christ. Their campaign with us will live long in our memory. . . . Trinity Tabernacle, Portland, Oregon, April 29–May 14, 1945

Three-year-old Sharon especially enjoyed these months of travel. With her dark hair carefully arranged in finger curls and her bright eyes full of laughter and fun, she was the darling of everyone in her mini-mobile world. She dearly loved the Eurekas and the Sally Martin Singers. In fact, for many years her favorite doll was a black baby doll she affectionately called "Sally Martin Singer."

It was while traveling in the east that Daddy first heard about an exciting new work designed to reach youth. Youth For Christ (YFC) was just getting off the ground, and Daddy was tremendously encouraged to find other young men who shared his vision and burden to reach young people for Christ.

Attending the first YFC conference in Winona Lake, Indiana, Daddy was greatly impressed by Torrey Johnson, the organization's founder and president. Torrey's dynamic magnetism attracted a whole band of enthusiastic young followers, including Billy Graham, Cliff Barrows, and David Morken.

Shortly after his return to California, Daddy was contacted by Dr. N.A. Jepson, a Christian businessman from Seattle who had heard him speak during his youth campaign in Oregon. The Christian Businessmen's Committee of Seattle wanted to sponsor a YFC rally in their area, and they asked Daddy to direct it.

MAN OF VISION, WOMAN OF PRAYER

Seattle in 1945 was a city perpetually in motion. Huge grey troop ships floated in the harbor, waiting to transport their battle-ready cargo. And thousands of lonely, sad-eyed boys in uniform roamed the streets, desperately searching for something to take their minds off the hell into which they would soon be sent. Separated from friends and loved ones, some found refuge in the many bars and girlie shows that lined the busy streets of downtown Seattle. But others found their way to the Moore Theater, its neon marquee brightly inviting passersby to attend the YFC rallies each Saturday night. Many wandered in out of curiosity or boredom, but once inside they were hooked! The music and singing, the hand-clapping and foot-stomping fully and uninhibitedly expressed the joy of the Lord; Seattle had never seen anything like it, or anyone quite like the energetic young dynamo who kept the whole thing going.

With wit and contagious enthusiasm, Daddy endeared himself to each Saturday night crowd. He would lead them in the joyous youth choruses of the day, surprising everyone by taking his mike into the aisles to catch a few solos from the audience. When he discovered which serviceman was farthest away from home, Daddy would invite the nervous young man to the platform, hand him a telephone, and tell him to call home "on the house." An expectant hush would fall over the crowd as with a trembling finger the number was dialed and an unsuspecting "Hello?" was heard over the public address system.

"Hi, it's me, Joe." The names would change, but the reaction was always the same—disbelieving stammering followed by shrieks of joy as, for a few minutes at least, a family was reunited by phone. After the first heartwarming words, the young man would be led backstage to finish his conversation.

The evenings always culminated in a powerful presentation of the gospel. Many times Daddy would speak; other times a guest speaker would deliver the message.

Daddy brought many up-and-coming young speakers, such as Torrey Johnson, Billy Graham, and Merv Rosell, to

SEATTLE

the Northwest. In order to make it financially practical for these men to make the long trip, Daddy would have to arrange a week of meetings in surrounding towns. As a result, my parents spent two or three weeks each month traveling the "Pierce Northwest Evangelistic Circuit." Unwilling to do anything halfway, Daddy would borrow a truck, load it with sound equipment, a portable organ, and other musical equipment, and recruit local musicians to provide appropriate music for the services. The three- or four-car caravan would then make a whirlwind tour of the smaller cities between Seattle and Vancouver, Canada.

Daddy thrived on the hectic schedule, finding the constant demand on his mind and body an exhilarating experience. God was stretching him, challenging him to grow and develop in areas of leadership and creativity, and each progressive step brought blessing and new awareness of even greater possibilities.

But Mother, although she never missed a Saturday night rally and always accompanied Daddy when he traveled, found it difficult to define her position in the midst of the continuous hubbub. Daddy was constantly stepping up the pace, and Mama's efforts to keep up with him left her breathless and with a feeling that in some indefinable way she was losing him.

Chapter 7

A SEASON OF NIGHT

Mother and Dad had been in Seattle a little over a year when Daddy excitedly announced he had been asked to become YFC's Vice-President-at-Large. Mother was greatly impressed by the title until she learned what "at-large" meant—travel, travel, and more travel!

Sharon was ready to start school, and Daddy felt that since he would be gone so much of the time it would be best for his girls to be close to Grandpa Johnson. So the family prepared to move back to Los Angeles.

Several hundred people attended a lovely farewell dinner to express their love and gratitude. Mother knew she was expected to say a few words, a prospect that always left her palms sweaty and her throat dry. But this particular night her nervousness seemed much greater than usual.

As the dinner plates were cleared and the speeches began, Mama felt her body begin to tremble. Her legs were shaking so violently that she began to doubt they would hold her weight. She sat rigidly in her chair, asking the Lord to keep her from falling flat on her face when she stood.

And God was faithful. When the time came, Mother stood and graciously expressed herself, appearing perfectly poised and confident before the large banquet room of people. Never before had Mother experienced such an extreme attack of nerves, but any alarm she might have felt was immediately lost in the flurry of moving. Daddy was scheduled to start traveling immediately, school was starting, and there simply

A SEASON OF NIGHT

was no time to hunt for a house. So when someone told them of a house for rent, they took it, sight unseen.

The little house in Glendale proved to be old and badly in need of repair. The roof leaked, the pipes roared, and the floor was partially eaten through by termites. Mama could see she had her work cut out for her.

Daddy had barely unloaded the furniture when he was off for an extended tour of the States. In his new position, he was responsible for visiting the many YFC rallies across the country and for organizing one-shot rallies to introduce YFC to cities that had none. Since he was dependent upon these meetings for the financial support of his family, he wanted to waste no time.

Mother put Sharon in school and tackled the enormous job of redecorating. Each night she fell into bed exhausted from the day's vigorous activities. Endowed with her mother's fastidious nature, Mama demanded perfection. She was unwilling to paint an unscrubbed wall or settle for anything less than an exact match between the curtains and the wallpaper. This was Mother's first opportunity to express her own style and flair, and she was determined to provide Daddy with a home he could be proud of.

In today's world of amateur psychologists and soap-opera watchers, it would not be hard to recognize the warning signals. Mother's frantic activity fairly screamed of the hysteria building up inside her. She lost herself in work, subconsciously refusing to deal with her growing panic.

Ever since her youth, when she had watched her parents' relationship deteriorate and her family tear apart, Mother's greatest fear was of being left alone. When she married Daddy she had equated his hunger for adventure with his youth. She was happy to share the excitement of travel and change until he found his niche and settled down to raising a family and pastoring a nice church somewhere.

But Daddy's drive to keep on the go seemed to increase, not lessen.

MAN OF VISION, WOMAN OF PRAYER

There was the time when they were still in Seattle and Sharon had just come down with the measles. In those days this was not something to be taken lightly, and Mother was understandably taken aback when Daddy announced he was leaving for Alaska. He had an invitation to speak, and he felt it would be a once-in-a-lifetime opportunity to take some movies.

This was but one of the many times my parents would have a serious conflict of priorities. Mother felt he had no business leaving her alone with a sick child. Daddy felt the opportunity too great to pass up. After some heated arguments, Daddy packed his camera equipment and flew off, leaving Mama angrily hoping his camera would freeze in the snow!

The situation worsened when Sharon developed complications, and Mother was left to face several very difficult days alone. But once again God was faithful, making His loving presence known by sending a young girl Mama hardly knew to the door to say she "just felt led" to offer her services while Daddy was away.

In retrospect, it is easy to see how God used situations like this one to gradually prepare Mama for the far greater testings of the future. Hindsight also often discloses that God turns even those things that appear foolish to His glory and purpose. After seeing the film Daddy took in Alaska, a young man named Willis Shank decided to repeat the journey Daddy had made. Flying in some of the very same planes, he was killed in a crash.

His tragic death brought attention to the fact that the thousands of Eskimos scattered across that icy wasteland had no adequate medical care. A wealthy Seattle businessman felt called to supply a hospital ship, and for years the *Willis Shank* sailed the Alaskan coast, bringing doctors and medicine to otherwise isolated areas.

It was the first time Daddy had left Mother for the sake of ministry when she really needed him, and the experience had shaken her. Now with his new position, separations were inevitable; the future promised nothing but one good-bye

A SEASON OF NIGHT

after another. Mama was unprepared emotionally to cope with the situation, and the demands of the move had exhausted her physical resources. Ever watchful, Satan grabbed the opportunity to strike a crippling blow.

The morning sun streamed through the bedroom window, bouncing off the freshly painted walls and dancing on the rose-covered ceiling. Somewhere in the distance, Mother heard the insistent voice of her young daughter announcing that she was hungry and that if Mama didn't hurry she would miss her bus to school.

Mama had the strange sensation of being outside of her body as she seemed to watch herself get out of bed, put on a robe, and walk unsteadily into the kitchen. Pour the milk, butter the toast, wipe Sharon's mouth. Kiss her good-bye. Slam!

The sound of the closing door reverberated in Mama's ears, echoing through the house until it faded into quiet. For a long time Mama stood in the middle of the kitchen floor. Her eyes darted from one object to the next as she desperately tried to find something familiar and safe. She became aware of the loud, uneven rhythm of her palpitating heart, its broken cadence releasing unnatural surges of adrenalin into her system to produce stomach-wrenching chills of panic.

Forcing herself to move, she walked into the living room. Sitting at the piano, she timidly touched first one key, then another, relieved to hear the notes ring out strong and clear. Next she moved to the typewriter, seeing each letter typed as irrefutable proof that she was a part of the world from which she felt so distant.

For the next couple of days Mama attempted to carry on, finding great comfort in Sharon's presence. But finally the last string snapped, and she could go on no longer. Calling Papa, she was barely able to make herself understood as she brokenly sobbed, "Help me, Dad. I'm sick."

Only those who have actually experienced an emotional breakdown can truly understand the agony of the distant no-man's-land into which one is exiled. After a thorough physical examination, the doctor could find nothing to explain Mother's strange symptoms. Thirty years ago, little was known about this kind of illness, and each person was left to fight his own way out of the pit.

Finally, against Mama's wishes, Papa sent for Daddy. He came home to find Mother frightened, disoriented, and unable to leave her bed. At a loss as to what to do, Daddy simply stayed close for the next several weeks, trying to be encouraging and constantly covering Mama in prayer.

During the nightmarish days that followed, Mama found God's Word the only antidote for her sickness of fear. Drawing strength from 2 Corinthians 10:5, she attempted to cast down "imaginations, and every high thing that exalteth itself against the knowledge of God, and [bring] into captivity every thought to the obedience of Christ." Philippians 2:5 said that she could have the mind of Christ, a comforting thought for one whose own mind was being used against her. And Isaiah 43:23 promised: "When thou passest through the waters, I will be with thee; and through the rivers, they shall not overflow thee: when thou walkest through the fire, thou shalt not be burned; neither shall the flame kindle upon thee. For I am the LORD thy God, the Holy One of Israel, thy Savior."

During this time and through the ensuing years, God also used the daily devotional *Streams In The Desert* to minister to Mother's heart. So often it seemed Mrs. Cowman had written the day's message with Mama in mind, and the book was a constant source of encouragement.

After several weeks of complete bed rest and quiet, the fog began to lift ever so slowly. Mama still couldn't face the world outside her bedroom door, but her body no longer felt like a throbbing exposed nerve, and she could tolerate an occasional visitor.

It was during this stage of her recovery that Torrey Johnson and another YFC evangelist, David Morken, came to see Mama. Seating themselves on either side of the bed, Torrey explained that YFC had been invited to hold a series of youth

A SEASON OF NIGHT

campaigns in China. It was an extraordinary opportunity, one that in the uncertainty of the times might never come again. David would be heading the team. With a deep breath, Torrey continued. "Bob refuses to even ask you himself. He knows how hard it would be for you to let him go. But I feel very strongly that he's one of God's men for this mission, and I'm taking it on myself to ask you. Please, Lorraine, release Bob to go to China!"

Mama's eyes registered the shock and disbelief she was feeling. Surely the man wasn't serious! She realized that no one truly understood the hell she had been through, but God did, and she was certain He would never ask her to face this alone. No! Absolutely not! It was too much to ask. This was man speaking, not God!

The next few days Mother agonized over the decision she had made. She knew Daddy wouldn't go without her consent, and she felt perfectly justified in not letting him go. Yet she had no peace inside.

Unable to shake the uncomfortable feelings, she spent hours in prayer, searching her heart and waiting before the Lord. Finally, deep within her spirit, she felt God's answer. "Trust Me. Let Me have him and let Me show you what I will do for you."

Two weeks later, Daddy left for China.

Chapter 8

CHINA—ONE STEP AT A TIME

Passport, visas, shots, last-minute shopping and packing . . . the next two weeks flew by in a blur of activity.

Daddy needed to meet David Morken in Shanghai by the second week in July for a series of meetings in the prestigious Moore Memorial Methodist Church. In order to pay his way, YFC agreed to give Daddy some money from a rally they were holding at the Hollywood Bowl. As the end of June approached and the promised money didn't materialize, Mother agreed that Daddy should use their small savings to fly as far as Hawaii. Daddy was sure that by that time YFC would be able to wire him more funds.

Honolulu, Hawaii, June 26, 1947

My most precious lover,

Just a note to tell you I love you with all my heart, and have never been so proud of you in the Lord; you are a better soldier than I.

I am already lonesome and homesick, but am conscious of His blessed presence, and have been praying all day that you may be strengthened and helped too. I know He will not fail.

When I came to check in at Pan American here, one of the girls came up to me and said, "Aren't you a youth worker?" I said, "Yes." She said, "I saw you in Nome, Alaska, when you came in there to speak." I was amazed that she remembered, but it goes to show you never know what impressions you make or who is watching you. . . .

CHINA—ONE STEP AT A TIME

Tell my darling Sharon how much Daddy is thinking of her and praying for his little Christian daughter constantly too. Give her a hug and kiss for me.

As soon as I get some money, I'll send you some. . . .

I love and adore you,

Bob

Stranded on the islands, Daddy called Wilbur Nelson to ask when he could expect some money, only to learn that the expenses of the rally had devoured every penny, and there was no money to send. I'm sure Daddy entertained a few second thoughts.

Finally Wilbur was able to send Daddy enough money to reach the Philippines. Landing in Manila, Daddy was warmly greeted by John Sycip, president of a Philippine airline and also YFC's business representative in the Philippines. Boarding one of Mr. Sycip's planes, Daddy then flew six hundred miles south of Manila to the island of Eohol. In a letter dated July 4, 1947, he enthusiastically described his welcome—by fifty delegates—to one of the most famous mission hospital communities in the Philippines. Speaking first to the students and faculty of a nonreligious college and then to a packed auditorium "with government officials all over the audience," God gave him favor with the people and liberty to speak the gospel. "At the invitation, even knowing the Catholic officials were watching them, 16 were gloriously converted and over 50 more came on the call for consecration to service. So we're praising God."

The Philippines gave Daddy his first real taste of the "pleasures" of overseas travel and introduced him to the beauty and fascination of the new world he was entering.

> As usual, I'm lying on the cot, "sweating bucketfuls." Man, the humidity! And the bugs! Mosquito bites all over me! And ants, and a thousand other little bugs and flies I never saw before. And lizards! Crawling on the walls and going "tick-tick-tick" all night long.

MAN OF VISION, WOMAN OF PRAYER

But in it all, God has been very near, and the people most hospitable and anxious to do for you.

This country is fabulous. It's just like a dream. The people actually live everywhere here in the little thatched houses on stilts. And as I write now, across the street children play under the house, with a pig and a cow sharing the same shade with them. Of course, I'm getting all the pictures I can—I borrowed a movie camera for my stay here in the Philippines and am trying to get as much of a picture for you as possible.

This Monday I leave for China, God willing. I expect to be two days in Hong Kong and then fly on to meet Dave in Shanghai Wednesday at China Inland Mission there.

In the meantime, please write me! I'm so lonely, even in the midst of the crowd. For I'm different. And I miss *YOU!* I love you darling, with all my heart and pray for you constantly. Have everyone remember me in prayer.

Love to all. I'm yours eternally, loving you always,

Bob

Daddy left the Philippines with a crisp new hundred-dollar bill in his pocket, enough money to get him from Hong Kong to Shanghai. By the time he arrived in Hong Kong, the money was gone! Dropped, lost, stolen—Daddy didn't know what had happened to it.

Daddy spent the next two days doing a lot of walking and praying. There had been so many barriers to overcome and now this. The doubts came flooding in. "Lord, I'm here because I believed this was Your will. I still believe it, but right now I could sure use a little reassurance!"

Working his way through the ever-growing throng of people, Daddy was totally amazed to hear someone call his name. A young man grabbed his hand, pumped his arm enthusiastically, and exclaimed, "I thought it was you! You probably don't remember me, but I used to attend your YFC rallies in Seattle."

Daddy had dinner with that young man, talking about the

CHINA—ONE STEP AT A TIME

good old days in Seattle and the wonders of the Orient. At no time did he utter one word about the lost money or his present financial predicament. At the end of the evening the man said good-bye to my father and handed him a plain white envelope. It contained a hundred-dollar bill.

My grandfather loved to quote the old saying, "Faith steps out upon an empty void, then finds a rock beneath its feet." That's exactly how Daddy got to China—one step at a time!

While Daddy was experiencing God's faithfulness on his side of the world, Mama was receiving equally good care on hers. Although her physical and emotional battle continued, God constantly made His loving presence known through His Word, His people, and His unfailing provision.

The China meetings provided great blessings but no income, and while Daddy's needs were being met by periodic offerings from the States and other YFC funds, Mother and Sharon could not have paid the rent or put food on the table if it hadn't been for a wonderful group of Christian businessmen who believed so strongly in what God was doing through my dad that they were willing to invest in his ministry by helping to support his family. It was by this means, with Papa's occasional help, that Mother and Sharon were cared for.

During the next four months my parents kept the post office in business. My father's journalistic letters provide not only an account of God's working through his ministry and in his life during these days, but they also paint a vivid picture of a China that exists today only in history books. The following letters have been edited, but the story remains intact.

July 14, 1947

China Inland Mission, Shanghai, China

Dearest Treasures on Earth,

I'm thrilled to see the power of God and to see the beauty of heaven in your letters. Never have I felt the oneness of *our* ministry as now. I feel your prayers—and oh, how I need them.

MAN OF VISION, WOMAN OF PRAYER

We have been worked almost to exhaustion. It has been hard on me because I was dumped into the middle of this humidity and heat with no period of adjustment. But God has wonderfully sustained.

I arrived here in Shanghai last Monday, with Dave preaching the first night and then being sent to the hospital for eight days rest. I've had every bit of the preaching to do. Broadcasts at 7 A.M., morning and night rallies every night in Shanghai's largest church, Moore Memorial Methodist—but God has gloriously blessed. Overflow crowds every night and about 900 saved these first six days. The missionaries seemed thrilled, saying they've never seen such results among youth here. And the crowd is 90% youth too. Glory!

Oh Sweetheart, this pace is killing—and my energy goes so fast—and everything here moves so slow—it seems my whole day is taken up going to or coming from or getting ready for meetings. But God is mightily blessing. Preached last night and God gave us over 100 again seeking to be saved. All my preaching and invitations so far have been just for salvation. And still they come. . . .

What a country! You never saw such hordes of people. Living where they happen to drop at night. Whole families—mother, children, and babies suckling at the breast—all sleeping on the sidewalks, while thousands step around them. Filth, smells, and sweat—beyond belief. Yet many live in luxury. I can't describe it all but am trying to get pictures so I can show you when I get home.

Darling Wife, I love you more than ever in all our lives. Oh, if I could only have you with me part of the time. Some of the time would be too hard as your little system and nerves couldn't take it but it is so very interesting. . . .

Soochow, July 18, 1947

My Own Precious One,

Well, here I am; out in real China for the first time. No cars on streets here; just rickshaws everywhere. A city of 150,000—one

CHINA—ONE STEP AT A TIME

of the old walled cities, the wall still standing. I am staying at the Southern Baptist compound. I am fairly comfortable but oh so lonely. . . .

The train ride from Shanghai here was interesting, through beautiful country, all looking like one big park every inch under cultivation. This is the most fertile soil in China, I guess.

Glorious meetings last night—heavy rain before meeting so only about 800 present but almost 80 conversions. Hallelujah! Many of the missionaries here are under liberal influences, so pray much. But the people are hungry, really hungry for revival. This morning's meeting was about twice as large as yesterday's and as I preached on price of revival, there seemed to be mighty conviction. Oh, do pray for us, Darling, the need is so great, the field is so large, the opportunity enlarging before us constantly. More cities pleading for us to come. When Andrew Gih and I visited Shanghai's mayor at his office the day before yesterday, he offered the city's largest auditorium seating 4,000 if we will return in September. Other pastors made the same request. So we may arrange it, as universities and schools will be in session then.

Another sidelight of Shanghai meetings: this coming Monday night the pastors are having a big welcome meeting just for the 1,000 converts of last week and they insist I return for that one night as speaker. I am amazed. You and I know how useless I am, and yet such has been the goodness of God in giving us favor and power, Praise His Name!

Wish you and Sharon could walk the mile to church with me—narrow streets, masses of humanity everywhere. Everyone here curious about the foreigner, calling the one word they know—"Hal-lo!" Look in the shops—eight-year-old boys wielding sledge hammers ten hours a day, filthy hands chopping meat, chopping vegetables, scratching open sores, back to kneading bread. Little children naked, urinating in the streets. Every mother with child suckling at breast, adorable babies. Skilled craftsmen making furniture, making metal pots, making shoes, making wicker, making clothes. Buddhist temples. Every step a rickshaw boy grunting for you to get out of the way. Every direction someone squatting with chop sticks, eating rice—oh, I give up. It's indescribable. I'm trying to capture it in the pictures, but that, too is almost hopeless.

. . . The letters I get from you are still my chief morale. I love you so much, dear; oh so very, very much.

You should see me. I'm laying on the bed, every window wide open, covered all over with red, itchy prickly heat, perspiring from head to toe. A spider the size of a dollar is crawling on the ceiling overhead, but I have never felt so needed in the Lord's work before in my life. And it is a glorious experience, all of it. Oh, pray that God may be able to continue to pour out his Spirit.

Again, kiss my adorable girl for me. Know that I have never been so constantly conscious of you both as now, praying for you, loving you, and missing you constantly. I'll write again in a day or so. I adore you.

Bob

The more Daddy saw of China, the more excited he became by the open, hungry hearts of the Chinese people.

Hangchow, August 3, 1947

My Precious Darling, My Very Own,

I love you more than I can tell and am thinking of you a great deal. Dave and I have just had a good season of prayer, and I have been praying for you—for the physical needs, for the financial needs, and just that our Wonderful Lord may be very near and very real and very precious to you.

I feel your prayers. I have been very conscious that you have been in the thick of the battle with me, and know that Heaven is going to have some glorious surprises for you when you receive your share of the rewards.

I preached in the Presbyterian Church here this morning and at the close made no altar call, yet over 50 came forward and ten were converted, while the others reconsecrated their lives or claimed other victories!

CHINA—ONE STEP AT A TIME

Dave and I have three main services a day here: 9 A.M., 4 P.M., and 8 P.M. The church is one of the largest in town, a Christian Church, and as usual we cannot get the crowd in. Last night we had about 2,000 in and many outside. Dave preached and God gave a great response. So far in China there have been over 4,000 conversions in our meetings. Hallelujah! . . .

Also Dearest, pray for *me*. When I come home I want it to be in His beauty and power. And I've asked God to do a work in my life, deeper than any ever experienced in my heart before.

It is still warm here. I'm sitting stripped and dripping perspiration. But Hangchow is one of the beauty spots of China. The hotel looks over a beautiful lake. And last night after the meeting Dave and I went out in one of the boats and looked at the full moon, and thought of our sweethearts and children.

Honey, I get so homesick sometimes.

Honey, you are not getting some of my mail. I wonder if you got my letters written and mailed in Shanghai the day before yesterday? You have no comprehension of the postal system in China. You cannot just drop a letter. You have to find the proper Post Office, have the letter weighed, pay for the proper amount of stamps and then maybe you will have it delivered but oh, Darling, keep writing frequently. Your letters do something nothing else can do for me. And the pictures! I carry them constantly and show them to everyone. The Premier of China and his whole family thought you both beautiful, and want you to come with me next time. We still have official approval and our appointment with the Generalissimo and Madame Chiang Kai-shek, but have not had the opportunity yet.

Darling, be praying much for God's revelation of Himself for our future. I don't know what He has in store, but feel He is definitely preparing something. . . . I have never been more wholly in His will than now, and am confident He will see us through.

God is blessing. This is God's time in China and *if you were here*, I don't think I would want to leave. These people are so *needy*, so hungry for the Gospel that even a nobody like me can, under God, do *so* much that I doubt if I'll ever be willing to just "go through the motions" of evangelizing in America again. But I know one thing more too. I need *you*. You *are* my partner and co-laborer together with God. And I do love you with all my heart.

And Sharon, Darling, Daddy is proud to hear that you are being a good girl. Help Mamma all you can, and keep praying for Daddy and China. I love you both more than life,

Bob

Chapter 9

GOD'S TIME IN CHINA
•

My father's reports confirm that China experienced a deep movement of the Holy Spirit during those twilight years, but he says little to indicate that he was aware of how fast the night was approaching. The powers of spiritual darkness that had ruled China for centuries had been soundly shaken, and they moved swiftly to put an end to the threat. But while the dragon of communism closed in on its victim, God continued to build and strengthen His church. He was providing China with an inner source of truth and hope against the day when the Bamboo Curtain would fall, shutting out all outside sources of Light.

Sian, China, August 8, 1947

My Dearest Beloved,

Well, here we are, way out in the middle of old ancient historic China, a thousand miles from the security of the coast. The atmosphere is different here and you feel you are really a foreigner in a foreign country. A thousand years ago, near two thousand I guess, this was the capital of China. A city of about one million in population. No cars, the most primitive elements of life. It is really quite an experience.

This has been the scene of much Communist activity. Eleven missionaries were massacred right here in this mission, the Scandinavian Alliance Mission, in 1932; and in the area just six miles from here, there have been eighty-five Christian martyrs in the last eight months. You really begin to realize some of the missionaries' sacrifices when you get out here.

Traveling any distance in China in 1947 required patience, ingenuity, faith, courage, and an iron-willed determination to get where you were going.

We were unable to reach the village for our rally last night because the rain makes the roads impassable, and we had quite a rain night before last. And last night, two of the American missionaries arrived here by train, after a trip that should have taken 24 hours and took two weeks. A bridge was washed out, and with their two-month-old baby they had to travel for days in an open roofless freight car to get here, after having to cross the river in a rickety boat, carrying the luggage with them to a train on the other side. Just before they crossed in the boat, another had capsized and drowned 40 people. And yet that little wife came into supper as though she had just run down to the store for a loaf of bread. Darling, you never saw such wonderful, heroic people as some of these doing the job for Christ out here in the pioneer spots of the world.

We had planned to go to Kaifeng next. It was there Dick Hillis was to meet us, but the rains have rendered the railroads useless, and we have no way of going. Romans 8:28. . . . For there is fighting near there. In fact, Dick Hillis' city is, or was last week, in the hands of the Communists. However, don't worry about us. We are not taking any chances, and though the nearness of the Reds sounds dangerous, it really is not because their activities around here are confined to small raiding bands, and there is a large army garrison here. So they pretty much avoid Sian at this time. . . .

Next we go back to Nanking, and then by car and chair to the mountain summer capital, Lushan. We are expecting to visit the Generalissimo at that time. . . . I am praying that God will give me the privilege of really speaking to him about spiritual things.

Well, Dearest, there is not much other news now but I love you with an up-to-the-minute devotion. You will never know what your letters and words of love mean to me. . . .

GOD'S TIME IN CHINA

Keep up your wonderful battle behind the lines for me dear, and I will try to do the same for you in your battle front there. I love you both with all my heart.

Forever,

Bob

Stopping in Nanking on his way to Shanghai, Daddy wrote explaining that the scheduled meeting with the Generalissimo had been canceled at the last minute, but that he and Dave expected to have some time with his wife in the next day or two. He then went on to describe their last meeting in Sian, where 22,500 attended.

> . . . In all probability this was the largest religious gathering in China in missionary history. The Chinese were packed in like sardines. Jammed in together with no aisles, no seats, no altar space; just one solid pack of hungry, ignorant, yet wonderful people. And they stood attentively for two hours and fifteen minutes. Dave spoke, then I spoke, and then Andrew drew the net. There was no way to call them forward, but conservatively at least two thousand responded to the invitation, raising their hands high and earnestly, repeating the sinner's prayer as Andrew led them. Oh, it was something to see. And God really works in the hearts, too. One of the pastors told us that after the last meeting some weeks ago, twenty-eight people had as a result come to his church, of which twenty-two were still coming regularly. So you see, even though we cannot get them forward, God is really doing the work. Hallelujah!

Shanghai, August 16, 1947

My Own Dear Precious Ones,

I'm very homesick and long for you both, oh so very much. You are in my mind day and night, and each of you fill my heart with love to the bursting point. . . .

Well, we had the honor of a lifetime yesterday. Dave and I had the privilege of being entertained by Madame Chiang Kai-shek in her own home here last night. She gave us almost an hour—something undreamed of by people here, and she was surely gracious. She is a woman of superb poise and charm. She is sharp as a needle, has a mind which grasps a picture in a moment. Her home here is an oriental dream, and she herself is most attractive for a woman her age. She must be 47 or so. We told her briefly about Youth For Christ and she immediately showed interest, but Dave and I were a little disappointed at her lack of real spiritual insight. She rather thinks of Christianity in terms of Christian and social betterment, I fear. But she has had some real experience with God, I believe. It is just that right now their government is in its greatest crisis. And they are thinking constantly in terms of that which will immediately help China. We tried to tell her of the power of the Gospel—and she agreed, saying that China's greatest problem was its "spiritual bankruptcy." After giving us several suggestions for the work here, I presented her with the Bible and she seemed genuinely moved, thanking me over and over again. Then Dave led in prayer and we left. I had wanted in the worst way to get pictures, but it was impossible. Well, pray with us that some of the Scriptures and the testimony we left may be used of God in their lives. She and the Generalissimo surely need prayer.

Daddy's next letter, dated August 18 from Shanghai, expressed his frustration with the Chinese postal system. It seems mail didn't travel any faster or easier than people did, and he would go for weeks without word from home. Then two or three letters might catch up with him at once.

From Shanghai it was on to Peiping, a city Daddy described as the one place in the Orient, more than all others, where he wished Mama could be with him.

. . . It is perhaps the most famous old Chinese city. Full of ancient history! And packed with the most interesting of old Chinese culture. It is the loveliest and most naturally beautiful too. And, of course, since it was the most famous capital city, it is full of beautiful palaces and temples. I have taken many color movies hoping to bring some of its loveliness to you. Also, the

GOD'S TIME IN CHINA

climate is marvelous and the mountains around remind me of southern California.

This is also the home of China's most beautiful silks, and embroidery and lacquer carved boxes, too. The delicacy and beauty of the work is exquisite. All of China's silver jewelry, loveliest vases, best silks, etc. come from Peiping. So I have done *all* my shopping here. I believe you will love everything.

God is good to us, Dearest! Staying here at the Oriental Missionary Society compound (Mrs. Cowman's work—she wrote your "Streams In The Desert") has been my pleasantest experience in China. The people are all wonderful. It has been like home. One reason is most of the missionaries are young couples and all have been in southern California at one time or another.

This is the most beautiful compound of any missionary society in China, I'm sure. Chinese architecture, beautiful landscaping, lovely chapel, and fine equipment. They are doing fine work.

But I have left the best for the last—the meetings have been glorious! And God seems to have given me unusual favor. The meetings are held in the largest church—again the Methodist. But all the churches—Presbyterian, Salvation Army, Assembly of God, Episcopalian, Plymouth Brethren, Congregational—all are cooperating. We have had hundreds standing. And best of all—over 1,000 conversions in the five days. . . .

One of the most invaluable characteristics of Daddy's letters is his faithfulness in supplying statistics. His letter goes on to relate his schedule of meetings for the day and the glorious results: Spoke at girl's high school, 900 present, 175 at altar. Boy's high school, 1,100 present, 192 converted. Preached evening service, 1,700 present, 92 first-time decisions. He concludes, "In five days God gave me 711 at the altar for conversion. *All* of the glory belongs to Him! But I know *you* have a great share, too, Darling!"

Daddy's letters constantly reflect his awareness of the daily battles Mother faced and his appreciation of the considerable part she played in his ministry.

En route to Chungking from Shanghai he wrote a letter that

MAN OF VISION, WOMAN OF PRAYER

Mother has carried in her Bible thirty-two years. It began, "To be read whenever you are discouraged."

My Very Own Sweetheart and Co-Laborer in the Gospel,

At very best, no doubt, I can only dimly imagine the heartaches, the fears, the conflicts, the loneliness, the discouragements, the desperate battles you must face again and again—alone, save for our wonderful Lord. In tears again and again I have drawn aside to cry out to God for you. I am such a poor husband, and so inefficient and ineffectual both in my ministry to my home and my Lord, that it is a constant source of wonder that either of you care for me.

But my Darling, I am thinking of you constantly, and my heart is hourly mindful of the fact that you are paying a price, making a daily consecration, bearing a cross. Our loving Savior is noting it too. And it is the fact that these struggles are not easily won which lends them value in His sight. If the price was easy to pay, it would be no proof of devotion. So, do not be discouraged because you must battle to win. "And in nothing terrified by your adversaries—for unto you it is given on the behalf of Christ, not only to believe on Him, but also to suffer for His sake." It is out of our sufferings that we begin to discover our true motives. We discover whether we are serving self, or truly serving Him for His pleasure alone. Time and again these weeks God is testing me. And I am not happy over what is revealed. Too often I find that mixed with my purpose to serve Him is some hidden serving of self. I am trying to go down. I am crying out for sanctification in its true sense.

Do not be dismayed if out of your suffering, my Precious, He prunes and digs about, sometimes painfully. I recall time and again the words you passed on to me from someone . . . "This painful experience too is from the loving Hand of God. It is the best and choicest gift His love can find to give you. If He knew a more generous token of love and care to present you, He would surely give it. This hard thing, this infirmity, this distress, this pain, is as much His *love* gift as was the richest pleasure He ever permitted you!"

GOD'S TIME IN CHINA

These words have come to me again and again. Let them comfort your heart now, my Darling, "For it is God which worketh in you, both to will and to do of His good pleasure" Phil. 2:13.

The victories out here have been the most glorious I have ever dreamed of. In Tientsin the pastors said the meeting God gave us was the greatest revival in that world-famous city in 20 years. Missionaries in city after city, noting how ordinary is our preaching, have been dumbfounded at the tremendous response and results. Old-timers again and again exclaim they have never seen the like in China. God *is* working. But there has been suffering too. The physical drain is greater than anyone can realize. But the point is, our victories are not won without wounds, even out here. . . .

. . . And so it must be with you, Dearest. You must look to our God for the compensations. I get much of the excitement of the battle. But you are earning a "crown with an eternal weight of glory." And the only thing that counts is that which is accomplished or suffered with this one single motive—*His pleasure!* The memorizing of the first chapter of Ephesians has revolutionized my thinking in these matters. Everything there is centered around "the good pleasure of His will." The motive for everything must be "the good pleasure of His will"! We do not understand what is happening, but we must rest confident "that it is God which is at work in us." And no matter what happens, "Satan means it to us for evil, but God means it to us for *good*"! And "all things are working together" . . . . I have never been so confident of God's blessing, never been so positive we are in His will. I am only anxious that we both may obtain to the full all of the God-offered advantages to be gained through whatever suffering or corrections may come our way these days.

It may well be that the greatest thing God is doing is not the glorious meetings He is giving so miraculously here in China, but is rather the work He is doing *in our own hearts.*

So, my Darling Sweetheart, "Chin up!" We are on the winning side. And I'm proud of you. Proud of your fighting spirit for the Lord. Proud of your courage in the battle. Proud of the fact that out of all the better men in the world, you love me. And I love you more and more and more, every day I live.

Yours always,

Bob

Daddy arrived in Chungking with a swollen throat and lungs so congested that he feared pneumonia. He was physically exhausted and, in his own words, the excitement had worn off.

The city of Chungking did little to lift my father's spirits. It had been heavily bombed during the war, and for the most part it still lay in broken disrepair. Only one church building was left standing, and it was there that Dave and Daddy held their meetings. The little sanctuary only seated 300, but 102 people responded the first night and 60 the next!

From Chungking it was on to Chengtu.

Chengtu, Tuesday Night, September 9, 1947

My Own Precious Darlings,

Well, this is the close of our third day in Chengtu! And what glorious days of ministry they have been! You will remember that my interpreter, Andrew Gih, and I are here alone, as Dave has gone to visit Biola School in Changsho. Andrew and I are guests here in the manse of the Anglican (Episcopalian) bishop, and have never been treated more royally. The bishop, his dear wife, and the entire staff are some of the most genuinely spiritual people I have ever met. . . .

Of course I'm tired, Dearest, but I feel your constant prayers. I'm only sorry you cannot be here to share the thrill of seeing God's work. There are some aspects you would not enjoy, however. There was no way of evading an invitation to a Chinese feast given by the Methodist pastors this evening in my honor. They are the most generous hosts in the world, these Chinese! But I doubt if you would have enjoyed it. At all their meals everyone eats with chop sticks out of a common bowl.

GOD'S TIME IN CHINA

Courtesy demands that you partake of everything. Tonight we had stewed eel, and frog legs, and sea slugs (like great big snails), together with stewed chicken, heads and legs and toenails all included in the stew. Very tasty, I must admit, seasoned wonderfully (really), and I managed to get along with my portions of each. But I did think of you as I ate, and wondered how you would have enjoyed it. I'll admit I'd rather have had a hamburger!

In my last letter I told you I was going to speak that afternoon in the great government high school in Chungking. Well, God gave us almost 500 who came out for Christ before the whole crowd! Oh, Dearest, this is the most wonderful harvest field in the world! And this is God's time! Missionaries have never seen it like this before! And the opportunities are so great, "pray ye therefore the Lord of the harvest that He will thrust forth laborers into the fields." Ask the people everywhere to keep praying for us and for me. The pace is wearing. It's hard for me to get enough rest. But "His strength is made perfect in weakness." Hallelujah! . . .

Two days later Daddy added this postscript:

We are on our way back to Shanghai to stay overnight before leaving for Hong Kong in the morning. We left Chengtu yesterday morning after a glorious climax to the meetings. One of the missionaries came to me at the close and said God had done more through our visit in three days than all the church and missionaries had done in a year. I do know God gloriously revived the whole city. New Bible classes are being founded in the universities to follow up the student converts. Some of the preachers who were on the fence of liberalities have been revived. . . . We've now had about 11,000 accept Christ! In fact, I believe it's over that figure. And they are really being followed up. They say that never in China has there been such enthusiasm over the follow-up work of personally contacting each one who accepted Christ. There is no explanation of these things except that God is sovereignly showing His power—"calling out a people here for His name." I didn't know it until the last night in Chengtu, but each service we had a group of

lepers from the leprosarium present in a side room. Several were gloriously saved. At the close I spoke to them personally. You should have seen their faces, alight with the joy of heaven.
. . .

Bible classes in the universities . . . each one who received Christ personally contacted and followed up . . . eleven thousand new converts! As I read this letter now I wonder what happened to those thousands of radiantly transformed young people. How many denied their newfound faith as soon as it became politically unacceptable? How many lost their lives refusing to be drawn back into spiritual darkness? And how many survived to become part of the underground church recent events have unearthed?

"There is no explanation of these things except that God is sovereignly showing His power—'Calling out a people here for His name.' "

Chapter 10

CHINA CHALLENGE
•

Daddy spent four months in China on that first trip, and as the end drew near Mother looked forward to his return with as much anticipation as he did. Each day had presented a fresh challenge of survival as she had slowly crept back to a semi-normal state. One week she would overcome her fear of the telephone, the next her terror of the supermarket.

These were battles she was to fight many times in the following years. And they were battles she would for the most part keep to herself, knowing that it was nearly impossible for anyone who didn't have a similar problem to understand her fears and limitations. How could she explain that although her whole life had revolved around the church, now suddenly the idea of entering a crowded sanctuary robbed her of breath and turned her knees to jelly?

Oh, people tried to be sympathetic, but when she wasn't back on her feet in a few months the situation became awkward. Even close friends were uncertain how to react. Most chose to avoid the problem, and they quietly faded out of the picture. Others decided that what Mama needed was a good pep talk. "This has gone on long enough. It's time you stop babying yourself and pull yourself together." But when it became obvious that their well-intended advice was not producing the desired results, they too backed off.

And so this was a lonely and confusing time for Mama. Her world was reduced to Sharon, Papa, and one or two good friends who had suffered similar difficulties and who knew what she was going through.

MAN OF VISION, WOMAN OF PRAYER

But although Mama had little emotional strength, she had no problem coping with Sharon's daily demands, constant though they were. Children have a wonderful way of accepting people just as they are, without pointing out their flaws and weaknesses. Mother never felt on the spot or pressured with Sharon and her little friends; rather, she found their company refreshing and most enjoyable.

One of the things Mama hated most about her illness was that it prohibited her from ministry. She was a woman with love and spiritual insight to share, and she wanted to give, but her condition seemed to make that impossible.

One day, while watching Sharon at play with a group of neighborhood friends, she had an idea. Calling the local Child Evangelism office, Mother arranged to open her home to neighborhood children. She used the Child Evangelism material and a flannelgraph board to teach the youngsters about Jesus. For years Mother was faithful to that ministry, starting a class wherever she moved and leading many precious little lives to Christ, including her own sweet Sharon.

It's lovely to me the way God tied Mother and Daddy together in ministry even in this way, sending Daddy to minister to a whole world of lost children across the ocean, and burdening Mama for the equally lost little ones in her own backyard.

And so, despite Satan's vicious attack on her nerves, it was during these months that Mother was released into a significant expression of ministry. Of course, Satan didn't rest on his laurels. He kept up a tiresome campaign of harassment in the area of finances. But in the midst of this continual warfare came wonderful times of refreshment as God made His Word alive to Mother's heart.

One day while reading in Ephesians 6, it became quite clear to Mother that the only way she could continue to release Daddy and be victorious over loneliness and constant emotional attacks was to daily "Put on the whole armour of God, that ye may be able to stand against the wiles of the devil" (v. 11). The power and reality of that Scripture verse impressed

CHINA CHALLENGE

her so deeply that for years Mother began each day by kneeling beside her bed and mentally placing the "helmet of salvation" on her head, putting on "the breastplate of righteousness," girding her loins with truth, and shodding her feet "with the preparation of the gospel of peace." Then, "taking the shield of faith, wherewith ye shall be able to quench the fiery darts of the wicked," she felt prepared to face another day.

Daddy invited Mama to meet him at Winona Lake, Indiana, and she gladly accepted. Just the thought of being with him again endowed her with an energy and confidence she hadn't felt in months. And once they were reunited, Mother's whole being relaxed. She had been obedient, Daddy had gone to China, God had richly blessed, and now her long, lonely ordeal was over. Yes sir, the next time Daddy went anywhere she was going with him! And she did.

Youth For Christ was to hold its first International Conference in Beatenburg, Switzerland, with youth leaders to come from all over the world. Mother and Daddy made the trip together, leaving Sharon with Grammy in Chicago. My grandmother had remarried some years before, and she and her new husband had both experienced deep, sincere conversions. Under Rev. Billy McCarrol's strong ministry at the Cicero Bible Church, they began giving much of their time to evangelistic work in Chicago's skid-row areas. Grammy's new relationship with Jesus had resulted in a slow but sweet reestablishing of the love relationship between Mother and her, and by this time they were keeping in close touch.

The trip to Switzerland was a refreshing break for Mother and Daddy. They saw Europe for the first time together and enjoyed some much-needed time alone. But soon after their return to the States, Daddy began talking about returning to China. He had received many invitations to return for meetings, but his main concern was a film he wanted to put together. He had taken some footage the first time out, but he felt more was needed to complete the project.

Needless to say, Mother wasn't thrilled with the idea, but

by this time she knew that asking Daddy not to travel was like telling an eagle not to fly. She also had a feeling that they were involved in some plan, some purpose designed and decided before the foundation of the world, and she knew she could not interfere with what God was doing. And so, in May of 1948, Daddy returned to China.

En route to China, Tuesday, May 18, 1948

My Dearest Precious Darlings,

As I write this we are far at sea out of Honolulu on our way to Wake Island where I hope to mail this tonight during the refueling stop. . . .

Darling, my memory of your brave good-bye and courageous strength all day Sunday has been inspiring to me. Never have I loved you so much! Never have I been so proud of you!

Keep praying for me that God may make this whole trip all He would have it to be. Let's agree together for 20,000 souls! Oh, that sounds presumptuous—but it's just that this trip must count for His purpose. Never have I felt less adequate, smaller, weaker, nor more dependent on our Lord. We must have His sovereign guidance, power, and strength. I am claiming it for you there at home. Keep claiming it for us over here.

Never forget for a moment that I adore you, I miss you, and after this trip, God willing there will be no more long partings. . . .

Shanghai, Wednesday, May 26, 1948

My Sweetest Precious Ones,

I suppose you have read in the papers about the students here in Shanghai threatening anti-American riots—several big anti-foreign rallies being held and attended by thousands of Chinese. But so far, we have seen nothing out of the way, and no one here is feeling any concern.

CHINA CHALLENGE

In the meantime, our time is taken up with photography—we've been getting some good shots in the side streets. And by the way, God worked a miracle to get my camera and film into China.

The Customs Official on our arrival impounded all my film. Next day we went to the Customs House, where they advised me that it was too much and could not be brought in. They also said any we did bring in would cost 35% duty. We had been working on the red tape about two hours when a Chinese rushed up to me bursting with cordiality. He was a fellow I met here last year—*not* a Christian. I told him of our difficulty—he immediately went to the man he had come to see at the Customs House—his warm personal friend—who turned out to be the Commissioner of Revenues! The Commissioner immediately put one of his men on the job, got my entire 10,000 feet of film through ($1,200 worth) and the duty was only $50! Here at China Inland Mission they can't believe it! Getting my camera in was also a miracle—the man ahead of me at Customs desk in the airport had his taken away from him. They looked at mine—(worth three times what his was), the official said, "This is evidently an old, used camera, for see how broken with age it is!" And so he let it through! Another miracle. . . .

Kunming, May 31, 1948

My Most Precious Darlings,

Well here we are at the end of our first city-wide campaign, and how our God has blessed and answered prayer! The city is 200 miles inland from Shanghai—it is the end of the Burma Road—a city of over a half million people. The meetings were held in the city's largest movie theater seating 1,500. We held two meetings nightly, one at 6 P.M. and the other at 8, and night after night more were turned away than could get in! The first night I preached the crowd was so great, those turned away almost started a riot and three people were injured, although not seriously. Police, with fixed bayonets, guarded all the doors every service after that—and in the five nights 1,300 people were at the altar for salvation. Hallelujah! . . . Mission leaders said that

MAN OF VISION, WOMAN OF PRAYER

probably more souls were saved in this campaign than in all the past twenty years in Kunming! Praise God! . . .

Shanghai, Monday, June 7, 1948

My Precious Beloved,

Well here I am back again back in Shanghai. . . . And God is continuing to bless. We spent two days up in Kuling—and I do mean up. But what an experience. You go out about eight miles from the city of Kiukiang to the foot of some of the most rugged mountains you ever saw, and then get in sudan chairs—a chair with two long poles, one fastened on each side—and then six coolies carry you almost straight up the mountain side for six miles—along a trail carved out of almost solid rock, with sheer precipices which drop for thousands of feet straight down around you on all sides. The trail is not over four feet wide most of the way, and often on a turn your seat is swung out over sheer nothingness! Oh boy! What a sensation. However, it was more than just an experience, for from the top of those mountains you see some of the most lovely scenery in the world. It is here that you discover that the strange paintings you have seen the Chinese do are not imaginary, but are actually existent— waterfalls, streams, stunted trees, rocky peaks and all.

Kuling is so famous that in spite of the chair ride, it is the summer capital of China and the Chiang Kai-sheks make it their summer home. Which brings me to one of the wonderful privileges God gave me there. I was invited to speak at the high school there and we had a great time. Among those present were some generals and top officials. As a result I was invited to preach at a specially called meeting in the Chinese Church. When I arrived at the church, the people of the community were slow in coming because the time announced was a little too early for them to get away from their work, etc. So when the captain in charge of Chiang Kai-shek's bodyguards arrived and the church was only partly full, he visited with me a few minutes and then suddenly disappeared. I was just getting ready to preach a little later, when in comes the captain with his entire company of soldiers marching behind him! He had gone back to quarters, commanded the men to fall in, whether they wanted to or not, marched them to the church, packed out the auditorium for me, and God gave me 19 of them at the altar to be saved, including the captain. Hallelujah! . . .

From Shanghai it was on to Hangchow, where three hundred more people received Jesus in four days' time. But while the great number of young people receiving Christ was cause for rejoicing, their decision to follow Jesus was not without sacrifice.

. . . In each of our meetings, young people are getting saved at the cost of being thrown out of their homes by their Buddhist parents. With the boys it's bad enough, but with these young girls it is tragic. It would break your heart to talk with them as they bravely pour out their troubles through tears, all the time purposing, nonetheless, to live for Christ at any cost! These are not isolated cases. We have had several of them. So pray for God's provision for them.

It was during this second trip that Daddy visited a mission school and orphanage run by a group of German sisters in a small village close to the Tibetan border. While viewing the facility, Daddy's attention was drawn to a forlorn little figure, her razor-thin body hunched resignedly at the bottom of the cold, stone steps. Although the child couldn't be more than nine or ten, her gaunt little face and coal black eyes reflected a lifetime of hardship and pain.

Deeply touched, my dad asked one of the sisters about her.

"Oh, she comes and sits there every day. She wants to come to school. But we have no room." The sister wasn't unfeeling in her response, but the ease with which she seemed to accept the situation irritated my dad.

"Surely one child won't make that much difference," he reasoned. "If she wants to come so badly, couldn't you make room for just one more?"

The sister turned sad, searching eyes on my father. Her voice was tightly controlled as she patiently explained, "We have made room for 'just one more' time and time again. We already have four times the number of children we were originally prepared to care for. We have stretched our food as far as it will go. I myself am feeding three others out of my own rice bowl, as are all the other sisters. If we don't draw the line somewhere, there will not be enough rice to keep the children we already have alive. We simply cannot take one more child!"

The brutal, ugly reality of the situation filled Daddy with indignation. "That's crazy, ridiculous! A child can't come asking for help and be turned away at the door. Why isn't something being done?"

With one sweeping movement the sister picked the little girl off the ground and thrust her into Daddy's arms. "What are *you* going to do about it?"

For a brief moment Daddy was taken aback by her forthright question. He knew he could dig in his pocket and give the sister the money it would take to support that little girl until he could send more. And this is exactly what he did.

But Daddy realized there was a far more important principle involved. Many of us self-righteously cluck our tongues over all the suffering and injustice "they" allow to happen in the world, while we place ourselves somewhere outside that circle, in a safe place of unaccountability.

Jesus said, "Go *ye* into all the world," not "send them." The whole point of the story of the Good Samaritan is that man has a natural tendency to avoid the unpleasant, depending on someone else to clean up the world's messes. But Jesus said, "I was [hungry], and *ye* gave me meat: I was thirsty, and *ye* gave me drink: I was a stranger, and *ye* took me in: Naked, and *ye* clothed me: I was sick, and *ye* visited me: I was in prison, and *ye* came unto me. . . . Verily I say unto you, inasmuch as *ye* have done it unto one of the least of these my brethren, ye have done it unto me" (Matt. 25:35,36,40, italics mine).

Long after Daddy continued his journey, the sister's words rang in his ears. "What are *you* going to do about it?"

Chapter 11

THE WRONG DIRECTION

Bob Pierce was never the same after his trips to China. In one of his letters he wrote, "These people are so needy, so hungry for the Gospel that even a nobody like me can, under God, do so much that I doubt if I'll ever be willing to just 'go through the motions' of evangelizing in America again." Those words did not reflect unconcern for this nation's spiritually lost; rather, they expressed his shock and outrage that such extreme suffering and spiritual darkness could go unchallenged.

I believe my father was a man of destiny, designed and fashioned by God to do a specific work. His compassion, energy, enthusiasm, strong will, imagination, temper, gentleness—all that he was, was carefully blended and seasoned to prepare him to see and respond.

Picking his way through China's crowded, filthy streets, he didn't see a faceless mob of subhumans who come from nowhere, who fight all their lives merely to exist, and who then finally lose the battle and fade into nothingness, to be replaced by other equally faceless, hopeless beings. Daddy saw people—mothers, fathers, children—human beings who love and care and feel as we do, people trapped in the naked ugliness of a world without God.

With each passing day he found himself more inextricably involved, unable to simply observe from a safe distance. My father went to China a young man in search of adventure. He came home a man with a mission.

Upon arriving home, Daddy immediately set out to do

something about the needs he had seen. Armed with the film he had taken, he traveled from church to church, proclaiming, "This is the reality of life for half the world's population—hunger, sickness, filth, poverty, death, topped off by total spiritual destitution." Then he would close with the razor-sharp challenge that still echoed within his own heart. "What are *you* going to do about it?"

From the content of his letters, I'm sure Daddy intended to go back to China. But within weeks of his return to the States, the Communists overthrew the government, forced the missionaries to flee, and closed the Bamboo Curtain. I can only imagine his feelings of disappointment and confusion as a seemingly wide-open door was suddenly slammed shut in his face.

In an attempt to regain a sense of direction, he threw himself back into Youth For Christ, taking the temporary directorship of the Los Angeles rally. The job gave him an opportunity to be at home with Mother and Sharon, but compared to Shanghai and Peiping, Los Angeles had all the zip of flat Seven-Up.

One day Daddy got an inspiration. Each year the famed Hollywood Bowl held an Easter sunrise service. Why not do something similar at the Rose Bowl in Pasadena?

It was just what he needed—a project to sink his teeth into. He anticipated a mighty work of the Holy Spirit as great as any he had seen in China! With the energy and imagination of Cecil B. DeMille producing *The Ten Commandments*, Daddy set to work planning an impressive program that would insure a large turnout. Movie stars, Ralph Carmichael and his orchestra, radio spots, billboards—each day he had a new idea to explore or a new problem to overcome.

Finally the day came, and as the Easter morning sky gradually blushed from a whisper of pink to a deep, dusty rose, cars lined up for six miles as twenty thousand people inched their way into the Rose Bowl parking lot.

Only God knows why things happened the way they did. Daddy may have had a tendency to get carried away with his

THE WRONG DIRECTION

own sense of style and his insistence on professionalism. Certainly the program was planned not only with great care but with much prayer. And God received his offering, allowing this Easter sunrise service to become a Pasadena tradition for over twenty-five years.

But when the altar call was given on that Easter morning, not one person responded. And when the offering was counted, Daddy found himself $10,000 in debt.

The Rose Bowl fiasco was a staggering blow, and it marked the beginning of another walk through the valley for my parents. The initial sting was so painful that Daddy disappeared for a few days, unable to face his family and friends. When he finally surfaced, Mother whisked him off to Palm Springs to lovingly comfort and encourage him and to help him sort through his feelings. His anger needed to be faced, and the feeling that God had let him down had to be confronted and confessed before healing could begin.

Palm Springs provided my folks with a much-needed rest. But the fiery darts of the enemy were poised and ready, waiting to take advantage of Daddy's weakened condition.

In the summer of 1949, Daddy received an invitation from the Kilbournes, Oriental Mission Society (OMS) missionaries he had met in China, to come to Korea. Daddy's immediate response was positive, partly because of his memories of China, but also because a deep stirring within his spirit told him he was supposed to go.

On the other hand, Mother had no such stirrings, and she seriously questioned the necessity of the trip. She had just discovered she was pregnant with me, and she didn't relish the idea of being left alone for an indeterminate period of time without any reliable income or the support of Daddy's presence.

But the conviction that he was called to go outweighed Daddy's sense of obligation to his family, and despite Mother's objections he left on a YFC tour of speaking engagements, hoping to raise money for his trip. Torrey

MAN OF VISION, WOMAN OF PRAYER

Johnson had promised to help him make some money contacts after the annual Winona Lake conference.

Angry, hurt, and unable to cope with her feelings, Mother escaped to the next-door neighbor's as Daddy prepared to leave. Later she discovered a note written on the back of an envelope, dated 1949, 2:40 P.M.

Darling,

I love you far more than my own life.

Floyd tells me you do not want to be here as I leave. I shall be back soon. Please love me.

I will keep you informed by letter as to what happens these next few days. In the meantime, I will not phone you if you do not want me to. As you know, I'll be at Winona through next Friday, and at Minneapolis on the next Saturday.

I have only five dollars, so will mail you money after tonight's meeting.

Forever yours,

Bob

Two weeks later he was back, frustrated and deeply discouraged. YFC's most effective fundraiser was now unable to raise the money he needed for himself. A small amount had been pledged in different meetings, but it wasn't enough.

First the Rose Bowl, now this. Daddy sat like a deflated balloon on the living room sofa.

"But I feel I'm *supposed* to go," he said in a voice heavy with weariness.

I'm beginning to think God allowed many of these early points of crisis for the purpose of knitting my parents more closely together. In the end, it was my mother who got the rest of the funds Daddy needed. Still dreading the separation but sensitive to the signs of God at work, she got the money from a friend. Mama's only request was that Daddy return as soon as possible.

Things started to go haywire the day Daddy announced he was going to Korea by way of Paris. For reasons I have not

THE WRONG DIRECTION

been able to ascertain, his camera was in a repair shop there, and he needed it for his trip.

Mother quickly pointed out he'd be going in the wrong direction. It would probably cost less to buy a new camera than to fly to Paris. But Daddy was adamant and off he flew.

Paris proved troublesome from the very beginning. When he arrived at his hotel, Daddy discovered his reservation had been lost and no rooms were available. However, he was able to locate a small room at another hotel.

Next, he found that the only person who knew where his camera was no longer worked where he could reach her. It took two days to track her down. Finally, camera in hand, Daddy prepared to leave for Korea by way of Cairo and Bombay . . . "as soon as the camera is cleaned and fixed."

A letter dated August 6 begins: "Boy, is Paris a jinx!" First, the camera repair was delayed ("something about there being no electric power at the repair plant"). Then he was put flat on his back with the Parisian version of Montezuma's Revenge. Nauseated, weak, depressed, Daddy wrote on August 11, "I have to 'grow up,' I guess, but somehow it's always hard for me to tell you when things are going rough. Each day . . . I've been sure I would be better and on my way. . . . But, Darling, I've really had a time."

He goes on to describe repeated problems with his camera, and his discovery that in order to take film into India he would need to put up a cash bond. Everywhere he looked there were problems and his sense of isolation increased as the days passed and he had no word from home. For while Daddy sat delayed in Paris, Mother was sending her letters on to Bombay.

His last letter ended: "When I don't hear from you, it's hard on me not to know how you are feeling and if all is well with you and Sharon. I'm praying daily that all is well. . . . In the meantime, I have been trusting God to somehow see us through. *And get His job done!*

"Oh, how I hope you've written so I'll have a letter in Bombay."

Daddy never got to Bombay to receive the letters Mama

wrote. One day his letters to her stopped coming. Only he could explain just why and how the bottom dropped out, but somehow he lost contact with "homebase" once again.

In the meantime Mother waited at home, her concern approaching panic as the days passed and Daddy's silence continued. Assuming he had gone on to Bombay, she finally wired the American embassy there to see if her letters had been picked up. But before she received an answer, a friend called to say Dad had been seen in Paris. An acquaintance had run into him in a camera shop. Their conversation had been awkward and brief, but the message had come through loud and clear. He had given up, and he wasn't coming home.

I know it's hard to understand how the author of the letters you just read could find himself in such an ungodly predicament. But then, why were Adam and Eve compelled to do the one thing God told them not to do? How could the children of Israel rebel against God and build an idol in the wilderness after witnessing the parting of the Red Sea and being fed every day by manna from heaven? And how could David—a man after God's own heart—stoop to such treachery and deceit to obtain Bathsheba as his wife? David battled the same temptations and weaknesses we all encounter and lost more than one spiritual skirmish during his lifetime.

I don't know why God allowed these painful experiences. I do know God is not dependent upon our perfection to get His work done; rather, we are dependent upon Him to work wholeness and health in us so that His Spirit can work through us in purity and power.

Perhaps God was giving Daddy some rein to remind him of his own fallibility and to refresh his awareness of the source of his strength and ministry.

"God gently leads His children along. Me, He *yanks!*" Daddy used to candidly observe. No one was more aware than he that his iron will constantly needed breaking and humbling before the Lord. And God continued to yank and pull and push and chastise throughout Daddy's life, because deep in his heart he wanted God's way.

THE WRONG DIRECTION

And God was committed to him. One of my dad's favorite verses was Philippians 1:6, which says we can be confident that the work of grace God has begun in our lives will be continued until its completion, when we see Jesus face to face. Aware of his own weakness, Daddy depended on that promise. As a child, I often heard my father pray, "Lord, I give You license to interfere in my life any time You see me going the wrong direction. Slam doors, knock me down, do whatever You need to do, but *have Your way."*

And God did. But sometimes He used dramatic and frightening methods to do it!

For the second time in her life, Mother entered into spiritual travail. The news that Daddy wasn't coming home confirmed her worst fears and left her once again with no recourse but prayer. Spending hours on her face before God, Mama reminded Him of His many promises. The growing life within her was a constant reminder of the love she was in danger of losing. Her emotional buffers weakened by her physical condition, despair would engulf her at times, leaving her sobbing wordlessly before the Lord depending on Romans 8:26: "We know not what we should pray for as we ought: but the Spirit itself maketh intercession for us with groanings which cannot be uttered."

Finally, the intensity of her spiritual travail threatened to bring on physical labor. She began cramping, and Papa rushed her to the doctor.

After giving her medication and ordering complete bed rest, the grim-faced doctor took Papa aside. "Better get Bob home fast, or she'll lose that baby!"

Papa succeeded in cabling to Daddy in Paris. The realization that Mama might lose her baby was a big enough "yank" to bring him home, but the problems and doubts came with him. All of us at one time or another have experienced alienation to some degree from someone we love. Communication breaks down, barriers go up, and suddenly two people who have shared the deepest intimacy have nothing to say to each other . . . no common ground. And so it was with my folks. Satan had succeeded in placing them on either side of a raging river of hurt, accusation, and misunderstanding. Neither dared to step out too far for fear they would be swept away by the current.

There is no dramatic climax to this portion of the story. It's like healing. Sometimes instantaneous miracles occur, and other times there's a slow, gradual period of recovery. Both are legitimate examples of God's love and power to heal. One simply takes longer.

As the next months passed, Daddy inched his way back into a comfortable relationship with his heavenly Father. The closer he got, the better things were with Mother.

In the meantime, the two did their best to reassure Sharon. At eight, she was keenly aware of the fact that things were changing, and although she found ready asylum in the innocence of her youth, her ear was constantly tuned to the tic, tic, tic of the emotional bomb she hoped would never go off.

Christmas was coming, and since Daddy hadn't worked for a while the cupboard was pretty bare. Sharon had excitedly asked Santa for a bicycle, but there was barely enough money to pay the rent that month.

Daddy, still in the midst of a spiritual dearth, declined invitations to speak. He was unwilling to step back into what had become a hollow image, although he did agree to speak at a Salvation Army mission in downtown Los Angeles, explaining he felt he could relate to a congregation of "down-and-outers."

Christmas morning dawned to reveal a shapely little Christmas tree bravely displaying a scattering of balls and a few small packages carefully placed beneath its boughs. Sharon entered the living room with the studied cool of an eight-year-old, but she couldn't quite hide her disappointment when she saw no package larger than a shoe box. With a resigned little sigh, she sat down to open her presents—jacks, a box of paper dolls, new panties, a pair of socks, and of course, the annual bedroom slippers.

"Sharon, would you get my sweater out of the closet?" Mama asked ever so casually.

THE WRONG DIRECTION

As she opened the closet door Sharon froze. With eyes big as saucers she stared at a beautiful, fire-red two-wheeler. The house was filled with her delighted screams and with Mother's and Dad's equally delighted laughter. So what if the rent didn't get paid? It was a small price for their daughter's joy.

That bicycle was to come in handy soon. A recent accident had demolished the car, so when I made my appearance in January, Daddy pedaled to the hospital to visit us, balancing Sharon on the handlebars.

My arrival seemed to mark the end of Daddy's spiritual detour, but at the same time it left Mother vulnerable to one more attack of the enemy.

Two weeks after coming home from the hospital, Mother began hemorrhaging and had to be rushed to the emergency room. She had nearly died from the massive loss of blood. Once again she began the recovery process, getting back on her feet just in time to help Daddy pack.

In March of 1950, he prepared again to make his first trip to Korea, finally headed in the right direction.

Chapter 12

KOREA AT LAST!
•

My father had no special sense of destiny as he boarded that plane for Korea. He went there as he had gone to China, to preach the gospel. He had been invited by the Kilbournes, Oriental Mission Society (OMS) missionaries he had met in China who were now ministering in Korea. It had been arranged for him to hold a series of campaigns throughout South Korea with Gil Dodds, an Olympic gold medalist.

The trip went pretty much as expected. . . a mixture of great blessing and tremendous warfare.

> Taegu, Korea, Friday, March 31
>
> My Precious Darling Sweetheart,
>
> Well, the battle is on. Never have I been faced with so great an apparent opportunity. These meetings were set up on a colossal scale. Governors of each province to introduce us. Entire cities with populations of hundreds of thousands wide open to us, awaiting us, sending delegations ahead of time to confer with us.
>
> But Gil Dodds still sits in Tokyo. . . .

It seemed someone had suggested that Mr. Dodds not go to Korea because of a serious disagreement among the different church associations. Stadiums had been hired in all the large cities. Posters of Gil were placed everywhere. Receptions with the president of Korea had been arranged. Hun-

KOREA AT LAST!

dreds of churches, some with over a thousand members, had held five o'clock prayer meetings every morning for over twelve months, praying for revival and for the coming campaign.

> Taegu, Korea, Monday, April 3
>
> My Dearest Precious Treasure,
>
> How my heart is rejoicing. God is sweetly answering prayer—without my lifting a hand. Gil is here, without my asking him to come. God sent him. The serious rift between churches, while not in any sense settled, is being put aside for souls. And everyone here is aware that God is working. . . .

And so the marathon was on! A typical day for my dad might begin as early as 6:30 A.M., when he would preach to soldiers at an army camp chapel. Then he would go on to a girls' high school for a 9 A.M. meeting, a 1 P.M. high school assembly for boys, a 3 P.M. assembly for teachers and faculty, and a 7:30 P.M. evening service in the city's largest auditorium. In between meetings, Daddy might stop to visit a colony of lepers living among the tombs of a cemetery.

On such a typical day, Daddy would speak to four to six thousand people, seeing hundreds come to know Jesus. He described one invitation this way. "When I called them forward it was like a dam bursting—glorious!"

Daddy wrote that during the seven-day campaign in Taegu, more than fifteen hundred received Christ. On the last day he spoke at the Bible Institute.

> God poured out His Spirit in such power that classes were suspended for the rest of the day while students went to prayer. . . . It was glorious, but it is just the beginning. . . .

While Daddy's letters were full of the excitement of being

on the front lines, Mother's depicted the more placid life of the home front.

Glendale, California, April 12, 1950

My Dear Husband,

How thrilled I am at the wonderful reports of your meetings there. How thankful we should be every moment of living, to think God would chance to honor us with this ministry. How unworthy we are—I've spread the word as much as I have had the opportunity. Paul Meyers was supposed to announce it yesterday on his radio broadcast [*Haven of Rest*]. I wrote Bob Cook [President YFC] today, thanking him for the weekly support and also told him of your meetings. . . .

Sharon is fine. She had a bad cold which she gave to me, and I in turn gave it to Marilee. . . .

Marilee is so precious. She weighs 13 pounds and is one pound overweight. I got the buggy and she's enjoying her walks on these beautiful days. She's still so good and getting so pretty. You'll just love her. She keeps me hopping though. But that's good, for it doesn't seem possible you've been gone almost three weeks. Time really is whizzing by. . . .

From Taegu the campaign moved to Pusan, and then on to Seoul.

Seoul, Korea, April 18, 1950

My Darling, Precious Wife,

It is only 7:30 A.M. and I have just now preached to 2,000 people. God is gloriously blessing, and last night we saw our greatest altar response yet. Monday night it rained and we could only get a small part of the crowd under shelter. But our crowds have been running larger than 16,000 each night. . . .

We are all being worked to death. I have been going from 6 A.M. till midnight for days without rest. However, today and tomorrow I will only preach three times a day, and so can rest a little.

KOREA AT LAST!

Then I'll travel by train to the President's Assembly in Taegu on Friday and begin preaching there for one week on Saturday. It is a crucial hour in the church and their one hope is revival. Pray much for me. . . .

The meetings in Korea came to a marvelous climax in the city of Inchun, where they had crowds of almost fifteen thousand each of the last four nights, the largest on record. Reports from the cities where they had their first meetings began coming in, and it was not uncommon for a pastor to report as many as 250 new members in his church. When Daddy left Korea for Japan, a great crowd swarmed to the airport to see him off.

In a letter from Tokyo, dated May 24, 1950, Daddy described his first impressions of that lovely city.

> I really believe you would enjoy it here. This is the most modern city I have ever seen in the Orient. It will be a good place to "break you in," for the people are much cleaner, and the city is clean, and you can get almost any Western convenience you wish. If God wants us out here, I think this would be a good place for our headquarters.
>
> . . . I went with Dave and Tim Pietch to a great street meeting in front of one of the metropolitan railroad stations, and had one of the unique experiences of my life. I preached from the back of a truck for thirty minutes, gave an altar invitation, and between two and three hundred Japanese came forward before the thousands gathered around and knelt on the stone pavement while we prayed with them. We gave out thousands of Gospels and had the time of our lives. They do this several times a week. I thought of Harry and Mother and what a wonderful time they would have here. Testifying through an interpreter is fun, and besides the preacher, they have several testimonies each service, and give an altar call several times each night, and each time get a whole net full. You would love it!
>
> I gotta quit now, but more tomorrow. Pray for my needs here. Must have more film and am beginning to wonder about fare for

getting home. And many times each day I pray for all your needs. . . .

Your Bob

Evidently God supplied the needed funds and film, for by June 1 Daddy was home, safe and sound. Again he had incredulous stories to tell and reels of film to show. But within a matter of days, the stories were academic and the film outdated. Communist troops crossed the Chinese border of North Korea and the little country literally exploded into war.

First China, now Korea. Daddy certainly had a knack for narrow escapes! But he was deeply concerned about those he had left behind—missionaries and pastors he had worked with and had grown to love during his time there. And what was happening to the church, to the thousands of Korean Christians who would rather die than deny their faith?

Hours after hearing the news, Daddy was in Washington, D.C., pulling any string that happened to dangle within his reach and cutting through miles of red tape in order to obtain permission to return to Korea. Absolutely no civilians were being allowed into the country, but by arranging to file stories with the American Christian Press he could get in as an accredited war correspondent. The title gave him the rank of an officer and the right to fly with the military.

Upon returning to Korea, he was horrified to discover his worst fears being realized. This clipping from a December 30, 1950, Akron, Ohio, newspaper partially describes what he found.

> . . . Dr. Pierce said the Korean War already had cost 80 per cent of the Christian leaders in North Korea. The Reds have extended their exterminating tactics wherever they have gone, he said.
>
> He told of 47 leaders in Seoul tricked into assembling in one of

KOREA AT LAST!

the large churches by promises of cooperation. They have not been heard of since, said Dr. Pierce.

"One afternoon 3,000 Christians were murdered on the banks of the Han River, their hands bound by barbed wire," said the missionary.

He said 24 pastors were killed in the small town of Sonchon.

"I have testimony to this on my wire recorder," said Dr. Pierce, "from a man who escaped the Reds by burying himself for seven days under the filth of a pig pen."

He said a huge pit in Korea held 1,800 bodies of persons killed because "they went to church."

Dr. Pierce showed a one-reel color film taken in Korea on his first trip last spring. The film recorded scenes of peace that scant weeks later were embroiled in war.

"The cities you saw on film are in the headlines tonight," said Dr. Pierce. "One town was just retaken by the Reds."

"For every orphan you saw there are thousands today. Jesus cares about every dirty unwashed Korean."

He appealed for funds, for tracts to be distributed to the Koreans, for medicine needed by Korean lepers, and for the orphan children walking in the snow.

That brief clipping gives only a glimpse of the horror and pain Daddy encountered. If these homeless, terrorized, desperate people didn't become innocent casualties of the war that exploded all around them, then starvation or disease stood ready to fell them. If somehow they managed to scrounge enough to eat, they still had to contend with the icy winter.

Someone else might have been defeated at the onset by the magnitude of the need, but for my dad it was a call to battle. And one of the major weapons of that battle was his camera.

Back in 1948, when Daddy returned with his China foot-

MAN OF VISION, WOMAN OF PRAYER

age, he had formed Great Commission Films with a young filmmaker named Dick Ross. Daddy shot the film, then Dick edited it and put it together. Later, Dick and Great Commission joined the Billy Graham organization to become World Wide Pictures. But for the next several years, Great Commission worked exclusively producing films for my father. And what impact those films had! *China Challenge, Dead Man On Furlough, The Flame, This Gathering Storm*—these films went far beyond the typical missionary presentation. Dick Ross was a talented professional whose demand for perfection equaled my dad's. Each film was produced not only with a sensitivity to what God was saying, but with the high quality necessary to present that message effectively. *Dead Man On Furlough* and *The Flame* were among the first Christian films to use a scripted story and professional actors to present the gospel. And Ralph Carmichael's moving music always added greatly to the films' impact. (I've been told that today those films are studied by students of Christian cinematic history, and my father is considered by many to be an influential pioneer in the development of Christian films).

By the time Daddy got home from his second trip to Korea, Dick was already hard at work on that early Korean footage. The result was an emotion-packed film entitled *38th Parallel*.

It was one thing to stand before a group of well-fed, healthy people and describe the hell others were experiencing. It was something else to show them. The film *38th Parallel* brought people face to face with the atrocities of war and the unconscionable suffering of the innocent—whole cities constructed of cardboard and newspaper; families huddling together in a feeble attempt to find shelter from winter's savage elements; thousands of dark-eyed, helpless children, their ballooning stomachs a stark contrast to their toothpick arms and legs; a young mother tenderly embracing a tiny bundle, the child's weak cry leaving no doubt that soon her arms would be empty.

Night after night Daddy presented his appeal and people

KOREA AT LAST!

responded. The money came pouring in, and it became obvious that some kind of organization was needed. Prayerfully, Daddy sought the Lord for direction.

Chapter 13

BIRTH OF A VISION
•
In September of 1950, World Vision, Inc. became a legal corporation with Bob Pierce as president, Paul Meyers (First Mate Bob) as vice-president, and Frank Phillips (Director, Portland, Oregon YFC) as executive secretary. It was formed as a missionary aid organization to meet needs during times of crisis in the Orient, and it was headquartered in Portland, Oregon.

From its inception, World Vision sprouted arms of ministry in as many directions as there were needs. The initial priority was simply keeping people alive, so it provided food, clothes, blankets, and medicine for the thousands left homeless by the war. In 1951, Daddy became involved with the Tabitha Widows' Home, sponsored by the Yung Nak Presbyterian Church in Seoul. He was touched by the plight of these women, most of whom had lost their husbands because of their Christian witness.

One little woman with four daughters particularly touched Daddy's heart, and World Vision began sending the family monthly support. Of course, Daddy couldn't stop with just one widow, and soon World Vision was responsible for the support of the entire widows' home.

As the war progressed, another problem began to materialize—the GI baby. Considered outcasts by Korean society, many of these precious little ones were simply left to die in the streets. Some mothers tried to care for their illegitimate offspring, but when the fathers were transferred or shipped home there was no way to support the children, and

BIRTH OF A VISION

so they perished. Many were brought to one of the World Vision children's homes that began springing up throughout Korea. At first there were thousands of children and no organized method of sponsorship.

One evening in 1953, Daddy was speaking to a large congregation in the States. Afterwards, a young boy in his midteens approached my dad with a big grin and said, "You probably don't recognize me. I'm—"

With one of his world-famous bear hugs, Daddy embraced the boy. "Of course I do—you're Erv and Flo Raetz's boy." Daddy had met the Raetzes in China, where they had run a child sponsorship program for the Christian Children's Fund. "Where in the world is your father? I have a job for him."

A few months later, Ervin and Florence Raetz went to Korea to set up a child sponsorship program for World Vision. By the end of 1954, World Vision had more than 2,200 children in 27 homes in 2 countries. By 1958 there were 12,000 in 4 countries. By 1964 there were 20,000, and by 1966 there were 32,000 in 307 orphanages in 19 countries. Today, in 1980, World Vision sponsors more than 200,000 children throughout the world.

Another burden my father had was for the many pastors who were forced to flee the Communist invasion of North Korea. Having lost everything, these men bravely struggled to recover some sense of direction for themselves and for the Korean church at large. In an attempt to unify and strengthen the church, World Vision held a pastor's conference. Its success soon led to conferences in Formosa, Viet Nam, the Philippines, and eventually in other countries around the world.

World Vision supplied hospitals, clinics, leprosariums, schools, churches, medical equipment, jeeps, buses, trucks, and wheelchairs. Disaster relief, fifty-three hearing aids for students at Taegu School, payment for a missionary's surgery, life-saving blood transfusions for a sixteen-year-old girl, transportation for a missionary mother to her son's funeral—this is just a sampling of the services World Vision provided. And behind every bit of it was the compassion, the energy, and the vision of one man; in fact, to most people World Vision *was* Bob Pierce.

Within a few short years, his inexhaustible efforts made him a legend throughout the Orient. No need was too great for him to tackle or too small for him to bother with. My father never set limitations on his ministry or on God. He thoroughly enjoyed watching God accomplish the impossible and learned never to think too small. "Always leave room for the 'God space,' so that after you have done all you possibly can, God has room to work," he used to say.

During his thirty years of overseas ministry, Daddy was privileged to be a participant with some of the greatest Christian workers of his generation—people like Lillian Dixon in Taiwan, Rev. Walter Corlett and Beth Albert in India, Irene Webster-Smith in Japan, Dr. J. Christy Wilson in Afghanistan, and many others less renowned but equally important.

The missionaries loved him because he made them feel their significance. Despite his grueling schedule, he found time to get involved with their lives, to sit at their tables and know their families.

Daddy loved these people; in many ways he felt more at home with them than he did with us. They were on the same team, having a common call of God on their lives. They needed and drew strength from one another.

Between 1956 and 1964, Daddy would become one of the ten most traveled men in the world, receiving "one" and "two million miler" certificates from several different airlines. The walls of his office would be lined with awards, plaques, and testimonials for the work he had done. He would learn to be at ease with presidents and kings, as well as with lepers and jungle tribesmen.

But all this was part of the future; no one could have predicted these things when World Vision opened its tiny office in a corner of YFC's offices in Portland, Oregon.

Chapter 14

"CROSS THE OCEAN IN A SILVER PLANE"
•

I have no memories of my father during the three years we lived in Portland, partly because I was so young and partly because he was seldom there. World Vision and I were born the same year, and she was a much more demanding baby than I.

I do remember the special time each evening after dinner when Sharon, Mother, and I would kneel by the living room sofa for our family devotions. I was always allowed to pray first, and I took the responsibility most seriously. But I had little interest in any prayer other than my own, and after I had asked God to "bless my Daddy wherever he is" and "give him good souls," I was usually excused. Then Mother and Sharon could continue without unnecessary interruption.

Those times on our knees were not only spiritually significant; they also helped bind us to Daddy in a tangible, positive way. As we entered into his ministry through prayer, the family was united and solidified, and we were made conscious of the fact that we belonged to one another.

It is true I have no specific memories of my dad during that time, but I have no conscious awareness of his absence either, probably because Mother did such a beautiful job of keeping him involved and a part of us.

Shortly after we moved to Portland, my folks bought a machine which enabled them to make their own records. It was a rather tedious process, but in my mother's opinion it was well worth the trouble. In this way she could capture precious moments Daddy otherwise would have missed—

birthdays, holidays, family gatherings, Marilee singing "Jesus Loves Me" at eleven months, Sharon's first piano recital, "the cute thing Marilee said yesterday," thoughts and feelings and expressions of love that most wives share with their husbands in the quiet moments after the children are in bed but which are seldom remembered in the morning.

Of course, when Daddy was home he was the star performer. I still love to listen to the scratchy old recordings of Mother and Daddy at the piano playing "When the Roll Is Called Up Yonder." What they lacked in technique they certainly made up for in enthusiasm!

There is no denying that the Portland years were tremendously difficult for Mother. While I grew from an infant to a toddler to a "trusting three," she struggled to adjust to "marriage by correspondence." The complications after my birth had left her physically weak and vulnerable. Old fears began cropping up, and new attacks of nerves often left her hands clammy and her stomach queasy. But her greatest battle by far was against the constant, aching loneliness. During that time Daddy was gone an average of ten months each year, a statistic that would vary only slightly during the next fifteen years. This fact prompted a close friend to stop by on one of the rare days Daddy was home, to play a new song he'd just learned.

"This is *your* song," he announced, seating himself at the piano to sing.

> "Cross the ocean in a silver plane,
> See the jungle when it's wet with rain,
> Just remember til you're home again,
> You belong to me!" *

It was their song all right. Its lilting tune provided background music for Mother's more melancholy moments, for

---

* "You Belong to Me," by Pee Wee King, Chilton Price, and Redd Stewart. Copyright owned by Ridgeway Music Company, Inc. Used by permission.

"CROSS THE OCEAN IN A SILVER PLANE"

although she always took great pleasure in her children, she was a romantic at heart, and never lost the need to share life with someone special. She loved to communicate—to talk, touch, see, and hear. And although letters gave a certain release, they were poor substitutes for the sound of Daddy's voice or the feel of his arms holding her close.

There was never really any question that Daddy should go. The conviction that he was under divine commission to do exactly what he was doing far outweighed the yearnings of Mother's heart. But that didn't make it easy for her to let him go; it just made it possible.

One particularly nice thing that happened in Portland was my parents' reunion with Earle and Ruth Mack. They were living in the area, which made it possible for Mother to go with Daddy occasionally, leaving Sharon and me in the Macks' loving care.

But even with the Macks close by, Mother's physical condition didn't allow her to travel much. Daddy's work in Korea had opened doors of ministry worldwide, and when he was invited to hold a series of campaigns in England and Ireland he decided to take Sharon with him.

Mother packed Sharon's suitcase with great care, coordinating each outfit and tagging them accordingly. Daddy was a stickler about appearance, but he was also color-blind and would be no help in deciding what went with what!

Mother was thrilled that Sharon had the opportunity to go, and she had no doubt that she would make her father proud. Still, it wasn't easy to stand at the gate and watch her ten-year-old march across the field and up the stairs to the plane, head held high, off on the adventure of her young life.

Arriving in England in March of 1952 was like stepping into fantasyland for Sharon. Buckingham Palace, the Changing of the Guard, the Tower of London, the Crown Jewels—wonderful things thrilled her eyes and aroused her imagination.

On the Saturday before they were to leave London for

MAN OF VISION, WOMAN OF PRAYER

Belfast, Ireland, to begin Daddy's campaigns, Billy and Ruth Graham invited them to the Savoy for lunch.

"We arrived to be royally greeted by all of them," Daddy wrote. "Billy, Ruth, Cliff and Billy Barrows all made much over Sharon. Cliff immediately took her and bought her a corsage. We had a marvelous time."

Then it was on to Belfast, where Daddy described the campaign as "only four days long, but one of the best I've ever had." Every night the auditorium was packed with over three thousand people, and at the end of each service dozens came forward, although "here they do not believe in coming forward. So it is really phenomenal that we have had such results."

While in Belfast, Daddy and Sharon were guests of Major Neill, a member of the Irish parliament and minister of labor in the national cabinet. They also had tea with the prime minister.

On the last night there, Sharon gave her testimony in the service, and Daddy wrote back that she did "gloriously." He added: "The people really took her to their hearts. She is a marvelous trooper!"

The next series of meetings was scheduled in Liverpool, England. It was from there that Mother received a letter from Sharon.

Easter Morning, April 13, 1952
Liverpool, England

Dear Mommy,

This morning Daddy and I received your telegram. So now I am writing you. For about a week Daddy has been getting after me to do this and I say I will but never do. . . .

Here the weather is quite warm. But the sun don't shine.

Last night Daddy started the Liverpool campaign. It is being held right now in the Philharmonic. The auditorium is a brand new building which is beautiful. Last night we packed it out and

"CROSS THE OCEAN IN A SILVER PLANE"

turned people away. I think that is the way to start a campaign, don't you? I have been giving my testimony lots of places and have stumbled on my words quite a lot in front of small audiences, too. But last night I gave my testimony in front of a huge crowd and didn't feel nervous or scared, but right at home. I didn't stumble either. I said, "I am very glad to be here tonight and I love the Lord with all my heart and I have wonderful peace and joy since He has come into my heart." How do you like that? . . .

My birthday party was at the hotel where we stayed. Oh Mommy, I will never be able to tell you how simply beautiful the land around the hotel was or how wonderful the hotel was. There were millions of trees around the hotel because the hotel was just out of Cheltenham. Cheltenham was a clean, beautiful little town, the prettiest one I have seen; almost nicer than any town I've seen there at home in the States, except for any town in California. . . .

Well, Happy Easter, Mommy. I miss you both and wish you were here getting Marilee fixed in her Easter dress.

Love,

Sharon

As elated as Sharon was over her trip, no one was more thrilled than my dad at the opportunity to show off his charming daughter.

> I am sure that Sharon has never been happier in her life. She continues to eat like a horse . . . and she is having a good time in the meetings, too. Last night she signed autographs for twenty minutes. . . . in fact, in every city now she has been mobbed just like the rest of us, and does she love it! She signs some Psalm verse after her signature like an old trooper. . . .
>
> Everyone everywhere compliments us on her manners and pleasant little ways. So, I guess you gather from that that I am terrifically proud of her.
>
> The meetings are going along splendidly. As you know, the first

night England's finest opera house seating 2,500 was packed and hundreds turned away. . . . We are going to move to the Boxing Stadium seating 4,000+ beginning Saturday night. . . .

My heart is full of His praise. And, Darling, never, never have I loved you more. . . .

By May, Sharon was home and settling back into the routine of school and family life. But for Daddy, routine was airplanes, hotels, strange food, and one service after another. From the jungles of Formosa to the World Congress in Ireland; from the war-torn streets of Korea to the crowded streets of India, the schedule never let up, and neither did he.

Formosa, July 23, 1952

My Adored One,

God is gloriously good to us here. I am with Lil Dixon on the back side of Formosa among the jungle savages—the head hunters! What an experience! And today we came to one of the finest missionary enterprises in the Orient—a medical hospital packed with 200 terribly diseased babies, mothers, children, and just a young doctor and his wife busily at work. They have been here four months. Imagine my total delight and surprise to have them burst with pleasure at the sight of us! God had used me to break their hearts for missions and Formosa, and they had given up their $20,000 a year practice to come here! Oh, what a time of blessing it is! . . .

World Congress, Belfast, Ireland
August 11, 1952

My Darling,

It is raining, raining, raining! It begins to seem like winter in Portland! But this is unfolding as a truly great Congress. There is a marvelous group from all over the world here—and a glorious sense of God's presence. All the meetings, beginning

"CROSS THE OCEAN IN A SILVER PLANE"

with early A.M. prayer meeting, are filled. Every meeting I've addressed (four so far) has had people turned away. Sunday night the auditorium (2,500) where I spoke was packed way ahead of time. The overflow filled a church seating 2,000 across the street, and the overflow from that filled a church seating 500 three blocks away, and still folks were turned away!

Already people everywhere ask me about Sharon. She made a great impression here. I'm in the same hotel and all here ask about her. I miss my big daughter. Tell her I'm praying for her much, too.

Of course, you break my heart with the story of Marilee calling *her* "Daddy." I wept when I read it. I have never missed Marilee so much. But I've never missed you so much either! I guess I'm getting old—I need my wife, truly and deeply.

Keep praying for me, my Lover. I do have an unusual sense of God being with me. I feel "sovereignly sent" toward whatever it is that is just ahead. But I want you to be praying for me. In the meantime, not once, but uncounted times each day, I speak your name to Him. Keep the babies happy. Remind them that I love them intensely.

Forever yours,

Bob

Seoul, Korea, August 31, 1952

My Dearest Beloved One,

Well, here we are in Seoul. For several days I have been in Puson, then Taegu, now here. God has been good. This afternoon Dr. Han (pastor of Yung Nak church) took us to an orphanage. And I was delighted! The 200 wonderful, eager little ones put on an hour of singing and programs just for me. How you would have loved them—3 to 10 years old. But oh, how thin! The buildings are good, separate from the church (about 2 miles away on a nice, airy hill), the children are spotlessly clean, but need better nourishment and vitamins. God help us improve their lot!

MAN OF VISION, WOMAN OF PRAYER

Thursday we visited the children and widows in our widows' home. They are terribly grateful, but Darling, it would break your heart. Their lot is some better than average, but nonetheless, still awfully crowded and pitiful. They make rope out of old gunny sacks, and work hard. But they have so little. However, they were thrilled when I told them about your sewing machine promise! They can buy the kind they want right here. Singer machines and they cost $100 a piece. I told them they could buy two right away. They were thrilled beyond words. You will be proud when you know what it means to them.

Although she was seldom able to actually be at Daddy's side, Mother didn't let distance prohibit her active involvement in his ministry. By the time she heard of a specific need, it usually was already being met. But occasionally she would hear of something she could do, and Mother would make it her own special project. Such was the case with the sewing machines.

Perhaps in a letter or in conversation Daddy mentioned that if these widows had some sewing machines, they could earn enough money to live by sewing clothes and uniforms.

Mother immediately set out to raise enough money to buy the needed machines. Despite the fact that speaking in public had never been easy for her, she called churches in the Portland area, arranging to speak to several women's groups. With Auntie Ruth at her side as moral support, she spoke as a woman and a mother about the desperate need of these Korean widows to provide for their children.

In a few short months, Mother raised enough money to buy eight new sewing machines. And so Mother continued her battle behind the lines, doing what she could to help while learning to cope with having Daddy face not only spiritual artillery, but real live guns and bullets.

Seoul, Korea, September 1, 1952

Today we went to the front, right up into the action. Perhaps you've been reading of "Baldie," the mountain blasted com-

"CROSS THE OCEAN IN A SILVER PLANE"

pletely bare by weeks of bombardment—and death. Ninety men were killed here in one day recently. Both sides are so close to each other that men are being killed by hand grenades and sniping daily. We donned armored vests and helmets and got a close view—so close I personally got a glimpse of three of the enemy. It is some experience. The men are living solely with death. Four killed and five wounded—as near as I could get it today. In that sector, I mean. But it is something to see, the helicopters landing right in the lines to pick up wounded. However, don't worry. I take no chances. Mostly staying underground in the bunkers, and watching through periscopes.

Tomorrow I hope to go forward with the Korean Marines. I intend to do a story on our Korean chaplains under fire.

Unfortunately, I have no follow-up correspondence or printed material to verify whether Daddy got his story or not. Knowing him, I'm sure he did. I do know he got out of the bunkers without a scratch, for the beginning of 1953 found him in Calcutta, India. Evidently, finding him was not quite so easy for Mother.

Calcutta, India, February 1, 1953

My Own Precious Wife:

Late last night a wire came from Joe Weatherly stating he had a cable from you inquiring where I am. It is incomprehensible to all of us here in Calcutta why, as they have been with me as I have wired you several times and written you at least four letters this past two weeks. Surely by now some of them must have reached you. I love you so very, very much, and I don't want you to worry needlessly.

God continues to gloriously bless here in the meetings. Dr. Corlett, pastor of the leading church in the city, said in his pulpit this morning that Calcutta has never seen anything like this moving of God's spirit, nor crowds like these in all the memory of the oldest missionaries. . . .

There are some conversions among the hardest people to reach.

MAN OF VISION, WOMAN OF PRAYER

Last night a wonderful specimen of manhood, a turbaned, black-bearded young Sikh came forward and was gloriously saved. You cannot imagine how this thrills the missionaries. . . . My heart is so grateful. This whole experience is like a new beginning for me. I don't know how it is happening, but oh, how I thank Him! How I love Him! And somehow I've been pleading with God to let some of this joy and victory come through to encourage your heart. Day and night I am praying that God will do something to set you physically and spiritually free to experience these thrills with me. How glad I am now that I hung on to get there. I tremble to think that except for God's faithfulness when I was without faith, I would have turned back. . . .

Chapter 15

THE 38TH PARALLEL

One of the most extraordinary episodes in my father's life was his ministry to the soldiers and POWs during the Korean War. The following letters deal with those frenzied days in 1953, just before the war ended.

Kojedo Island, Saturday, June 16, 1953

My Own Precious Darling:

Here I am in the heart of the war prison camps. Within sight and sound from here are thousands of the men who desperately need our Lord. Harold Voelkel is doing one of the most amazing evangelistic jobs in history, I believe. But the enemy is opposing. Ray Provost and I arrived here yesterday to be greeted by the new commander in charge of the camps and were told that a new directive has come out prohibiting any civilians from participating in the camps. So at present an appeal has been sent to higher authority. I hope you are praying. But whether I get to preach or not, here is one of the greatest Gospel stories in the world. In one big camp here, the Korean pastors who are Voelkel's assistants have organized the Christians among the prisoners, and there are six churches now meeting in this one camp. Most amazing of all, they have their daybreak prayer meeting every morning, and even the unsaved attend, with often as many as two and three thousand present. Yesterday morning in a nine o'clock weekday preaching service, there were 60 decisions for Christ among these Communists. There are six Bible schools among the prisoners, with over 1,000 students studying the Word. As I came back from Tokyo, I brought

MAN OF VISION, WOMAN OF PRAYER

them 1,000 notebooks and 5,000 pencils, so great is the growing interest in their classes. They can't get Bibles enough, nor even Gospels, so they use these notebooks to write Scriptures in.

The preaching services on Sunday are terrific. The camps are divided into smaller groups now, but last Sunday Voelkel and his helpers had 18 services, with as many as 5,000 to 6,000 in several of the meetings.

Even though I may be stopped from preaching to the war prisoners, God sent me to supply some needs. I have just bought Voelkel's group ten folding organs, and ordered public address systems he desperately needed. And tomorrow I am going to preach in the morning in the main chapel for the GIs and officers. Then in the evening they plan to show *38th Parallel*. . . .

The prayers of my mother—and others—were answered when Daddy was finally able to preach to thousands of Communist POWs.

Korea, Monday, June 18, 1953

My Dearest Precious Darling:

Well, I have spent my first weekend among the prisoners of war—hereafter to be referred to as the POWs. And Sweetheart, it has been one of the greatest experiences of my life. The enemy did everything he could to forestall our getting into the camps, and even yet we are forbidden to take our cameras in. But Saturday the camp commander, who is a blasphemously ungodly man, was forced to let us in because I phoned headquarters in Pusan. So Saturday night we went to one of the enclosures, and there on ten minutes' notice had a meeting with over 3,000 attending. That day there were sixty decisions. We could have had hundreds raise their hands but they prefer to hand-pick the fruit through personal work by the hundreds of North Korean Christians who are among these POWs.

Then Sunday at 6 A.M. we went to one of the larger enclosures. I am not permitted to indicate the number of POWs in the camp,

THE 38TH PARALLEL

but Darling, there were actually 9,000 at least who were present at that hour for prayer meeting. I'll never forget hearing them sing "What can wash away my sin?—Nothing but the blood of Jesus." For a solid hour the meeting lasted, just singing and prayer. Then I preached to a packed chapel for the GIs, and 3 officers and 21 men responded in the morning worship hour to the invitation for salvation, something unheard of there. Oh, how my soul magnifies the Lord! Then at 2:30 in the afternoon, I was driven to a little harbor and taken aboard a Navy LST ship and held chapel for 105 men who had had only one other service since last January. Then at night, we showed *38th Parallel* to 1,800 GIs and God mightily moved! . . .

Danger and death were sickeningly near as my father wrote on Independence Day, 1953.

Korean Front, July 4, 1953

My Own Darling Wife;

How I miss you and long for you tonight! Just to be with you. Just to be home—to sprawl out on our own davenport with your precious hands to hold and to hear the voice I love more than any other sound on earth. Lorraine Pierce, I love you with all my body, with all my mind. And Sharon! And Marilee! Is she growing? Does she still run with jolting little steps? Will she remember Daddy? All the little children here heartbreakingly remind me of my darlings.

In the past few hours, we have stood very close to death. A little while ago, I was with one of our heavy artillery units at the front. While I held my ears at the awful sound, their huge shells rocketed over a nearby hill and in a few short minutes inflicted almost 200 casualties on the enemy. As our jeep jolted over the rough mountain terrain, just a little ahead of us, one of our trucks struck a mine and was destroyed. All day long we have had to pull off the road to let our ambulances pass, rushing our fresh wounded back to medical care. All this going on even as the radio reports peace and cease-fire negotiations are being talked about! In the midst of all this, however, I had a wonderful time of blessing and fellowship with Chaplain Stemple—a true man of God. And even this day have had Korean soldiers at the front tell me they heard me preach here or there a year ago. And everywhere there are invitations to preach. Many of these front-line troops haven't had a church service for weeks, and in every little meeting there are two or three who decide for Christ. . . .

As always the compelling needs of orphaned children constantly weighed on Daddy's heart. As this letter reveals, his concern for the kids did not stop with rice and sleeping quarters but included balloons and sporting goods as well.

Seoul, Korea, July 5, 1953

My Darling,

We are sleeping in the undestroyed portions of a former apartment building here. Everything here has been bombed and burned to nothing. This whole great city is one great ghost of twisted steel, tottering walls, and ashes. The few buildings that were left when I was here in December are mostly gone now. And the streets that were so jammed are empty even at noonday. You see, they are not permitting the civilian population to return yet because there is no water for the people. The reservoirs and pipes were all destroyed. And, of course, it's thirty minutes' jeep ride to some sections of the front where even as I write this, there are skirmishes with the enemy.

But we are fairly comfortable. The food is edible and we have mosquito nets to keep the malaria mosquitos off, and it is the center of things.

It rained all night last night and most of the morning, so instead of going to the front we drove down to Inchon, where the orphanage was which appeared in *38th Parallel*. I recognized three of the little kids who were there three years ago. The orphanage is running now, and little kids pouring in—picked up and sent there by GIs and chaplains. So we had a wonderful time. Gave them all balloons and then made arrangements to give them funds for two buildings to sleep in—desperately needed.

THE 38TH PARALLEL

I also began arrangements through Chaplain Stemple to provide some sports equipment for them, as they had nothing to play with. The only heartache was to look for some of the darling faces I remember and to find them missing. . . .

Chapter 16

HOME: COFFEE, FRIENDS, AND LOVE
•

In the latter part of 1953, we made the move to southern California. At the time, Daddy was gone, as usual, and Mother came down to spend a week house-hunting. The first house the realtor showed her was a lovely, ranch-style home in Arcadia, home of the famed Santa Anita Race Track. As they pulled in the circle driveway, the realtor quickly explained that she knew it was much more than my folks could afford, but it was so lovely that she wanted Mom to see it.

Mother fell in love with it the moment she stepped through the door, but after a tantalizing tour she walked out, prudently pronouncing it completely out of the question.

By the end of the week, Mother had looked at at least fifty houses and had seen nothing that could even begin to compare with the memory of that first house. Daddy flew in to see what she had found. Papa Johnson, who was living in nearby Altadena, drove Mother to the airport to pick him up.

"Well, what'd ya find?" Daddy inquired with his typical "let's-get-on-with-it" air.

Before Mama could speak, Papa answered, "She found a house she really likes but it's a bit expensive."

"Let's take a look at it."

The moment they drove into the driveway, Daddy squeezed Mother's hand and announced, "I like it!"

He walked from room to room knocking on walls, peeking into closets, and making all the appropriate "prospective buyer" sounds. But Mother could tell he was just going

HOME: COFFEE, FRIENDS, AND LOVE

through the motions; he wanted the house. They all knelt then and there on the hardwood floor to commit the house to the Lord and to ask that if it was His pleasure for them to have it, He would provide a way.

Then they called the realtor to let her know they wanted the house.

"Oh, I'm so sorry," the voice on the phone said. "I just finished typing up the escrow papers. The house is sold."

With a mixture of relief and disappointment, my folks went back to Portland, trusting the Lord that in His time He would give them a house.

A few weeks later the phone rang.

"Honey, I've got good news!" It was Papa calling from California. "The most amazing thing happened. I was in the market today when this woman stopped me and said, 'Aren't you Mr. Johnson?' It was your real-estate lady. How she ever remembered me I don't know, but she said the escrow fell through on the house and she's been desperate to reach you. If you want it, it's yours!"

And so God gave us our house on Santa Margarita Drive. It was a much more lovely house than Mother ever dreamed of having. In fact, for the first few months she battled feelings of guilt that robbed her of joy in her new home.

Then one day she was talking with Helen Morken, explaining her feelings. When she finished Helen said, "Lorraine, how do you receive a gift?"

"Why, I simply take it."

"Then what do you do?"

"I say 'thank you.'"

"Don't you see that all God wants you to do is receive His gift and say 'Thank You'?"

It was a simple truth, but it released Mother to receive.

That very day she walked from room to room, laying hands on every wall and window, praising God and committing every square foot of the house to His honor and glory.

A few days later Mama wrote:

MAN OF VISION, WOMAN OF PRAYER

My wonderful one,

It was rugged when you left—coming home in the car I had a real bad spell (that suffocation attack) and so when I arrived home, I went right to bed and Ruth took the children with her. Well, I lay on the bed and the past loomed so discouraging, and then the lonely future with this terrible nervous affliction—and Bob, I almost tried not to breathe. And suddenly God met my soul in such a triumphant way that I just started to cry out and praise Him. In what seemed the blackest night the light shone through and it was God. Well, of course, afresh I laid everything dear, and you, and myself upon the altar and wonderful peace came. I went from room to room giving the whole house to the Lord, and I'm feeling a great deal better about it. In the midst of all this the little pastor from up the hill came and I was able to witness to him of God's grace.

Well dear, I really took my stand and feel God's arms around me, and I'm not afraid. . . .

While Daddy was away, life was as relaxed and mellow as the Robert Goulet records Mama used to play as background music for her girlish daydreams of Daddy's return. Our home was quiet and comfortable, the large, sunny rooms extending a gracious welcome to all who walked through the door. My mother's Swedish coffeepot always stood hot and full on the stove, filling the kitchen with an irresistible aroma.

I seldom remember coming home to an empty house. Mama was always waiting, her cheerful greeting assuring my childish heart that all was well. Although there was usually no one there to feed her feminine ego, she was always immaculately groomed, taking pride in her appearance for her own sake. And she taught us to do the same.

Although most of the time we were a group of women alone in a big house, I seldom remember being frightened or nervous. I knew the house belonged to Jesus; each night we prayed for the angels to "encamp around about us." Many nights as a small child I fell peacefully asleep, envisioning heavenly beings linked wing to wing surrounding our home.

Florabell and Asa Pierce, parents of my father.

Floyd Johnson and Ethel Niemeyer, shortly after their engagement. They were to be the parents of my mother, Lorraine.

My mother at age 18, the year she met my father.

My father (in his early 20s) as he looked when he met my mother.

A Youth for Christ Conference, Lynn, Massachusetts, 1946. Many of these men later participated in far-reaching ministries. Top row, L to R: Bob Evans, David Morken, Bob Cook, my father, Billy Graham, Watson Argue, Walt Smyth, Emerson Pent. Middle row, L to R: John Huffman, Walter Block, Dick Harvey, Torrey Johnson, George Wilson, Chuck Templeton, Wally White. Bottom row, L to R: Rex Lindquist, Cliff Barrows, T. W. Wilson, Ed Darling, Bob Murfin, Ken Anderson.

Daddy went to Korea where God poured out His Spirit. Thousands received Christ.

Daddy's heart was broken by the plight of Korean war victims, such as this mother who would not leave her wounded children. He came home determined to do something to help.

In response to the overwhelming needs of children, Daddy founded World Vision, Inc., in 1950.

My sister Sharon, age 9, welcomed my father home from his first trip into the Korean battle zone.

Mother, Daddy, and I on the film set of *The Flame*, 1953. When Daddy returned from China in 1948, he formed Great Commission Films with Dick Ross.

Daddy and Mother, 1953.

Korean Children's Home. By the end of 1954, World Vision had over 2,200 children in 27 homes in two countries. By 1958, there were over 12,000 in four countries. Today (1980) World Vision sponsors over 200,000 children throughout the world.

In 1956 Daddy and Billy Graham met with Generalissimo and Madame Chiang Kai-Shek in Hong Kong. China was already closed to the gospel.

Here we are—a happy family enjoying a family conference at Maranatha Conference grounds in Muskegon, Michigan (1955). (This conference center was founded by Paul Radar and my mother's father.)

Daddy with little Robin, on the cover of World Vision's magazine in December 1959.

A big kiss for a Daddy who was always missed so very much (1957).

In 1960 Mother made her first trip to the Orient to celebrate World Vision's tenth anniversary.

Mother being introduced by Pastor Hahn to the Yung Nak Presbyterian Church, Seoul, Korea (1960).

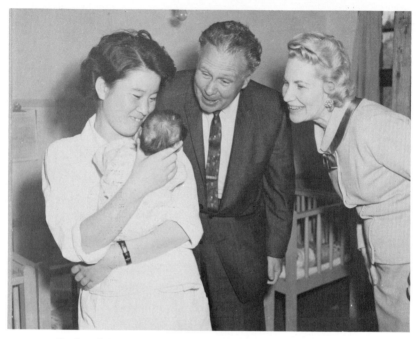

On her first Korean visit Mother saw firsthand the little ones Daddy had given his life to help. The years of sacrifice took on a new significance.

On May 6, 1960, Daddy received from President Syngman Rhee the highest honor Korea bestows on a foreigner.

The Osaka Crusade in Japan was unique—three weeks of meetings. Ralph Carmichael conducted the Osaka Symphony Orchestra and a 300-voice choir.

A few precious moments alone in Japan.

Daddy was surprised by Ralph Edwards' *This Is Your Life* television program in 1961. Grandma Pierce is on Daddy's right. In the background are Roy and Dale Rogers. Daddy had earlier brought back a little Korean orphan girl for them.

President Eisenhower greeted my father and the Korean war orphans in 1962. Sister Robin is in the foreground, and the Korean Orphan Choir ladies are standing with us.

Mother and Daddy returned to the States to tour with the Korean Orphan Choir (1963).

One of the most well-known portraits of my father. "Let my heart be broken with the things that break the heart of God."

Family portrait taken at Mother and Daddy's 30th wedding celebration. Sharon's daughter, Lisa, is standing in front of Daddy (1966).

Sharon was 25 when she accompanied Daddy to Vietnam and presented these sheets to be used for hospitalized Vietnamese soldiers. Accepting the gift from World Vision is President Thieu's wife (1967).

Groundbreaking ceremony for the new World Vision building (1964). Standing behind me is Dick Halverson (acting president World Vision) and Claude Edwards (World Vision board member).

In 1975 World Vision gave a lovely banquet honoring my parents for thirty years of missionary ministry. L to R: Dr. and Mrs. Ted Engstrom, Mama, Daddy, Dr. Richard Halverson, and L. A. County Supervisor Kenneth Hahn.

In May 1975, Daddy walked me down the aisle and I became Mrs. Robert Dunker. My wedding was the last time Mother and Daddy were together until "the miracle."

The night of "the miracle." Daddy's last photo. L to R: Sharon's daughter, Lisa, Daddy holding my daughter Michelle, Robin, Mother (back of Daddy) and myself.

"The brood," as Daddy, called us: L to R: Robin's husband, Victor Ruesga, Robin (holding daughter Christiane), Sharon's daughter Lisa Harfman, Mama (holding my daughter Stacey), my husband Bob, and myself (holding daughter Michelle).

Mother as she is today, painting at her easel.

HOME: COFFEE, FRIENDS, AND LOVE

And if one of us heard strange footsteps in the night or an unnatural rustle of leaves outside our window, Mother could be confident of our prayers and encouragement as we pushed her out the back door, flashlight in hand, to make sure the intruders were the four-footed kind—neighborhood pets and an occasional wild animal on the prowl, such as those furry little black "kittens" with the broad white stripes for which no investigation was necessary.

Mother worked hard to give us a sense of family unity and tradition. We might all go our separate ways during the day (with one girl in high school, one in elementary school, and later, one in diapers, there was little common ground during many of those years), but every evening the table was set with a brightly embroidered Korean cloth and we all sat down to eat by candlelight.

In 1956, when Daddy started his nationwide Sunday radio broadcasts (usually recorded in the States but occasionally taped overseas), we'd arrange to sit down to Sunday dinner just as the World Vision quartet would sing the opening theme "Send the Light" and we'd hear Daddy's friendly greeting, "Hi, neighbor!" It was nice, sort of like having him at the table with us. However, there were times when the sound of his voice would fill me with an overwhelming sense of longing and sadness that would erupt into wracking sobs and exclamations of "I want my Daddy!" Soon Sharon's lip would begin to quiver, and Mother's eyes would fill with tears, and for a while it would sound like we were having a wake instead of Sunday dinner. But most of the time we looked forward to those half-hour visits. They made Daddy seem closer, and also helped keep us abreast of what he was doing!

Life without a man around the house would have been far more difficult if it hadn't been for the wonderful men and women who felt led to help fill the void Daddy's absence created.

Robin (my younger sister) and I had a whole slew of surrogate daddies to choose from when the time for father-daughter banquets rolled around. And Mother knew that all she had to do was pick up the phone any time of day or night if the car broke down or the plumbing went haywire.

True, these people were World Vision employees, but their love and commitment to us went far beyond the call of duty. They were—and still are—family to us. Bill Price, Hal Stack, George Hahn, Norval Hadley—all were men who not only served my father with great devotion but who gave selflessly to the family he left behind. They all had families of their own who lovingly shared their daddies with us even as we shared ours with the world.

These gracious, giving people were God's special gift to us, along with all the office workers, orphanage superintendents, doctors, nurses, and field workers who made World Vision work.

From the moment we would get word that Daddy was flying in, the excitement would begin to mount. I could sense it in Mother's frequent laughter and her quickened step. Furniture that was usually only dusted was polished to a high sheen. The shag carpet, which had just been vacuumed, now was raked as well (and heaven help the first little foot to leave a print in the middle of that perfectly combed rug). With a good pair of gym socks you could slide the whole length of the kitchen on the high-glossed floor. The house smelled of lemon polish and fresh-cut roses, and it buzzed with anticipation.

Finally, we'd all pile into the car to make the familiar drive to Los Angeles International Airport.

I have no idea how many times through the years we stood at an airport gate, searching the travel-weary faces of passengers for the one we longed to see. But the first glimpse of my father's slightly rumpled figure never failed to put a lump in my throat and tears in my eyes. With cries of "Daddy" and "Sweetheart," all four of us would attempt to rush into one pair of open arms, hugging and kissing and talking all at once. In some ways it was as if the lights were suddenly turned on, the cameras started rolling, and someone shouted "Action."

Daddy was home.

Chapter 17

AT HOME WITH DADDY
•

Inevitably, we'd celebrate Daddy's homecoming by stopping at some nice restaurant on the way home. It didn't matter if it was morning, afternoon, or night—we'd just eat whatever seemed appropriate. After all, what's a celebration without food?

My family never ate a meal that wasn't blessed. At home, in a restaurant, on the beach—we always joined in prayer before we ate. When Daddy was home he usually said grace, and just as he rarely preached for less than an hour, so his prayers were of proportionate longevity. One thought would lead to another, and by the time he was through it seemed we had prayed around the world, country by country!

Eventually I learned to appreciate my father's table prayers. When I was eleven or twelve, a group of wonderful Korean pastors came to visit us. We all went out to dinner, and because there were twelve or fourteen of us, several tables were pushed together to form a long banquet table down the center of the dining room. This was one of those places where the lights are kept at a warm glow, dishes noiselessly appear and disappear, and the patrons sit quietly conversing in plush, cushioned booths.

When it came time to pray, Daddy asked one of our guests to do the honor. With tremendous dignity and pride the brother rose, closed his eyes, and proceeded to pray in Korean in a loud, healthy voice. When he sat down five minutes later, the entire room hung suspended in silence. No one even chewed. After that, I decided Daddy's prayers weren't so bad.

MAN OF VISION, WOMAN OF PRAYER

I realize now that Daddy was never home long enough to truly unwind. He was like a football player after a big game, exhausted but much too keyed up to come home and relax. After a twenty-four-hour snooze, he'd be up and rarin' to go, determined to make up for lost time with trips to Disneyland, Knotts Berry Farm, and nice dinners.

Robin and I loved it. It was like Christmas, and Daddy was our own special Santa.

Of course, there was also work to be done while he was home. Since the office was only a few minutes away, it was easy for folks to come to the house or for Daddy to spend time there. His correspondence alone was enough to keep someone busy full time. Then there were speaking engagements, the radio broadcasts, television interviews, and usually a film in the making. And there were always people—friends visiting from out-of-state or missionaries home on furlough.

One evening in the early sixties, Billy Graham came for dinner. During the evening's conversation he made this observation.

"Don't live close to your office, Bob. Make your home someplace apart and away, so that when you're home you're really home. Otherwise, you'll never have a real home life."

At the time, his advice made no great impression on any of us. But in years to come Mother would remember it and wonder if things might have been different had they taken it more seriously.

Some things stand out sharply in my memories of my dad—like the funny, high-pitched little giggle he had when something really struck him funny. And the way he had of pronouncing "Marilee!" when I'd done something wrong, reducing me to a glob of quivering, remorseful Jello! Then there was the time he brought home several large crates filled with minute, intricate pieces of wire and metal. Singlehandedly, he was going to transform this assortment into the best stereo system this side of Tokyo. To Mother's chagrin, he carefully laid the pieces out over two-thirds of the living room floor. Only then did he discover that the instructions were in Japanese.

AT HOME WITH DADDY

Surrounded by a sea of nuts and bolts, Daddy spent the rest of the day and much of the night attempting to decipher the diagrams. Periodically one of us would venture to see how things were going, discerning by his furrowed brow and sweat-soaked shirt it was better not to ask. Sometime in the wee hours of the morning, Daddy admitted defeat, piling the whole mess in one corner of the room until someone could be hired to put it together.

Our family loved games, especially word games, and the competition was tough. Both Mother and Sharon were word addicts, working crossword puzzles to keep in shape. And we all read voraciously. Language was one of Daddy's major tools, and his vocabulary was impressive. But occasionally he'd slip one in like "hyquinox."

"Hyquinox!" we'd all scream in unison. "What's that?"

"Why, a hyquinox is a small brown seahorse-like creature found in the China sea, which is dried and ground into fine powder as seasoning for some of the most exotic Mandarin dishes," he'd reply without blinking an eye.

Dragging out our two-volume encyclopedia dictionary, one of us would confirm our suspicions—there was no such word.

Dismissing our objections with a wave of his hand, Daddy would say, "That's not a *comprehensive* dictionary. There are lots of legitimate words that aren't included in that dictionary. And 'hyquinox' is one of them!"

"Oh, Daddy!" we'd all laugh, as he gleefully added sixty or seventy points to his score.

Although there was much excitement and joy when Daddy was home, there was also an awkward feeling—a feeling that he was visiting. Most of those years he never even bothered to unpack his suitcase, leaving it open and ready to go at a moment's notice. This was a real sore spot with my mom, who hated living with the constant reminder that her man was only home temporarily.

With Daddy gone so much, it was inevitable that we would fall into our own routines and habits. A household of women functions differently from a home where the man comes home every night.

MAN OF VISION, WOMAN OF PRAYER

Mother was used to making decisions and exercising a certain amount of independence while Daddy was gone. We children became dependent upon her for some of the things we might naturally have looked to our father for if he had been there.

Then Daddy would arrive. He was accustomed to being the person in authority, since he lived in a world where he was revered and treated with an awe peculiar to the famous and powerful. When he spoke, people listened. When he wanted something done, it was done. When he saw something he didn't like, it was changed.

After the first few days of homecoming, little conflicts would inevitably erupt. It was impossible not to step on one another's toes as we jostled around in search of our rightful positions. Daddy was a strong disciplinarian, perhaps because of his need to establish his headship in the home, and this caused us girls to feel resentful of his "interference" in our lives at times.

Mother would gladly hand Daddy the reins of control in most areas, enjoying her freedom from responsibility, only to find herself upset at some minor difference in opinion or change of plans.

Daddy always made it a point to be home for Christmas, relishing the holidays every bit as much as we did. One year Mother decided to decorate the tree with gold balls crowned with red velvet bows. She and Sharon spent many hours tying the bows on dozens of shiny gold balls that they planned to hang on a plain green tree.

Meanwhile, Daddy had envisioned a different Christmas tree. He chose a huge, pink, flocked beauty. He also bought a large assortment of decorations, in general overruling all of Mother's carefully laid plans. The ensuing blowup resulted in one of the few times Mother ever left. Checking into a nearby hotel, she managed to stay away one whole night before contritely returning home.

It sounds silly, but not altogether unexpected. How do two people who live in different worlds keep from losing touch with one another?

AT HOME WITH DADDY

I could always tell when Daddy was getting ready to leave—that's when the arguments usually occurred.

Lying in bed at night, my ears would perk up at the first sound of angry words, my heart pounding with dread. I suppose my folks fought a lot considering the amount of time they had together, but I think I understand why. The farther away you are from someone, the louder you must shout to be heard. And about some things, my parents were worlds apart.

Usually the fights had something to do with Daddy's leaving. Mother would ask, "Why do you have to go?" Sometimes there was an obvious answer, which Mother couldn't refute. Other times the reasons seemed vague and difficult to understand. Daddy seemed to be going simply because he wanted to, and Mother would feel hurt and angry.

Then, in the midst of the furor I'd hear Daddy say, "I know, Sweetheart," or "Honey, you just don't understand."

"Sweetheart." "Honey." It was alright. They still loved each other. My whole body would relax, and while the fight raged on I'd slip off to sleep, confident the angry words were no threat to my world.

Getting Daddy off on a trip was usually a hectic and suspenseful ordeal. He didn't believe in wasting time waiting in airports. The result was that he usually had five minutes to check his luggage, get his ticket, and run the long distance between the ticket counter and the gate, boarding the plane with the finesse of a baseball player sliding into home plate. The split-second timing never seemed to bother him, but for those with him the experience could be hair-raising!

Chapter 18

IN THE PRESENCE OF ROYALTY
•

My fifth year will always stand out in my mind, for it was then that a phenomenon called *The Mickey Mouse Club* first appeared on our television screen, catching me as well as three fourths of the rest of the under-age-ten population up in its magical spell. For the next few years my cousin, Dianne, and I lived in a world of Mickey Mouse ears and Mouskateers; a world where one could climb aboard a flying elephant named Dumbo and be transported to any place in the world in a matter of seconds.

Daddy, however, continued to insist on a more conventional means of transportation as he prepared to meet a queen. He had been asked to come to Washington, D.C., to speak at an International Christian Leadership Conference (I.C.L.), and then stop in Amsterdam on his way to India to report to the honorary international president of the I.C.L., Queen Wilhelmina, princess of the Netherlands and mother of Queen Juliana. Daddy wrote from Holland on February 7, 1955.

My Darling Wife and Children,

This day is one I wish you could have shared with me here. I arrived here from New York yesterday about 2 in the afternoon. . . . I was instructed to proceed to this lovely hotel, and shortly after arrival I was picked up and taken to the home of Holland's famous financier—Mr. Van Der Veen. . . . Her royal highness requested me to come to the palace at 10 this morning. A lovely Cadillac came and took me to that delightful old palace. There

IN THE PRESENCE OF ROYALTY

this old dear Christian saint, who was queen for 50 years, received me in her apartment and for an hour and fifteen minutes we visited alone. She herself served me coffee and cakes, and then pumped me with questions about the churches in the Orient. She is very alert, very charming, and treated me with the greatest imaginable courtesy. Our visit ended with a precious season of prayer. . . .

You are much, much in my prayers and I love you with all my heart. . . .

Bob

Four years later, in 1959, Mother met not only the queen mother, Wilhelmina, but also the reigning queen, Juliana. International Christian Leadership sent Daddy as their representative, first to Paris, where he would hold a series of meetings and make contact with several high government officials, then on to Amsterdam.

By this time Daddy was used to rubbing elbows with royalty, but for Mother it was a Cinderella experience.

In Amsterdam, Mom and Dad checked into a lovely hotel and were informed that their audience with the queen would be at two the next day. They had been granted an audience with Wilhelmina, the queen mother. But it just so happened that it was the day after Queen Juliana's birthday, and she would be with her mother at the summer palace just outside of Amsterdam. So Mother and Dad would see them both.

At the appointed time, the long, black palace limousine pulled up in front of their hotel. Its presence immediately drew a crowd of curious onlookers who were eager to see the honored passengers. Mama almost felt like saying, "Sorry, it's just us," as they were seated by the uniformed chauffeur.

As they drove leisurely through the countryside, Mama was struck by the clear, bright freshness. Everywhere there were flowers and greenery. The people seemed to take much pride in their country and displayed a friendly, joyful spirit.

That's good Lorraine. Talk about the country, Mother thought to herself. *And don't forget to curtsy and call the queen, "Your*

MAN OF VISION, WOMAN OF PRAYER

Royal Highness" and the queen mother *"Your Majesty"* . . . or is it the other way around?

Suddenly the car stopped outside the gates.

"Why are we stopping?" Daddy asked the driver.

"We're a few minutes early," the chauffeur replied.

With a wink, Daddy took Mother's hand and settled back in the seat.

"How do you feel?" he asked. "Are you nervous?"

She thought a moment and replied, "No, I'm terribly excited, but I'm not nervous."

"Now you know what it means to be commissioned."

Mother looked at Daddy. *What it means to be commissioned?* Suddenly she had an insight into a part of Daddy that had always eluded her. . . the reason he always had such confidence and seemed almost foolishly fearless at times. He felt commissioned, and when you are commissioned you function not with your own authority but with the authority of the one who has sent you. She had to admit that it was an exciting and wonderful feeling.

Finally the car drove past the massive gates and wound its way through the immaculate grounds. The front steps were strewn with thousands of flowers. It was a colorful and beautiful sight, and the chauffeur explained that it is customary for the people to bring flowers on the queen's birthday.

They were greeted at the steps by a gentleman who led them inside and through a maze of large and exquisitely furnished rooms. Finally they entered what can best be described as a small garden room. There, in this cozy, intimate setting, sat Queen Juliana and Queen Wilhelmina. All need for pomp and circumstance was immediately dismissed as they warmly greeted my folks and asked them to sit down.

The next thirty minutes raced by. Both ladies were extremely interested in Daddy's work, and they asked him many questions. Mother sat quietly, content to listen.

Then, to Mother's surprise, Juliana turned to her and began conversing, as she poured tea from a lovely silver tea set and served pieces of her birthday cake. At first Mother found

IN THE PRESENCE OF ROYALTY

herself repeating her carefully rehearsed comments about the country, but soon the queen's natural friendliness put her at ease and she found herself talking much as she would have with a dear friend. Both women had three daughters, and their motherhood gave them a whole world of common ground.

When Daddy saw that their time was up, he asked, "Would you mind if I pray with you before we go?"

"Not at all," came the reply. Mother was a bit startled to see Daddy kneel on the floor between the two queens. With a hand on each chair, he raised his head to heaven and prayed.

Who else but Bob would dare to do that and have two queens accept it as nothing unusual! Mother thought, amazed at the favor God had given him.

The prayer over, they rose to go. Wilhelmina took Daddy's arm and walked him to the door.

But Juliana took Mother's hand and said, "Can I ask you something, Mrs. Pierce? How do you live alone without your husband? And how do you raise your children without their father?"

Mother's heart went out to her. She had read somewhere that there was trouble between the queen and her prince; the woman was definitely troubled and hurting.

Covering the queen's hand with her own, Mother said, "I can do it only because the Lord enables me to do it. And He does."

The two women talked for several more minutes. Mother was amazed at the words God gave her as the queen wept quietly.

In the car on the way back to the hotel, Daddy held Mama close and said, "I'm so proud of you, Sweetheart. You had a real ministry to the queen."

Chapter 19

ELEPHANTS, MEASLES, AND MEMORIES
•

> These last ten days have in some ways been my life's busiest. But how God has blessed! No doubt this conference, attended by 3,337 pastors besides others, has been the greatest thing of its kind in the Orient, if not elsewhere!

That is how Daddy described his meetings in Seoul, Korea, in September of 1955. On the last day, more than 80,000 people climbed Namson Mountain to hear Daddy preach. The Korean army sent its band, and the university sent its orchestra. A choir of over 500 voices combined to sing praises to God for His transforming touch upon the Korean church during those days.

While Daddy was standing on a mountaintop ministering to 80,000 people, Mama was home washing my hair and reminding herself of 1 Samuel 30:24, which Papa Johnson often used to encourage her: "As his part is that goeth down to the battle, so shall his part be that tarries by the stuff: they shall part [share] alike."

Although the scriptural reassurance of her significance in God's eyes was comforting, there were times when she expressed her loneliness and her desperate need for a closer relationship with Daddy.

> Dear One,
>
> I picture you eating lunch somewhere in Korea. It's 8 P.M. here. I've just finished shampooing Marilee's tresses, so thought I'd write at this advantageous time while she dries her hair. . . . We are enjoying *Daily Light* together. I make Sharon read it every

night at dinner. It's so nice to know, too, that you are reading it there. Every tie means so much to me. I can't seem to shake this terrible loneliness. I'm trying not to show it, though, and haven't mentioned it even to Dad.

We pray for you each day together, and I remember you several times a day. I don't want a moment of any day wasted. I pray to that end. If all these days are counted in God's great plan for souls and His kingdom's work, then I want to keep breathing, living, waiting for you. Anything less than that, no. So, I'm praying for the picture and you these days. . . . not just one heart but two invested in this one.

Well, I don't mean to be morbid. If it bothers you, tear it up and don't read it again. But I told you I would be putting some things on paper that I'd been feeling for a long time. I have to. You do the same if you like. I want so badly for you to really know me—for me to know you. You seem so far from me at times and then again, you are so very much mine. . . .

Of course, it was always a special treat to go to the mailbox and find a letter addressed to me!

February 7, 1956
Maramon Convention, India

Darling Marilee,

My, how your daddy misses you! Many times every day I think of you, and wonder what you are doing. . . .

I have enclosed a picture of your daddy riding an elephant in India. . . . I thought of you and wished you could ride it. Perhaps someday you will.

We have had wonderful meetings everywhere. Sometimes there were more than 100,000 people attending in South India. The heat has been melting your daddy, though. It has been terribly, terribly hot!

I love you very, very much. You're very precious to me, my little darling. Please keep praying for me and for our meetings. I pray for you constantly. Before too long now, Daddy will be seeing you.

P.S. Lorraine, last Saturday Billy [Graham] and I had thirty minutes with Prime Minister Nehru. Very enlightening. Somehow one comes away feeling he is a good man trying to help India survive. . . .

I only remember two occasions when Daddy brought Korean orphans back to the States for adoption. Part of the reason the Korean government appreciated World Vision was because they didn't export the children they cared for; rather, they prepared them to be productive, responsible members of their own society.

But in 1956, Daddy did bring twenty-six children from Korea to the arms of loving, adoptive parents here in the States. Among them was a precious little girl who was adopted by Roy Rogers and Dale Evans. They named her Debbie. Some years later she died in a tragic bus accident.

The job of singlehandedly transporting twenty-six children halfway around the world was every bit as difficult as it sounds!

Wednesday, May 23, 1956
Tokyo, Japan

My Beloved,

Well, it's been some time! First, at the last minute, six children couldn't come because of the American embassy slip-up in mailing the necessary papers between Japan and headquarters in Korea. Then one child came down too sick to come. But we all got safely off. . . . One little Negro baby had a fever and runny nose, but we all thought it was just a cold.

After a five-hour flight we arrived in Tokyo, were 1½ hours getting cleared, and then taken to a hotel to stay overnight. We were to leave at 6:15 P.M. on PAA the next evening, May 22. But about noon I called the doctor because two or three had fevers and the little black baby especially worried me. Well, the doctor

ELEPHANTS, MEASLES, AND MEMORIES

took one look and said measles and that three others should go into the hospital for observation!

Hospital after hospital turned us down on admittance, but thank God for the Catholics. They were as crowded as any, but have done everything! They aren't even supposed to take contagious cases, but stuck their necks out to help. They have our room sealed off and are taking excellent care of all six.

And PAA is the most wonderful outfit in the world here. The head, Bill Ortwin, is an old friend of mine, and they got me nurses and Amahs (baby-tenders) who are with me around the clock. I have one nurse and two Amahs at all times. But they don't speak English, and they open windows, allowing drafts on the fevered ones, and congregate in one room while little sick ones are left alone and terrified in the other. So I don't dare leave them at all. Of course, I am quarantined also, but I'm not sure for how long. And also, I really don't know if I've had measles, and if I have, they say you can have them again! So, fingers crossed! . . .

It was a struggle, but finally Daddy got all the children safely to the States.

Daddy's arrival home with those children was a big event. Newspaper and television newsmen were going to be there, and many of the prospective parents also would be meeting the plane.

Now Mother has never functioned tremendously well at five in the morning, so to be sure we would not be late for the 7:00 A.M. flight arrival, we spent the night in an airport hotel. After instructing the desk to call us at six the next morning, we settled down for the night.

I was so excited I didn't think I would ever get to sleep. But the next thing I heard was Mother yelling hysterically into the phone, "It's 7:30! Why didn't you call us?"

Well, by the time we got there everything was over but the shouting . . . and I do mean shouting. Daddy was furious. No amount of explaining seemed to make a difference. All he knew was that he had just been through a week of nerve-wracking, exhausting pandemonium and he had looked forward to stepping off the plane and seeing his family waiting—and we had failed him. No one had known where we were, and finally he had been left waiting with nothing to do but worry that something had happened to us.

Of course, no one was more sick about it than we were, and Mother most of all. She had the opportunity of sharing moments like that with Daddy so seldom that it was a real disappointment.

Unfortunately, this is only one example of many incidents that resulted in hurt and resentment, despite our best intentions.

Even as we were contending with Satan's subtle attacks, the world continued to fall victim to his blatant assaults as once again innocent people were forced to flee warlike aggression.

> Tuesday, November 20, 1956
> Vienna, Austria
>
> I have just now arrived back from an eight-hour tour of relief stations along the Hungarian border, where the fleeing Hungarians are first gathered after they sneak across the line. It is a heartbreaking sight! Today about 3,600 have gotten across! The roads are all blocked by Russian tanks and these people waded through a shallow lake to escape. They are frostbitten in the feet, have no change of clothes, and the relief organizations are in chaos. They just can't get clothes, soap, towels, socks, etc. enough! It is bitter cold. The ground is frozen everywhere. No heat in the rooms. How they stay alive I don't know, except they are determined to escape from the Russians. I wrote a check for $5,000 just to provide warm underwear today. These people cannot survive without at least warm, long underwear. I guess this is all we can do. . . .

Never was Daddy's absence felt more keenly than on those special days families love to celebrate together. Birthdays. Anniversaries. Holidays. Daddy tried to be home on these days, but sometimes it just wasn't possible.

ELEPHANTS, MEASLES, AND MEMORIES

Such was the case in November of 1956, and we were all disappointed. It just wouldn't be Thanksgiving without Daddy there to carve the turkey. But his disappointment was even greater—where he was they'd never even seen a turkey!

November 21, 1956
Beirut, Lebanon
Telegram

My Darling Lover,

In a few minutes it will be Thanksgiving Day! How I wish we were together! You and the children will be in my heart and thoughts doubly through the coming hours. And in my prayers of gratitude to God.

When Daddy couldn't make it home for Thanksgiving, it meant he wouldn't be home for an even more special occasion.

November 24, 1956
Istanbul, Turkey

My Beloved Beloved,

Twenty years ago today, tonight rather, we began together! My heart floods with memories of all the warm and good things we have had together. . . . Remember our wedding night in Floyd's apartment? Remember the first apartment by the Forum Theater? Remember the first little apartment in Glendale? Remember our "campaign" in Ojai? Remember the days in San Diego with Earl and Eunice Anderson and Brother Will South? Remember Palm Springs and Banning? Will you ever forget El Centro and the dingy room and air cooler? Most of all I remember you! You, and all these things, and a thousand other places and times. I loved you then, but I love you more now. . . .

Forever Yours,

Bob

Chapter 20

THE EVANGELICAL SYNDROME

The year was 1957. Sharon was an independent sixteen-year-old, and I had just turned seven. For years Mother had stayed at home, fulfilling her obligation to her children. Her life had been an endless succession of hellos and good-byes. Deep down inside, she believed Daddy's ceaseless wanderings would come to an end someday. Papa used to say, "Let him go, Honey. Eventually he's got to slow down."

But the years passed, and Daddy showed no signs of slowing down. The work kept growing, and he became a man in perpetual motion. In January and February of 1957 he visited the Philippines. . .

> The opening night everything was packed out. One paper said 50,000. . . . this is the largest thing of its kind Protestants have ever seen in the Philippines. And how I want to thank God for His goodness; 388 decisions the first night. . . . Last night all seats were filled, the crowd was 9,000 to 10,000 and 245 definite, weeping sinners came forward. I praise God for His anointing and power. . . .
>
> . . .the Maramon Convention in India . . .
>
> Tonight is a great triumph for our Lord. I preached to 30,000 men, gave an altar call, and there was a wonderful response. Praise Him! This afternoon we dedicated a student center built by World Vision. These poverty-ridden students gave an offering of over $50 U.S. to build a fence around it. This represents several days' food for each of over a hundred students! . . .

THE EVANGELICAL SYNDROME

...Assam....

The days in Assam were a thrill. They live in such primitive conditions, but the Christians were so radiant and so thrilled to have us come. Rochunga Pudite's [Daddy's spiritual son and currently president of "Bibles For the World"] father and family all came to meet me. And the Bible School, mud-floored, thatched-roofed, mud-walled, already has 100 students attending it. . . .

...Afghanistan...

Afghanistan is "out of this world," like the most remote, primitive parts of China. But Christie Wilson, our missionary, is doing an historic work. About 125 people came to the meeting the night I spoke. A doctor, Herbert MacKell from New York, was there also, and Christie said that the three of us ordained ministers were the largest group of preachers ever in Afghanistan at one time in modern centuries. . . .

...Russia...

I thought of you again and again. Especially when I thought that on arrival in Moscow they might have time to ascertain who I am and might have detained me. Funny feeling the whole time, believe me. . . .

...and Austria, Greece, Italy, and France.

It became obvious that if Mother and Daddy were to have anything more than an occasional marriage, Mother would have to be the one to change. Now that we girls were old enough to do without her some of the time, she began to look forward to actively entering into Daddy's ministry.

God even provided the perfect babysitter. Grammy, my maternal grandmother, was now widowed and living close by. She and Mother had become very close in the past years, and we girls adored her. Mother knew she could leave us with perfect peace in Grammy's care.

MAN OF VISION, WOMAN OF PRAYER

But there were other obstacles to overcome. Occasionally an attack of nerves would leave Mother physically and emotionally incapable of handling large crowds of people—a real problem, considering that a good portion of Daddy's life was spent dealing with the masses. But these attacks were few and far between, and physically Mother was feeling strong and optimistic.

Another major obstacle was Mother's terror of flying. Satan is clever; he knew that if he could keep Mother grounded, he could successfully keep my folks apart. Daddy just didn't have time to always travel by train or boat.

In the very early years, Mother had had no great love of flying, but she had accepted it as an inevitable fact of life. Then, when Sharon was about three years old, she and Mother flew from Seattle to Los Angeles on a brand new DC-6. While flying over the mountains, the cabin pressure suddenly dropped; all passengers were required to don oxygen masks. Sharon panicked, and Mother had to physically wrestle her into the mask while trying not to show her own nauseating fear.

Shaky but in one piece, they landed in San Francisco, where they were grounded for several hours while the plane was repaired. Finally they took off for Los Angeles, but within minutes all the lights on the plane went off. Once again the captain came on the intercom to say they would have to return to San Francisco.

By the time they finally reached Los Angeles, the coastal fog had closed in, wrapping the whole city in a blanket of pea soup. This was before the time of sophisticated radar systems, and Mother was frighteningly conscious of the mountains just to the east. If she couldn't see the tip of the wing just a few feet beyond her window, how could the pilot see well enough to land the plane safely?

Looking at the sleeping little angel curled up on the seat next to her, Mother began praying aloud, oblivious to the other grim-faced passengers around her. She didn't care

THE EVANGELICAL SYNDROME

what people thought; she just wanted to get her child off that plane.

Finally the pilot announced they would have to land at Burbank. Mama groaned, thinking of poor Papa, who had been waiting since early afternoon to meet the plane in Los Angeles. From Burbank the weary passengers were bussed to the L.A. airport. The ordeal over, Mama collapsed in Papa's arms. "I'll never fly again!" she vowed.

And for nearly ten years she didn't. When she did fly again it was only because Sharon was attending school in Florida, and it was the only way Mother could see her. The flight there was uneventful, but incredible as it sounds, on the flight home the plane encountered a storm over the Gulf of Mexico. Lightning flashed threateningly all around, as the little plane bounced wildly on the churning air currents. Attempting an emergency landing at New Orleans, the pilot made two unsuccessful approaches, pulling up at the last minute like a roller coaster gone mad. Finally he found a break in the weather.

On another flight, Mother was flying from Denver to Los Angeles, and the landing gear wouldn't retract. They had to turn around and go back, landing on a field covered with foam and surrounded by a fleet of emergency vehicles with sirens screaming and red lights flashing.

Edith Rees, one of Mom's best friends and quite a world traveler in her own right, once told her, "Lorraine, I just can't believe all these things happen to you. One incident would be enough to scare me out of flying, but I've never had anything happen. I just don't understand it!"

Well, Mother understood it, and she was determined not to let Satan deprive her of being with her husband. So now, claiming Romans 8:39 as her very own, she prepared to see the world.

As a first step, she flew with Daddy to New York City for a Billy Graham crusade at Madison Square Garden. *Everybody* was there, and Mother loved seeing so many old friends and being a part of all the excitement. Mostly, she loved being with my dad. Everything would have been perfect if it hadn't been for an irritating touch of flu that kept her slightly nauseated all the time. She took some milk of magnesia and tried to ignore the discomfort.

After the Graham crusade, Daddy was to hold several meetings in Buffalo. But by the time they got there, Mother's flu had worsened, leaving her too sick at times to even get out of bed. Finally, Daddy decided she should go home.

Upon arrival in Los Angeles, Mother went immediately to her doctor. After a careful examination, he told her, "I'm afraid you have a tumor—nothing terribly serious, but I want you to see a specialist."

The specialist tested Mother thoroughly and then sat her down in his office. "Your doctor was right. You have a tumor. But you also have a baby."

On the way home her thoughts were spinning. All concern over the tumor was replaced by the thought of a baby. "I'm going to have a baby. At forty years of age! It just can't be! Why, Lord? Just when I was free to be with Bob some of the time. And oh! . . . what will Bob say?"

But Daddy's response surprised Mother. "Finally, the Lord is going to bless me with a son!" he declared most confidently. Seeing that Daddy was pleased made all the difference to Mama, and she too began looking forward to the arrival of a boy child. In fact, as her body began to change and she felt the new life within her, she positively glowed.

This time there was money to buy all the things she never had with her first two pregnancies—clothes, furniture, and the perfect nursery, decorated in blue, of course. But the one thing Mama wanted most was for Daddy to slow down a bit and share the joy and expectancy of those months with her. Her first pregnancies had been during difficult times; now she felt God was giving them a chance to redeem much of what they had missed before.

Daddy was torn. He loved Mother and truly looked forward to the arrival of this child. But he carried a great weight

THE EVANGELICAL SYNDROME

of responsibility, and he had been caught up long ago in what I have heard Dr. Jack Hayford describe as "the evangelical syndrome"—the misconception that a man can serve God to the fullest only if he is willing to put ministry before family. How many times I heard Daddy quote Luke 14:26, "If any man come to me, and hate not his father, and mother, and wife, and children . . . he cannot be my disciple." Daddy understood that Scripture to mean that he was obliged to put his ministry and the needs of the world before his own family. He used to say, "I've made an agreement with God that I'll take care of His helpless little lambs overseas if He'll take care of mine at home."

It surely sounded sensible enough, and Daddy sincerely believed it was right. Unfortunately, future events would prove that this was Daddy's agreement, not God's.

Chapter 21

ROBIN
•

It would be dangerous and presumptuous of me to judge what God required of Daddy, and what Daddy required of himself. Surely God blessed my father's endeavors because they were done out of a heart that yearned to please Him and see Jesus Christ exalted. And although Daddy would not seriously consider staying home, he was rarely insensitive to Mother's feelings. He did not consider her objections unreasonable; in his opinion they were merely impractical.

Such was the case in the latter months of 1957. World Vision had a series of pastors' conferences scheduled throughout the Orient, after which Daddy was to hold a crusade in Seoul. He could see no way to alter his schedule.

With the baby's birth only three months away, Mother received the following report. It didn't take all the sting out of Daddy's absence, but it certainly helped to have a clear picture of the wonderful things God was doing because Daddy had gone.

> News Report—World Vision Orient Trip—Fall, 1957
>
> Only eternity will measure the impact on Asia made during the last few weeks through the ministry of Dr. Bob Pierce and several internationally known clergymen working as a World Vision team.
>
> During these days of world tension, when Communism and nationalism are closing many doors in Asia to the white man,

ROBIN

Dr. Pierce has seen the urgent need to reach the pastors of the Far East with the Bible-centered message of Jesus Christ. . . .

To aid in this ambitious task of reaching the pastors in an unprecedented way, Dr. Pierce and World Vision gathered outstanding religious leaders from the East and West. . . . They included: Dr. Paul S. Rees, pastor of the great First Covenant Church of Minneapolis, Minnesota; The Rt. Rev. Alexander Mar Theophilus, Bishop of the Mar Thomas Church in South India, an ancient church believed to have been founded by the apostle Thomas during one of his missionary journeys; Dr. Richard C. Halverson, associate director of International Christian Leadership; and Dr. Enrique C. Sobrepena, Bishop of the United Church in the Philippines and chairman of the East Asia Christian Conference. . . .

The pastors' conferences began early in September with the first of such evangelistic efforts ever held in Indonesia. . . .

From there the team moved northward to the cities of Cebu and Baguoi in the Philippines. Then it was on to Formosa.

Before leaving Formosa, Dr. Pierce and the team were received by Madame Chiang Kai-shek, first lady of Nationalist China. She retold with beautiful sincerity her testimony of how God had worked in her own life, that of the Generalissimo, and in the lives of her people.

Two days of historic meetings were held in Tokyo, with several hundred ministers representing practically all denominations. . . .

The great climax to the conferences came in Korea, where separate conferences were held for 2,000 pastors and about 300 chaplains from the ROK Army. This may be the only such case in history when the chaplains of an entire army have been called together to study the Word of God and hear evangelistic messages. . . .

The pastors' and chaplains' conferences, with all their inspiring results, are now over, but Dr. Pierce is not through. He continues now in the midst of the biggest evangelistic campaign ever held in Seoul. . . .

MAN OF VISION, WOMAN OF PRAYER

Daddy was home from the crusade in time to help time the contractions, and on December 21 Mother checked into St. Luke's Hospital. The contractions were strong and regular, but it became obvious that the labor could go on for a while.

Partially sedated, it was all Mama could do to keep on top of the pain when she heard Daddy slap the doctor on the back and say, "Come on, Doc. Let's get this show on the road!" A few minutes later labor was induced, and within the hour Mother was wheeled into the delivery room. A few strong pushes later the child emerged, arms flailing and announcing to the world with a loud, healthy cry that it had arrived.

"Congratulations, you have a beautiful baby girl."

And she was beautiful—chubby and pink, her head a mass of dark, curly hair.

"Oh, Lord, don't let Bob be too disappointed," Mama prayed as she drifted off to sleep.

Sometime later Mama awoke in her room. It was the middle of the night, but Daddy was by her bed, tenderly leaning over her and stroking her hair. "Just wanted you to know," he whispered, "she's the most beautiful baby in the nursery." They named her Robin after her daddy ("Robin" is "Robert" in Scottish).

A few months later, Daddy returned from his first overseas trip since Robin's birth. Half the Orient had been praying for and awaiting with great anticipation the arrival of Dr. Pierce's son. For them, the news of a third daughter was quite a disappointment. "They said we weren't to worry, though," Daddy told Mama with a grin. "They say the *next* one will surely be a boy!"

Chapter 22

KOREA WELCOMES MRS. BOB PIERCE

•

The year 1960 marked the tenth anniversary of World Vision's involvement in Korea, and Daddy was to receive the highest honor Korea bestows on a foreigner. Immediately following, he was to go to Osaka, Japan, for a city-wide crusade. It was the perfect time for Mother to make her first trip to the Orient.

Flying over the rugged terrain outside of Seoul, Daddy pointed out the window and said to Mother, "Look, you can still see some pillboxes and other scars from the war in the landscape below."

Stepping off the plane was like stepping into another world. The Orient has a smell, a taste, and a feel all its own, and although Daddy had talked and written about it for years, nothing could adequately describe the things and feelings Mother was about to encounter firsthand.

There to greet them was a great crowd of people, with a huge banner—"Welcome Dr. and Mrs. Bob Pierce"—held high over their heads. Supervisors and missionaries from all over the country had been flown in for this special occasion. And there were children—dozens of beautiful, eager-faced boys and girls dressed in traditional Korean garb. As Mother and Dad approached, one after another shyly came forward, bowing as they presented their gifts of flower leis.

After endless bowing and hand-shaking, Mother and Dad climbed into a jeep with Erv and Flo Raetz, and Marlin and Kay Nelson, World Vision's directors in Korea. As they jolted along the dusty, pock-marked road into Seoul, Mother looked at Kay, who was seven or eight months pregnant. She was riding in the bouncing vehicle as casually as if she were riding down Fifth Avenue in a limousine. *How does she keep that baby inside her?* Mama thought with a mixture of awe and concern. It was her first real insight into the extraordinary character of the missionary wives she would meet.

Arriving at the World Vision House in Seoul, Mrs. Raetz led the way to the Pierce Room, a cheerful, immaculate room which had been Daddy's home away from home for years. The bed was covered with a beautiful, handmade quilt; the fireplace was laid and awaited a match.

Mother looked forward to a shower and a change of clothes after the long flight, but no sooner had she set her bag down when Daddy announced, "We've got to get going. They're expecting us at one of the children's homes, and we mustn't be late!" And that was the way it was for the next ten days—there was much to see and little time to see it.

The thrill of seeing that first children's home was overwhelming. As they pulled up, the superintendents and the little ones were lined up out front, waiting to greet them with a lively singing of "Jesus Loves Me." When the song was over, the children surrounded my folks, grabbing a handful of skirt or coat and raising their little arms to be picked up. They were starved for affection, and they wanted to be touched and held. Mother bent down to pick one up.

"Honey, don't even pick up one," Daddy warned. "If you hold one, you'll have to hold them all and we'll be here all day." It was heartbreakingly hard to ignore their outstretched arms, but Mother knew he was right.

The next day they went to an infant home, where newborns and small babies lay in row upon row of neatly kept cribs. Mother took one look, and her eyes filled with tears. They were so little, so innocent, so helpless. She looked at Daddy.

"Go ahead. These you can pick up," Daddy said as he settled back to wait as Mother went from bed to bed, tenderly cuddling each little one.

KOREA WELCOMES MRS. BOB PIERCE

As they walked into the next room, they were met with a pitiful sight. This room was filled with less fortunate children—many were weak and sick from months of starvation endured before their arrival at the home. One little boy was particularly pathetic; his baby arms and legs were little more than skin and bones, and his little body was twisted and crippled. Mother wanted to give him a comforting hug, but she was stopped. "I'm sorry, Mrs. Pierce," a nurse quickly explained. "You'd better not. He's terribly weak. You see, although he looks no more than two, this little boy is six years old."

"Oh, Jesus!" Mother prayed, as she wept over that precious little life. She saw many others in those next few days, and she realized that it was only by God's grace that her own children were spared such suffering and pain. No wonder Daddy hadn't been able to walk away. All the years of sacrifice took on a new significance as she saw for herself the good they had accomplished.

After the tour was over, the missionaries who ran the Children's Center asked Mother and Dad to lunch. The Severeids and the Skys were two wonderful Scandinavian couples who had given their lives to working with these children. Entering their home, Mother was again impressed, as she had been at the World Vision House, with how wonderfully these missionary wives succeeded in establishing their own sense of gracious living and tradition in their homes.

The table was beautifully set and laden with cheeses, cold meats, little cakes, and luscious cookies—a real feast, topped off with strong, hot cups of freshly ground coffee, an unexpected treat in this land of tea.

Afterward, Mother couldn't help commenting on how well the missionaries ate. "Oh, they don't eat like that every day," Daddy laughed, shaking his head. "They've known for months that you were coming, and all those cookies and cakes were sent in tins as Christmas presents from their families. That coffee is especially dear, as they only get a pound a year. They saved it all these months to serve to you as an expression of their love."

All during Mother's stay, there were many such loving expressions by the selfless and giving missionaries of Korea. It was a tremendously humbling experience, and Mother was all the more glad she had brought a little surprise for them. Aware that there was rarely money to spend on new clothes, Mother had brought a dozen stylish new dresses in assorted colors and sizes. For years afterward, she received letters from these missionary wives mentioning how much those dresses meant.

One night not long after they arrived, Mother awoke to the sound of hysterical, animalistic screams outside the windows. Waking Daddy, she asked what was wrong. "It's probably a Korean veteran," Daddy replied. "There are many old soldiers roaming the streets who suffer from shell shock or who were captured and tortured by the enemy. There are no insane asylums or government facilities here to take care of them, so they just wander about. We often hear them crying out in the night."

With fresh clarity Mama realized what a different world this was. It was a strange, frustrating, frightening world in some ways, but in other ways it was wonderful. And it was the people who made it so. The Korean people are a gentle, gracious lot, and their overpowering love and reverence for my dad was immediately extended to include my mother.

One Sunday, Mother and Dad attended Yung Nak Church, which at that time was the largest Presbyterian church in the world. They were warmly greeted by Pastor Han, and Mother noticed that all the women were seated on one side and all the men were on the other.

"It's their custom," Daddy explained. "Men and women never sit together in services."

During the service, Mother was asked to say a few words of greeting. It was the first time she spoke through an interpreter, and she did her best to express her great joy at finally being there after all those years. As she finished her short speech, she noticed that most of the women were weeping

KOREA WELCOMES MRS. BOB PIERCE

profusely. Tears were streaming down their cheeks, and some were hiding their faces in handkerchiefs to keep from sobbing out loud.

"What did I say?" she asked Daddy. "Did I say something wrong?"

"Not at all, Darling," he replied. "They're weeping with joy. They've waited ten long years to see you."

Later, the church presented Mother with an exquisite Korean gown in pale, soft pink, a color usually worn only by brides. It bespoke the highest possible compliment. Mother wore this gown to the grand reception given for Daddy and her at Korea House, the official government house used for entertaining guests. There she was introduced to Korean high government officials, army generals, and the entire missionary population of Korea.

On the day Daddy was presented the Medal for Public Welfare Service in "recognition of his exceptionally praiseworthy service to the Republic of Korea," Mother accompanied him to the palace in Seoul and stood proudly at his side while President Syngman Rhee made the presentation. It was a fitting and wonderful way to end her first visit to Korea.

Before they left for Japan, Mother and Daddy visited the World Vision office to say good-bye. Erv and Flo Raetz took Mother into their office and handed her a plain white envelope. Inside was a note that said, "Dear Mrs. Pierce, We are so happy that you have come, we would like to pay your way." It was signed, "The Superintendents." Accompanying the note was a check for one thousand dollars, every penny given out of their meager salaries and their abundance of love.

Now, it so happened that World Vision had already paid Mother's fare. (This was because she was to be actively involved in an official capacity both in Korea and in Japan. Daddy was always very careful not to take advantage financially. If we traveled with him, he paid our way—or perhaps a generous friend would help. World Vision never picked up our tabs unless we legitimately worked.)

MAN OF VISION, WOMAN OF PRAYER

Seated on the plane for the flight from Seoul to Tokyo, Mother held the check in her hand. Her thoughts went back to a day when Daddy had taken her high up on a mountain overlooking the Han River. "Some day a children's hospital will stand on this site," he had told her, and together they had knelt in the grass and dedicated that land to the Lord.

"Honey," Mother said to Daddy with great excitement, "I'd like this one thousand dollars to be the first money toward our children's hospital."

Later, when Mother arrived home, she was interviewed by several reporters who were eager to know about her trip. This gave her the perfect opportunity to say something about the pitiful plight of the children she had seen—and about their desperate need for a hospital. The article catapulted her into the spotlight, attracting much interest and many invitations to speak. She rented a post office box, and contributions began coming in.

When Daddy got home, Mother excitedly showed him one of the articles, sure he'd be pleased and proud. But his response was lukewarm at best, leaving Mama confused and uncertain. Everything came to a head one night when Daddy burst out, "I don't need you to build a hospital! If I want to build a hospital, I'll do it myself."

Mother was stunned beyond speech. Perhaps she should have checked with Daddy first, she thought. But she had come home from Korea so full of emotion that she had to do something constructive about what she had seen. She had felt so much a part of the work that she had never dreamed Daddy would feel she was out of line. The opportunities had presented themselves, and Mother had stepped out with the confidence that it was God's time for her to be counted.

But Daddy obviously felt she had intruded upon his territory. In his mind, the years of separation had placed Mother in one box and him in another, and he felt comfortable with Mother in a more passive role. Although he admired other women who exhibited a more aggressive nature, he found it very hard to accept in his wife.

KOREA WELCOMES MRS. BOB PIERCE

Having participated actively in his early ministry, Mother found Daddy's gradual change of attitude disturbing and painful. Early in World Vision's development, Mother had formed the Women's Auxiliary, a group of World Vision wives who came together to pray and to get to know one another. Soon the group began taking on special projects like sewing for the children overseas and holding luncheons to honor visiting missionaries. Through the years, Mother could tell Daddy was not overly enthused by her endeavors, but it wasn't until the hospital incident that she began to understand why. What he found admirable in others he was threatened by in Mother. Instead of counting her on his team, Daddy felt she was competing with him.

Daddy's growing inability to accept Mother's help or take pride in her accomplishments brings to light a very sensitive but significant point. Although his highly esteemed and influential position should have produced an increasingly healthy self-image, Daddy constantly contended with feelings of insecurity and a curious lack of self-confidence in certain vulnerable areas.

Sadly, this situation is not uncommon in marriages such as my parents'—where one partner is gifted, dynamic, and self-motivated, and the other is quieter, less self-assured, and needs encouragement to develop her natural gifts. Mother let Daddy's disapproval quench her ambitions to achieve outside of the family sphere, and she received it as confirmation of her own doubts about the significance of what she had to offer. This resulted in a certain amount of criticism from others toward Mother for not participating more actively in Daddy's ministry.

I am certain Daddy didn't recognize this weakness in himself, or its negative impact on Mother, for it was his nature to champion those who stepped out aggressively in the name of Jesus, whether they be male or female.

But one thing was certain—he was proud to have her by his side as they arrived in Osaka to begin the crusade.

Chapter 23

HEADING INTO THE STORM
•

For months, Christian businessmen and pastors had worked together to prepare the way for the Osaka crusade with much prayer and a huge promotional campaign. Daddy was already well-known because of his pastors' conferences, and now he was coming to do what had never been done in Japanese history—to hold three weeks of evangelistic meetings in the beautiful new convention center.

The sight was overwhelming as Mother and Daddy stepped off the plane. People were everywhere, crowding against the restraining arms of officials who were instructed to allow only the press on the field. The security was so tight that even World Vision men weren't allowed through. In desperation, Larry Ward (then editor of *World Vision* magazine, later the founder of Food for the Hungry) went up to a guard and flashed a gasoline credit card, hoping the man knew no English and would assume it was a press card. And so it was that the first thing Mama and Daddy saw was Larry's smiling face waiting at the bottom of the steps to help guide them through the throng and into a large black limousine, the first of a twenty-car procession that leisurely wound its way from the airport into the city of Osaka.

Arriving at the hotel, they were once again met by an army of reporters and flashing cameras. Daddy was placed on a small platform, and it was announced that a great man of God had come to that city.

Mother has described the Osaka crusade as one of the greatest thrills of her life. Every day the people would line up

HEADING INTO THE STORM

hours ahead of time, filling the large convention hall to capacity. The majority were students and young people, and although some missionaries considered them the hardest to reach, they were irresistibly drawn by the Spirit of God.

Each night Mother would sit next to "Sensei"—Irene Webster-Smith. This true saint of God had left her upper-class family in England as a young girl and had become a missionary to Japan. Now at a lively seventy-plus, she sat with Mother each night, praising God and saying over and over, "I've never seen anything like this." *

Each evening Ralph Carmichael conducted the Osaka Symphony Orchestra and a three-hundred-voice choir in a soul-stirring program of old hymns and contemporary Christian music. Then Daddy would stand up, his beloved interpreter Mr. Kita by his side, and present the simple message of the gospel. Daddy would speak several lengthy sentences, his voice filled with emotion. Mother was amazed to hear Mr. Kita repeat those words in Japanese, with exactly the same emotion. The Holy Spirit had come upon them both, unifying them so that the flow of the message would not be interrupted.

When the message ended, Daddy would give the altar call. First there would be a hesitation; then, as if in response to some heavenly signal, people would begin to rise—men and women, the young, the old, students, businessmen, housewives—an irrepressible wave of people would fill up the front of the auditorium and overflow halfway up each aisle. Thousands of weeping, broken, repentent sinners were casting off the bondages of darkness and entering into the freedom of life in Jesus. Each night the response was the same, as God continued to bless.

During the day, Mother was usually left to herself, as Daddy was kept busy from early morning until after the services. But one night no service was planned, and Mother

---

* The story of Irene Webster-Smith is told in detail in the book *Sensei*, by Russell Hitt, published by Harper & Row.

MAN OF VISION, WOMAN OF PRAYER

and Daddy decided to get away alone for twenty-four hours. They and a couple of World Vision men boarded an express train for Kyoto, one of the most beautiful and historic cities in Japan.

Arriving in Kyoto at midnight, they drove through the quiet darkness to a beautiful Japanese inn, nestled among trees and spotlighted by an enormous full moon.

Pointing to the moon, Daddy gave Mom a hug and whispered, "Special order, just for you." The inn was totally Japanese style, designed to cater to rich Japanese, not to the tourist trade. Upon entering their room, Mother saw their beds were *tatamis*, straw-like mats on the floor accompanied by thick, quilted comforters. The tables and mirror were all close to the floor, and not a chair was in sight.

After settling their things in their room, the World Vision men picked them up and took them to a geisha house. Traditionally, women are not allowed in geisha houses, but this had been specially arranged for Mother. They were greeted by several beautiful girls and were seated in a private room and served tea while the geishas danced and played instruments.

A little later, several of the girls gathered around her, talking and giggling. "They're fascinated by your blond hair," one of the men explained. "They'd like to touch it, if you don't mind." And so the East touched the West.

After an hour or so, the men took Mother and Daddy back to their room. "You haven't really experienced Japan until you take a bath Japanese style," they explained to Mother. They told her the custom included the help of a geisha girl if you are a man, or a geisha boy if you are a woman.

Petrified, Mother entered the bathroom, reassuring herself that if it was the custom and if Daddy was doing it, it must be proper. Relieved to find she was alone, she looked at the large, high-walled wooden vat of steaming water. "If I can get in before the geisha boy comes, I'll be all right," she thought to herself. "But how do I get in? The walls are so high."

HEADING INTO THE STORM

Just then she spotted a small wooden stool. She had just stepped up on it when she heard the door opening. She froze. Her towel was on a bench halfway across the room.

"Combowa. I am your geisha boy," Daddy said in his funny pidgin English, bursting with laughter at the look on Mother's face. He explained that the whole thing was a joke the boys had thought up. Then he asked, "Woman, what are you doing?"

"I was just trying to get in the tub."

"You don't get *in* the water. That stool is to sit on. You suds yourself up and then use that pan over there to scoop water out and rinse yourself off. That bath water is for the entire inn!" he exclaimed as he began lathering her back.

The crusade in Osaka ended, and Mother and Dad prepared to fly home. Their farewell was even greater than their welcome, for the whole city had been touched by the hand of God during those three weeks. The papers and media had been full of glowing reports. The churches had experienced revival and an explosive increase in attendance.

But mostly it was the young people who had so wholeheartedly responded to the message of salvation. Passing through the hotel lobby on their way to the train station, Mother and Daddy were mobbed by an enormous crowd of weeping, eager students, pressing in to say good-bye, arms reaching out from all directions just to touch my folks as they passed.

At the station they were greeted by more than a thousand people who filled the station to see them off. Once again a path had to be cut through the forest of bodies. Mother and Daddy smiled and touched as many as they could while still walking ahead. It would have been wonderful to hug everyone, but they had to make their train.

Finally they boarded the train, standing at a window as the train pulled out. One girl who was close to the window slipped off her class ring and held it out to Mother. Mama couldn't understand what she was saying, but she could tell by her face that she wanted her to have it. As she took the ring, Mama felt tears rolling down her own cheeks as the young girl's face lit up in a glowing smile. "Thank you," she said in halting English. "Thank you!"

The next year a crusade was scheduled for Tokyo. After the thrill of Osaka, Mother looked forward to returning to Japan. The people there extended many invitations for her to minister to the women.

Mother and Daddy decided to go by ship, joining Paul and Edith Rees for the two-week voyage. About two weeks before they were to sail, Mother caught one of those imported flu bugs. Too weak to do the hundred and one things necessary for such a trip, Mother lay in bed, staring miserably at the piles of clothes that refused to fold themselves into the waiting suitcases. For a few days, Mother seriously considered not going. At the last minute Daddy talked her into it, saying she needn't even pack. They simply moved the piles of clothing from their bedroom to their stateroom, and off they sailed.

The trip promised to be pleasant and restful. Mother had never met Edith Rees before, but the two hit it off well. The only thing Mother didn't like was being totally cut off from home for days at a time. Although she had total peace about leaving us with Grammy, it would have been comforting to know that in case of emergency she could pick up a phone or jump on a plane and be home in hours.

After five days at sea the ship docked in Hawaii, and Mother called home the first chance she had. Grammy reassured her that all was well, and Mother began the twelve-day voyage between Hawaii and Yokohama with only minor trepidation. After a few days she and Daddy both began to really relax, enjoying the lazy, leisurely days away from the pressures that had become a way of life.

One morning Mother was sitting at her dressing table, thinking how glad she was she had come. Her flu was gone, she and Daddy were getting along famously, she really liked the Reeses, and after this refreshing break they had another

HEADING INTO THE STORM

Osaka experience to look forward to. She hummed as she brushed her hair, realizing with a smile that she was singing one of Grammy's favorite hymns, "God answers prayer in the morning, God answers prayer at noon, God answers prayer in the evening, so keep your heart in tune."

Grammy was always singing. Her love for the Lord and for people and for life in general kept her far younger than her sixty-seven years. *Hope I look as good as my mother when I'm her age*, Mother thought, inspecting a previously unnoticed wrinkle.

The door opened and Daddy walked in. "Good morning, Sweetheart," Mother cheerfully greeted him. "Be ready in a minute."

"Lorraine." The way he spoke her name should have alerted her.

"Lorraine, I'm going to tell you the way I'd want to be told if it were my mother. Your mother's gone. She died this morning."

Mother was incredibly shocked, and her pain was almost unendurable. Faced with seven more days at sea, she did her best to carry on, dressing for dinner each night but spending most of her time in her room. After a couple of days she could stand it no longer.

"Please, Bob. I've got to know what's happening at home. I don't know who has the children or when Mother's being buried. I don't even know how she died!"

Daddy went to the wireless room to try to send a message. "Sorry, sir," he was informed. "We're heading into a typhoon and already have received a couple of S.O.S.'s. We have to keep our set clear to receive emergency calls."

And so the ship braved the typhoon. At one point the waves battered the ship so fiercely that the porthole in my parents' cabin was blown out. As Mother watched in astonishment, water poured in through the gaping hole, soaking the carpet and beds. Their things would have been ruined if Daddy and a half dozen stewards hadn't rushed in to transfer everything to a dry room.

MAN OF VISION, WOMAN OF PRAYER

But even the fury of the storm didn't really bother Mother. Numb with the pain of loss, she was far less concerned than poor Edith, who had no such emotional anesthetic to ease her fears. Nevertheless, every morning Edith would knock at Mother's door, bringing hot coffee and a cheerful word to help her face the day. For the remainder of the trip, Edith was her constant companion. During those emotional hours, the foundation of a lifelong friendship was laid.

Finally docking in Yokohama, Mother and Dad discussed what they should do. Daddy offered to fly home immediately to conduct the funeral. He felt Mother should stay, since we girls were well taken care of and there was nothing she could do. And Grammy had wanted her to come on this trip.

So Mother stayed in Tokyo while Daddy flew the many hours home, settled things there, then made the weary trip back to open the crusade.

Within two years of Grammy's homegoing, God took both Papa and Grandma Pierce to be with Him also. All three had been powerful prayer warriors on my parents' behalf—praying through the various crises, supporting the ministry, and generally providing a consistent covering of prayer. It's significant to note that once those prayers were silenced all hell broke loose.

Chapter 24

THE GATHERING STORM
•

The play-by-play description of the disintegration of a life or a family is neither easy to write nor easy to read. Certainly it was a nightmare to live.

Years of eighteen-hour days, sleep caught on planes, unsanitary food, and eternal jet lag had begun to take their toll on my father. Not only did he begin to experience a constant string of physical difficulties and exhaustion, but his emotional reserves were depleted. The temper that he had battled all his life to control got the upper hand more and more often, and the mind that had once operated with computer-like accuracy began short-circuiting occasionally, causing a growing erraticism in his behavior.

Others had stood by for years shaking their heads and making ominous predictions to one another on the inevitable outcome if Daddy didn't slow down, but they were too intimidated by his position and his ministry to deal with him directly about it.

If only my father had learned in the early years to say no occasionally, or perhaps to delegate more responsibility instead of trying to carry the full back-breaking load himself. Looking back on those years it's easy to say, "If only things had been different."

I'm sure that some who read this account will feel that the work would have suffered had Daddy done any less, but I find it hard to believe the Father's heart takes any pleasure in seeing His children used up like old shoes.

How often I heard Daddy say, "Just let me burn out for

MAN OF VISION, WOMAN OF PRAYER

God." But we are to be the light of this world, and a candle that burns out sheds no light. As surely as I know my father's ministry was ordained of God for His honor and glory, I know the following events grieved the Father's heart and were not in keeping with His will for my family.

The first rumblings of the coming storms were heard in 1963. Daddy had come home and had gone directly into St. Luke's Hospital for a series of tests. He needed a cure for a body that was beginning to fall apart piece by piece.

He left the hospital just in time to attend a World Vision board meeting, totally unprepared for what was coming.

His radio broadcasts had been airing for seven years. Next to his travels overseas, they were his most cherished extension of ministry. The radio was his direct line to the people . . . his pulpit. He foresaw his broadcasts as a stepping-stone to a television program that would bring a missionary challenge to thousands of people every week.

When the board voted to cancel Daddy's broadcasts, it cut him to the core, not only because he'd lost something very dear but because he had honestly expressed his desire to stay on the air and still he had been overruled.

There is no denying that Daddy felt betrayed. For the first time his authority and control had been challenged, and the experience left him shaken and deeply wounded. Seeds of suspicion and bitterness had been planted, and Mother watched anxiously as he began to walk an emotional tightrope.

Toward the end of that year, Daddy was overseas and we were preparing for the holidays when Mother received a letter saying he had decided not to come home. He was ill and in need of complete rest, and he had decided to spend some time in seclusion.

Sick with concern and dissatisfied with the sketchy explanation, Mother found a friend willing to lend her the money to fly to Daddy—if she could find out where he was. She planned to place calls to several major cities throughout the

THE GATHERING STORM

Orient. Miraculously, she reached Daddy on the first call—at the World Vision House in Korea.

Mother waited apprehensively as they called him to the phone, expecting to find him weak and perhaps critically ill. She was totally unprepared for the anger in the voice that greeted her.

"I don't understand," Mother said, relieved that he wasn't on his deathbed. "What's happened? Why aren't you coming home?"

"The board has told me not to come home until I pull myself together." (Later Mother would be told by board members that Daddy had flatly refused to come home. The truth probably lies somewhere in the middle.)

"I'm coming at once. Just tell me where to come," Mother said.

But Daddy didn't want her to come. Rejecting her outstretched hand, he chose to go it alone.

World Vision put him on medical leave, and Dick Halverson became the acting president.

Daddy rarely wrote during the next nine months, and he talked very little about them afterwards, but the following communications give us some insight into the pain of that period.

Hotel Okura, Tokyo, May 1, 1964

My Darlings:

I love you. With all my heart. More than life.
In the stormy seas through which I have sailed alone since Christmas the visibility has been so low I have been unable to see my way, much less announce it. And I cannot see ahead now. But you have not been one moment out of my heart and mind. I know that you are cared for, and recent months revealed you will therefore not miss me too much.

God bless and keep you.

MAN OF VISION, WOMAN OF PRAYER

I am in my fifth week of abcesses [boils] on my face. I have five now. But I am getting better. I hope to return to Saigon next Tuesday. I love you.

Bob

Tokyo, Japan, May 1, 1964
(Form Letter)

Beloved Friends:

Our Lord calls me aside to rest awhile.

For some months now I have served in the heat of His work with increasing impaired health.

But what a wonderful Savior! "He who promised is faithful" Heb. 10:23.

Almost thirty years ago He began my Gospel ministry on radio. Twenty years ago this summer I began a life of strenuous travel in the service of Christ.

Seventeen years ago next month I set forth for China with David Morken, and thence an average of twice around the world yearly in obedience to our Lord's assignment to seek and serve emergency needs in crisis areas.

We have proven that "faithful is He that promised Who also will do it" 1 Thess. 5:24.

Now, prayerfully, I am impelled to ask the World Vision board of directors for one year's medical furlough that during this time both body and soul may be renewed for the tasks exploding before us all.

I remain the president of World Vision.

The Board and I have agreed that one year from now I shall return, God willing, to the duties of presidential leadership. . . .

Please! More than ever NOW, stand by the care of our orphans, lepers, and pastors' conferences.

THE GATHERING STORM

Pray for us. And for me.

I do not abandon the battle. The gifts and callings of God are without repentance. I only "come away" for a little while that our Lord may restore me.

My wife and family join me in thanking you for your love and continuing prayers.

His, therefore lovingly yours,

Bob Pierce

Western Union Telegram, May 21, 1964
Thank you for your assurance of your love. Only now beginning to realize how sick I have been and continued need for rebuilding health. This is first week infection shows improvement. Emotional resources still depleted. I want to see the family before too much longer. I love you. Bob.

While Daddy was gone, Mother carried on as normally as possible. Most of the time she had no idea where or how Daddy was, so once again the only way to touch him was with arms of prayer.

For the family, those months were always shaded by a hazy covering of fear, like a thin layer of smoke curling around the edges of our consciousness, giving everything an unnatural tint.

In the summer of 1964, World Vision held a conference at Winona Lake, Indiana. With Daddy gone, Mother had no desire to go. She dreaded the inevitable questions for which she had no answers, and she felt totally incapable of displaying confidence and optimism. But Daddy's absence made her presence all the more essential, and so she prepared to fulfill her obligation as "first lady."

From that week in Winona, two images stick in my mind. One is of my mother standing in a reception line next to Dick Halverson at the president's reception, shaking an endless succession of outstretched hands, greeting many by name and all with a warmth that belied the great effort it took her.

The other image is of a fourteen-year-old girl holding a telephone receiver to her ear and listening to her father's voice. World Vision had set up a booth where people could hear a prerecorded greeting from my dad, including his regret at not being there. I'll never forget the feeling in the pit of my stomach as I heard my father's voice for the first time in eight months. He sounded so close. I remember talking to his voice, telling him how much I loved him and wanted him home, then weeping uncontrollably because I knew he couldn't hear me.

Later, during a main service, a call was put through to my dad so he could speak directly to those gathered. Then the phone was brought backstage and Mother, Robin, and I each had a chance to say hello. Afterward I felt confused and deeply saddened, realizing it had been easier to express my heart to the recording than to my father.

In October, Mother received a telegram from Daddy asking if he could come home for his fiftieth birthday. The fact that he asked permission shows the insecurity and alienation he was battling.

Once again the house was filled with that special buzz of anticipation as we prepared for the reunion. Daddy was coming home!

Chapter 25

SHARING THE SPOTLIGHT
•
The next few years passed with only occasional tremors. Daddy eased back into an active role with World Vision, concentrating his efforts on film projects like *The Least Ones* and *Viet Nam Profile*, slowly gaining momentum until he would resume his position as acting president once again.

In 1965, when I was fifteen, I made my first and only trip to the Orient. Seeing the work firsthand made a tremendous impression on me, as it had on my mother. I felt my own heart break over the desperate need and despairing hopelessness of a world that was both familiar and alien to me, and I was captivated by the mystical beauty of the Orient.

But I think the greatest benefit of that trip was seeing my dad in action. In the States he was well-known and respected, but the Orient was full of people who had not only *heard* of World Vision, but who were *alive* because of it. My father was not just a celebrity there; he was a hero whom God had sent to touch their lives.

Nowhere are heroes treated with greater respect or honor than in Asia. The awe and reverence that constantly surrounded my dad was a revelation to me. Everywhere we turned there were people smiling and bowing, not only out of tradition, but out of their great love for my father. And the missionaries were no less demonstrative, taking precious time out of their busy schedules to be with my dad and to make me feel welcomed. We stayed in the finest hotels, where we were always greeted with the warmth accorded to highly preferred guests.

MAN OF VISION, WOMAN OF PRAYER

At airports we would often be met by airline officials who would stamp our passports and whisk us through customs before most of the other passengers were even off the plane.

I remember arriving in Korea from Hong Kong by myself. Daddy had returned to the States for a few weeks, leaving me to stay with the Kilbournes. For the first time I was hustled into the customs line with all the other passengers, terrified that they would find something wrong with one of the half dozen trinkets I'd bought in Hong Kong. I watched with growing panic as they opened my suitcase and began rummaging through my clothes, finding a small box wrapped in brown paper suspicious enough to investigate. The box contained a pair of jade cuff links for which I didn't have the proper papers (to prove they hadn't come from Red China). I held my breath. Just as they were about to open the box, a customs official appeared, chattering officiously and speaking the magic words "Dr. Pierce."

"Oh, so sorry! So sorry!" my two inquisitors repeated over and over, quickly rewrapping the small box and stamping my suitcases "cleared." My rescuer escorted me through the airport and delivered me into the Kilbournes' waiting arms.

"Sure pays to know someone!" I remember saying, as with a shaky voice I told them what had happened.

I had known since I was very young that my father was different from the average dad. I remember the first time someone was impressed by my parentage. I was in first or second grade, making the monotonous bus journey either to or from school with the same kids I had ridden with every day since my limited academic career had begun. I found myself talking to a girl who looked familiar but whom I'd never talked with before. Somehow, the subject of our dads came up.

"What's your dad do?" she asked.

"Oh, he just travels a lot and preaches. He's president of World Vision," I answered.

"World Vision! Is your dad Bob Pierce? We listen to him on the radio every Sunday, and I have two 'brothers' in Korea!

SHARING THE SPOTLIGHT

Hey," she yelled, excitedly poking another kid in the side, "Did you know that Marilee's Bob Pierce's daughter?!"

I don't remember anyone else getting particularly excited by her announcement, but I was deeply impressed with her extraordinary behavior. After that, I would occasionally find a way to casually mention my dad's name, throwing it out to see if it got any reaction.

It was fun being the daughter of someone famous. Of course, it would never do for me to appear impressed with the fact myself; often I would don a facade of false modesty. "Oh, you've probably never heard of him," I'd say, protecting myself from the embarrassing possibility that someone never had heard of him. But as many times as not the name rang a bell, and it was a warm, special feeling to find myself illuminated by a corner of the spotlight in which my father lived.

Only later did that spotlight become a little annoying, as I attempted to establish my own identity rather than always being "Bob Pierce's daughter." I didn't battle any great resentment or feel anything but pride in being a Pierce, but more than once I remember teasing my dad with the threat, "Someday you're going to be introduced as 'Marilee Pierce's father,' and we'll see how you like it!"

While Daddy had been on medical leave, Mother, Sharon, Robin, and I had participated in the groundbreaking ceremony for the new offices World Vision was building in Monrovia, California. When Daddy came home he was furious to discover the architectural plans had been altered during his absence. The changes seemed to be symbolic of inevitable organizational changes that were also taking place.

Chapter 26

END OF AN ERA
•

I liken my dad, in those final years of his association with World Vision, to the last of the great dinosaurs—an endangered species struggling to survive in a changing world.

My father was a maverick, an innovator, a pioneer, a visionary. The key to his whole ministry was his unhesitating responsiveness to need. If he saw a need that no one else was meeting, he met it. That's why World Vision was created—to organize and finance the fulfillment of the commitments my father made. While they were small the supply and demand balanced out, although not without God's miraculous intervention time and again. But that was what made the ministry so exciting and satisfying.

But as World Vision expanded, the projects became larger and the sums of money grew astronomically. Millions of dollars passed through the office each year, and every penny had to be scrupulously accounted for. The government required detailed expense accounts, and of necessity the World Vision board began placing certain restrictions on Daddy's authority to commit money without their voted approval.

He did his best to comply, but my father was a free spirit, accustomed to checking only with the Holy Spirit before making on-the-spot judgments and instantaneous commitments. Asking him now to function by a different set of rules meant a whole change in his approach to ministry, a change he resented and resisted. Consequently, he had a number of confrontations with the board concerning unauthorized expenditures of money.

END OF AN ERA

The board's concern was understandable. None of them had Daddy's extraordinary backlog of experience. They functioned with prayer and good business sense, but Daddy had found that the two didn't always mesh.

For instance, in 1958 Daddy produced and released the film *Cry in the Night*. It was a tremendously moving film, shot with care, creativity, and cinematic style. It also had the largest budget of any Christian film produced to date, a fact that raised a few eyebrows and made people particularly jumpy about getting the money back.

Just before the film was to be released, Daddy called everyone together and made the startling announcement that the Lord had told him to lend the film out for free. The only stipulation he made was that whoever asked for the film would pay the postal fees and take an offering for their own missions projects.

No one could believe Daddy was serious, but at that time Daddy still had the final word. Within one year there were two hundred copies of *Cry in the Night* working around the clock all over the country, and the increase in sponsorship and giving from people who saw the film were greater than from any other single project up to that time.

But Daddy's track record didn't make his unorthodox methods any easier to accept, and to the board he often appeared as impetuous as he had to Mother thirty years before when he had dropped their rent money into the passing offering plate. In all fairness, I know there were times when God used the board to keep Daddy from stretching things too thin. Among other things, the Rose Bowl fiasco is proof that his vision was occasionally impaired.

But the fact remains that the growing operational disparities seemed to put Daddy on one end of a tug-of-war rope and the board on the other.

My father never handled confrontations well. Bill Price, my dad's personal assistant and constant companion for nearly eight years, said recently, "Your father's single greatest flaw was his explosive temper. But other than that—his morality, his vision, his dedication, his faith—for all these things I don't know any other man I respect as much as Dr. Bob. Countless times I watched him reach out, heedless of his own personal safety, to embrace the untouchable, the unlovely. He would always choose the most disfigured lepers, throwing his arms around them as an extension of Christ's love reaching out physically through his body.

"I remember so clearly our last trip together. We were visiting a hospital in Formosa. Our schedule was tight, and as usual we were in a rush when Dr. Bob spotted a ten-year-old boy with meningitis. There was nothing more they could do for him, and he was lying in the corridor waiting to die. He watched us approach with large, frightened eyes, too weak to raise his head or wipe away the tears that slowly rolled down his cheeks. Dr. Bob stopped and, without a thought as to how highly contagious the disease was, wrapped the boy in his arms and prayed with him. I watched the child's body relax as Dr. Bob held him, and we left him peacefully at rest in the Savior's tender care.

"It was such a paradox to see the same man who gave so lovingly explode over the most unexpected things."

Daddy's unpredictable moods had always caused us to step lightly; we were never certain what might set him off. It is not uncommon for someone who lives under high stress to use minor irritations as an excuse to blow off steam. But even when Mother understood the basic cause of such outbursts, it was hard not to take the attacks personally.

Being so well acquainted with his volatile temper, it was with a deep sense of dread and fear that Mother watched Daddy walk out the door one day in 1967. Once again he and the board had butted heads over several issues, and the day promised fireworks of the most spectacular kind.

Daddy had talked while he dressed. "I'm going in and tell them this is the way I operate . . . the way God has blessed me . . . the only way I know to work. They knew that when they signed on. I haven't changed. I can't face a hungry, dying world and tell them to wait while I go home and check

END OF AN ERA

with my board. There is no way I can come home and get board approval for every little thing!"

Mother had heard everything Daddy was saying countless times before, and so had the board. But there was something different about this time. With sudden clarity, Mother realized that Daddy shouldn't be facing those men that day. He needed physical rest and emotional refreshing, a time to get alone with the Lord and be spiritually refueled. At the moment he was flying on empty, and any strong winds of opposition could well cause him to lose control.

"I'm going to tell them to either pull with me or get off the ship!" he declared as he slammed the door behind him.

The next hours crawled past at an aggravatingly slow pace. The meeting went well past its scheduled duration, each additional minute adding to Mother's foreboding that something was wrong.

Finally, late in the afternoon, Mama heard his car pull into the driveway. She rushed to open the door.

"Well, I let them have it all," he said in a tense, unnatural voice that slapped the air with each word.

"What do you mean?" Mother asked. "What are you talking about?"

"I gave them everything—my films, my office, my work. I told them if they wanted it so badly they could have it. I started with nothing; I'll leave with nothing!" As he spoke, his voice trembled with the uncontrollable rage and indignation that had left no room for discussion or thoughtful reevaluation of the situation. Mother desperately tried to make him see what he was doing, but he was blind and deaf to anything but his own fury.

Mother rushed to the phone and called one of Daddy's most trusted friends, hoping his voice could call Daddy back to reason. For the moment, however, everyone was the enemy; Daddy told his friend to stay out of his business, and he hung up the phone.

The next day World Vision presented him with legal documents of agreement, and Bob Pierce signed his life's work away.

Chapter 27

"WHO ARE WE NOW, MAMA?"

The closest I can come to describing the next few months is that it was as if someone had died. Things continued in a seemingly normal pattern. We ate and drank and breathed and slept just as we always had, but everything was different. Life had taken a sudden and unexpectedly sharp turn, leaving us all painfully off balance. We were convinced it was a temporary condition, certain to right itself momentarily. Only it didn't.

As the days passed into weeks and months, each of us attempted to adjust. I think ten-year-old Robin expressed it best the day she asked, "Who are we now, Mama?" Suddenly there were no clear-cut definitions, because the thing that had controlled and defined the purpose of our existence—the ministry—had suddenly been removed.

I'm not saying God had forsaken us. Jesus was still the foundation our lives were built upon, the solid Rock which is the same yesterday, today, and forever. But the support beams of that foundation had been the work God had given us. Everything had emanated from that—our friends, our family relationships, our attitude about ourselves. We lived in that quiet assurance that we belonged to something truly remarkable, something that exalted Jesus Christ and served mankind and gave our lives a special meaning and purpose. Now, suddenly, we were outside that warm, magical circle, no longer a part of the family that God had given birth to through us. It was crazy, impossible, ridiculous, and totally terrifying.

"WHO ARE WE NOW, MAMA?"

For Mother, the following year was a kaleidoscope of emotions. Unable to believe that the situation was beyond salvaging, she called two board members whom she particularly trusted, begging them not to accept Daddy's resignation. "Put him on an extended leave of absence. Stipulate any conditions you deem necessary, only don't take his presidency away. Don't allow him to cut himself off like this. He's sick, and in no condition to make a decision he'll regret as long as he lives!"

But there was nothing they could do, and Mother was forced to helplessly watch their world fall apart. Her mind would rage with indignation when she thought of how Daddy had thrown away their life's work in a fit of temper, the way a petulant child might throw away a toy he can't work properly. It may have appeared that the board was taking advantage of his irrational behavior, but no one had asked him to resign. He had done it himself, without considering Mother, the family, or the overwhelming implications.

Mother's anger would usually melt into teeth-grinding sorrow as reality would come flooding in, followed by incredulous disbelief that such a thing could happen. During that time, Mother fought hard to hold on to the knowledge that God was still in control. It was now that the years of tenacious prayer and disciplined faith held her in good stead. She believed God because she knew no other way to survive, and that faith gave her the one thing essential to life—hope. And hope breeds expectancy. So Mother lived from day to day, waiting to see what God would do.

I cannot tell you all that my father must have felt during those days. He would express raging anger one minute and a flippant "I-don't-care" attitude the next. Sometimes he would be fine, appearing strong and in control of the situation. During those times he would talk enthusiastically about continuing his work on a smaller scale without the complications of a large office, which inevitably depersonalized things and, to his way of thinking, made the rules more important than the people. Mother would take heart, thinking that perhaps this was God's way of slowing Daddy down, of taking him back to the basic essentials that would allow him to continue ministering without killing himself.

But then something would happen . . . a word, a thought . . . and he would seem to crumble before our eyes, retreating into a world of incredible pain and anguish beyond comfort or reason. He was like a mother bereft of her only child, or a king dethroned and exiled from an empire of his own making. He mourned his loss with angry bellows and stormy silences, and we all watched with growing concern as his inward turmoil began to manifest itself in uncontrollable shaking and choking spells.

No one else was particularly aware of our situation or our battles. People were more than willing to accept the simple explanation that Daddy had resigned for health reasons, and while occasionally someone would express their shock and dismay over the turn of events, most people placed us on a shelf labeled "inactive" and moved on.

This truth struck home with me about a year after Daddy resigned. I went to Westmont College for my freshman year, a school attended by many P.K.s (Preachers' Kids) and missionary offspring. During the first few days we were all getting acquainted, and I was inevitably introduced as Bob Pierce's daughter.

"Oh," said one touchingly sincere girl, "I was so sorry to hear about your dad. When did he die?"

Her question smacked me in the face like a bucket of icy water, leaving me sputtering for words. Finally, I explained that "the reports of my father's death are greatly exaggerated," making light of what to me was tragically unfunny.

Daddy's disassociation with World Vision didn't happen with the slash of the pen, but rather it came gradually over a period of months. In the spring of 1968, he and Mother went overseas on a "Good-bye Tour," visiting Korea, Formosa, Hong Kong, and Japan.

As the time drew near to return home, Daddy began talk-

"WHO ARE WE NOW, MAMA?"

ing about making an unscheduled stop in Viet Nam. Mother argued against it. Not only would she have to fly home alone, but she had a gut feeling that he shouldn't go. But Daddy was adamant; he was uncertain when or if he would have another opportunity.

Still together on their trip, one evening the phone rang. Mother heard Sharon's distant voice.

"Hi, Mama. Is Daddy there?"

"Yes, Darling. But what is it? Is something wrong?"

"No. Yes. I love you, Mama. But can I please talk to Daddy?"

Mother handed the phone to him.

"Hello, Baby," Daddy said. "What's the matter?"

For the next several minutes, Mama watched the intensity on Daddy's face as he listened, sensing from his expression that he was battling within himself.

Finally he said, "Honey, I just can't come home right now. I feel I've got to go to Viet Nam now while I have the chance. I promise I'll get home as soon as I can, and your Mother will be home in a few days."

With that Mama took the phone. "Sweetheart, I'll catch a flight tomorrow and I'm sure your dad won't be long. Are you all right?"

"Oh, I'm fine. And don't worry. It's all right. I guess I knew he wouldn't come." Sharon's voice was strangely flat and hollow. As soon as she hung up Mother made reservations to fly home.

In the hours between the phone call and her departure, Mother tried unsuccessfully to convince Daddy to come home. He was officially retired now, and for once in his life he was free to put his family's needs first. But he was caught up in a desperate struggle for his own survival. Somehow the Orient represented the best part of him, a part he felt in danger of losing, and his own need to hold on was greater than any outside influence.

As it turned out, Mother's dark premonition was justified, for while in a remote part of Viet Nam Daddy contracted paratyphoid. He lay in a coma for seven days before the Lord miraculously touched him and he was able to be flown to a hospital in Hong Kong.

But any fear Mother had felt for Daddy was long forgotten in the light of her concern for Sharon.

Arriving home she found Sharon weak and depressed, her wrists bound, recovering from an unsuccessful attempt to take her own life. "I know you love me, Mama," she said, "but I just needed to feel Daddy's arms around me."

Chapter 28

SHARON
•

Soon after Sharon was born, Mother had presented her to the Lord at Papa Johnson's church in Los Angeles. This was during the time Daddy was away trying to find himself, and Uncle Floyd stood in his place at Mother's side.

Because Mother's prayer life was so active, Sharon grew up talking to Jesus like an old family friend. Each night at bedtime she would earnestly pray, "And bless my Daddy's mystery." Mother knew she meant "ministry," but she couldn't bring herself to correct her. When I first heard the story (I was four or five), I didn't get the joke. I often didn't know exactly where Daddy was or what he was doing, and "mystery" seemed an appropriate description of the situation.

Sharon asked Jesus into her heart when she was five years old, after hearing the Easter story in one of Mother's Child Evangelism classes.

The following Sunday evening Daddy was speaking at a church in Los Angeles, and Mother and Sharon attended with him. At the close of the message, he asked those who wanted to make a public confession of their faith in Christ to raise their hands. Sharon lifted her hand, as did many others, but somehow it was hidden from Daddy's view. Later, as they were driving away from the church, Sharon asked, "Daddy, why didn't you point at me tonight when I raised my hand?" Then she burst into tears.

Immediately Daddy took her in his arms and said, "Darling, I didn't see your hand, but Jesus did." He prayed with her, and while she was still in his arms she said, "Now,

MAN OF VISION, WOMAN OF PRAYER

Daddy, I want to be 'baptitized.' " Since Daddy was leaving for China soon, a baptismal service was held the following Sunday for one small child. Papa and Daddy shared the joy of immersing her in the waters of baptism, and of hearing her declare as she rose, "I love Jesus very, very much!"

Yes, Sharon loved Jesus, and her heart's commitment to Him never could be questioned. Her copious notes and the well-worn pages of her Bible testify to her love and knowledge of God's Word. She knew she was a child of God, and she truly desired to serve Him.

But as this book illustrates, a commitment to Jesus Christ is no guarantee of immunity to the disease and pain of the world. In fact, those who are most greatly used are often most viciously attacked. And what better way to wound the heart of a parent than through his child?

Sharon made her fairy-tale trip to Europe when she was ten, and had an equally lovely trip to the Orient at fifteen. She was a people-lover, and her gregarious personality and natural charm endeared her to everyone she met. The little autograph book she was given in Liverpool is a "Who's Who" of the Christian world, containing an amazing number of lovely tributes written to one so young.

No one who knew Sharon would ever have believed the terrible insecurity and sense of worthlessness she battled. Even Mother and Daddy didn't comprehend the seriousness of her struggle until it was too late. It is only as I read her many diaries, notebooks, unmailed letters, and poems that the true picture emerges.

The Sharon I remember was a bright, funny, spontaneous extrovert. She was a talented artist and a gifted writer. She loved music and would play the piano for hours. I loved to be with her because she made me laugh. She could find humor in almost any situation, and we would laugh till our sides ached. As we grew older, the nine-year gap between us seemed to narrow.

When she was thirteen, my folks sent her to one of those elite Christian schools where gangly girls and boys are sup-

SHARON

posedly transformed into graceful ladies and gentlemen. At the time, "everyone" was sending their children there, and Daddy felt the social benefits would be invaluable. Mother hated to be deprived of Sharon's company, but she didn't want to keep her at home selfishly. So off Sharon went, a frightened, awkward little girl with painfully ingrown toenails, a brand new set of braces on her teeth, and freckles.

That year away did accomplish some good, but Sharon's diary reveals that it was a traumatic experience for her. There was no discussion about her going back for a second year.

During her early teen years, Sharon coasted comfortably as far as spiritual things were concerned. She knew more Scripture than most, she never missed church, and she ran with a healthy, clean-cut gang of kids. Mother and Dad wisely didn't push, allowing the Lord to move in His own time. And He did.

It was another routine Sunday morning. Sharon and her friends sat in the back of the small sanctuary in the same seats they occupied every Sunday morning, whispering and doodling and passing notes back and forth the way seventeen-year-olds will when they are in church out of duty rather than desire. The choir began to sing the hymn of the morning, one Sharon had heard hundreds of times before. But this particular morning something extraordinary happened. As the music began and the choir burst out with one voice, the well-worn words struck something deep within Sharon's spirit, sending a chill down her spine and causing her to lean forward in her seat. Suddenly the words were not the cliché of a religion, but the expression of ageless, wondrous truth revealed with incredible freshness. She felt as if she were seeing Jesus face to face for the first time, and the confrontation left her both broken and magnificently together and alive.

Unable to wait until the end of the service, Sharon slipped downstairs and knelt on the cold basement floor. Tears of repentance streamed down her cheeks as she rededicated her life to her Lord.

MAN OF VISION, WOMAN OF PRAYER

Two weeks later, Sharon obtained permission to testify to what God had done in her life. Before the entire congregation, her shining face and unquestionable sincerity made it evident to everyone that God indeed had laid His hand on her young life.

Sharon had a marvelous mind, full of curiosity and clever ideas. And she had a compassionate heart. Her own failures and insecurities made her incredibly sensitive to other people's pain, and far less judgmental of their weaknesses. Like her father, Sharon never hesitated to get involved. She was always opening her home to those in need, taking in a young unwed mother one month and perhaps a friend down on her luck the next. She once said, "It's not what's in your hand that's important, but the reaching out, the touching, the caring." Sharon cared.

But she also inherited her mother's extremely romantic nature, and that, combined with her father's strong will, led her into an early marriage. When she was nineteen, she married her high-school sweetheart—a quiet, gentle boy whom she loved but with whom she had little in common. It surprised no one that their relationship quickly deteriorated. The marriage lasted four years and produced one beautiful little girl, Lisa. Sharon was totally delighted with her fair-haired baby. She would often say to Mother, "She's beautiful, isn't she, Mama? I can't believe I made such a wonderful, beautiful child!"

But despite the great love and pride she felt for Lisa, the failure of divorce scarred Sharon deeply. She never again saw herself as a person of great value or potential. As far as she was concerned she was "used goods," no longer a candidate for God's best. Her self-deprecating attitude resulted in a disheartening series of unsuccessful relationships. It seemed that every time she reached out she was burned, and each bad experience destroyed a little more of her self-respect, leaving her all the more desperate for the love and approval that stubbornly eluded her. Sharon began to fight waves of overwhelming depression and hopelessness while fiercely

SHARON

clinging to her dreams of what might be. During this time she wrote incessantly, penning the world of thoughts she couldn't speak.

Then, when Sharon was twenty-five, Daddy took her to Viet Nam as a war correspondent. She was to write human interest stories from a woman's perspective for use in *World Vision* magazine, and she was heady with anticipation. Finally she had a chance to use her considerable talents to do something worthwhile.

> Take one average American girl, age 25, sweep her out of her average southern California secretarial existence, place her in the middle of bustling Saigon, and you have me.
>
> In this modern age of jets, it is possible to board a plane, take a nap, and wake up on the other side of the world. The danger in traveling in such a manner is that I become so excited to see and learn, I often end up disappointed that things are not as glamorous and thrilling as I had imagined.
>
> But such was not the case in Saigon. I had been here barely a day or two before I was told I was invited to tea with the wife of Viet Nam's Chief of State. I am what the British describe as a "commoner." I usually don't have tea, but I do have lunch with my girl friends at Rod's Drive-In. I wasn't sure if I should curtsy or what, but I was thrilled and honored to have the opportunity to find out.

Daddy had only himself to blame for Sharon's uninhibited spirit of adventure. She thrived on the danger and excitement of this strange new world, likening her first helicopter ride in a combat zone to a roller-coaster ride. "At first it is frightening, but then the thrill surpasses the fear and it is marvelous. . . . Of course, [avoiding enemy fire] is not a game, but each adventure is such a thrilling experience that I can't help looking forward to every moment."

Occasionally there were times when her sense of adventure overcame her common sense, and things got a bit too "thrilling." One day, she and a friend decided to "hitchhike" via

MAN OF VISION, WOMAN OF PRAYER

"Military Air Lines" to the town of Dalat. They arrived to discover the terminal was nothing more than a large tent pitched in the middle of some rice paddies. They could find no transportation into town. At the time, the Viet Cong were not exactly competing for the American tourist trade, and Sharon found herself stranded in what was definitely unfriendly territory. The situation went from bad to worse when they learned that the plane would not be able to return for them until the next day.

Unable to safely leave the tent or communicate with anyone back in Saigon, there was nothing left to do but wait and pray. I'm sure Sharon laughed when she saw God's answer to her fervent prayers—not a plane, not an armored car, but a simple horse-drawn wagon, driven by a friendly farmer who was willing to bury Sharon and her friend under his load of vegetables for the short but nerve-wracking journey into town. Once in Dalat, Sharon made her way to a missionary school, where she was lovingly cared for until she could be flown out safely the next day.

Having been the subject of Daddy's wrath a time or two myself, I'm sure Sharon seriously considered surrendering to the V.C. when Daddy found out about her little adventure. But, evidently, the incident did little to dampen her enthusiasm, for shortly thereafter she wrote:

> In the weeks that I have been here the most wonderful and exciting things have occurred. I came with Big Daddy and while he was here, it was a storm of activity. He was only here a week and I can understand why the people in Viet Nam say they are glad to see him come . . . and glad to see him go. We met with numerous government officials regarding proposed projects, flew out to the "fighting," inspected orphan sights, and enjoyed social invitations. When he departed, I began to get around on my own a little. Having my press credentials, I have hitchhiked with the military and even got stranded one night in Dalat. It's quite a tale. . . . The worst part of my trip is that the writing I'm supposed to be doing just doesn't come easily. Some days I can

SHARON

sit down and write off page after page; on other days each word is born out of sweat and tears. . . .

Daddy enjoyed having Sharon with him, and he felt her contributions significant enough to bring her back to Viet Nam that same year. But even this time in Sharon's life was shaded by gnawing fears and feelings of inadequacy. In a letter to Mama she wrote:

> I have been constantly praying that God will do something new. . . . I don't really know what to ask for or how to pray. I just know I don't want to be useless. In just this one week I have seen and felt many things that have deeply moved me. . . . I don't know yet whether I'm a help or hindrance, but I'm trying to be a help.

Sharon returned from Viet Nam full of anticipation and enthusiasm about the future. But her high hopes didn't last long. For reasons I don't understand, nothing was ever done with the articles she worked so hard on. By January of the following year, she wrote to a friend confiding that she felt she was dying of boredom and frustration. She had had "the chance of a lifetime" to go overseas, and in her opinion she had done nothing with it. Now she was back where she started from. "I feel so trapped, as if all my opportunities are quickly passing me by. . . . I concede failure! What do you feel I should do? I'm dying. . . . Help!"

Sharon's personal papers and diaries are full of that desperate cry for help, a cry she found impossible to communicate outside the privacy of her own thoughts. Only God knows the damage that was done when suddenly she lost her daddy to a work that demanded all his thoughts, energy, and time. Robin and I never knew what it was to have Daddy home all the time, but Sharon was eight when Daddy started traveling, and she suffered a very real sense of loss. Effective communication was replaced by shallow dialogues that kept the peace but seldom expressed the heart.

MAN OF VISION, WOMAN OF PRAYER

At a particularly difficult time in her life, Sharon wrote the following. She was twenty-three or twenty-four, had just lost a job, and was feeling desperately alone. Mother and Dad had just arrived home from overseas.

> I had been so upset anyway. The last week had been all the worse, with no job, no money. . . . there was a comfort that they'd be coming home. When they did, Mom was only able to say she was sorry about my job . . . but it probably meant a better one was coming and that was that.
>
> Like he always does, Daddy said something about it being too bad I hadn't received severance pay—and he'd pay my employment fee—and that was that. Daddy always volunteers to pay something but, as he will tonight, leaves for the other side of the world and it's forgotten. I know it's not because he doesn't want to help or love me, but he's too preoccupied with other things. . . .
>
> He told me that he loves me and I'm not insignificant, etc. I know that, but he makes me feel terrible. We are going to have dinner tonight. I'll tell him what I need because I have to. But generally I'll tell him everything's OK—I have what I need, when really I'm dying. This is because I know I've been an awful problem for them for years and I don't want to be! As I will tonight, if I tell Daddy what I need, it only makes me feel like one of the large groups of problems he already has. He looks on me as just one more pressure he has to meet—one more person pawing him and that he has to give money to; just part of the rest of the little people who scratch and he feeds. God, how awful.
>
> Mom loves me too and I know she resents it when I turn to Daddy. But some things a woman just can't give—one being the comfort of a man, yes, a father even, when he puts his arms around you and says "everything will be O.K."

The feelings Sharon expressed were at times common to all of us kids, and Mother too. It was hard for us to believe that Daddy really understood our needs. Although we knew he

SHARON

loved us, he was gone too much to be involved with our everyday lives, and it was impossible to fill him in on a month's worth of life during two dinners and a trip to Disneyland. He was always careful to verbalize his concern and interest, but the life-and-death situations he was constantly dealing with must have made the problems of his healthy, well-fed children difficult to take seriously.

None of us was adequately sensitive to the seriousness of Sharon's situation. Even Mother, whose life revolved around her children, was totally shocked when she arrived home to discover her daughter had slashed her wrists in an attempt to end a life she found too painful to endure.

During the next few months, Mother and Dad tried desperately to understand Sharon's problems and to find someone to help her. She spent several weeks in a sanitarium, where she appeared to pick up and take hold once again. But Satan had planned his strategy carefully. Just as she began picking up the pieces of her life, her relationship with the man she deeply loved and hoped to marry ended in an extremely cruel and devastating way.

It was the final blow. Her overwhelming need for love and approval from the men in her life and her need to feel useful and significant drove Sharon deeper and deeper into the pit of despair. Her whole life had been spent like that little girl of long ago, earnestly waving her hand with a desperate desire to be acknowledged, but somehow always being overlooked in the crowd.

The only One who never hurt or disappointed her and in whom she had total confidence was the Savior she had accepted as a small child. Never in any of her writing did Sharon ever blame God for her failures, or depict Him as anything but a loving heavenly Father. Her deepest desire was to serve Him, and she struggled with the conviction that here too, she had failed. Her last thoughts were a testimony to that fact.

I love you Jesus. Oh, how I beg your forgiveness for each and every time I failed you or sinned. The biggest sin of all is my omission to witness for you. Even tho I am salt which has lost its savor, let me be one of the least in heaven! And if you find this last act a sin, please dear God, please forgive me for my final weakness. I love you, as you know.

Who can say why Sharon wasn't able to cope with life? She was a woman of great strengths and courage in so many ways. And yet, when it came to those last months and weeks she seemed to drown in a sea of hopelessness. It was during this time that she wrote this poem.

> Tonight the air is hot; hot to the senses and the emotions. The crickets are singing a friendly consolation. But the loneliness is so loud it overpowers.
>
> Somewhere on the edge of consciousness are sounds of life. But they are not related to me.
>
> There is a sadness so deeply penetrating that there is no use for tears or anger.
>
> It is a limbo of such nothingness that it numbs pain and joy.
>
> It is a night in which I simply exist. How do you fight Nothingness?

On November 30, 1968, Sharon chose to be with Jesus. She was twenty-seven.

Chapter 29

THROUGH THE LOOKING GLASS

•

Of all the heartaches our family has endured, losing Sharon was the most painful. I'll never forget the look on Mama's face when she was told her baby was gone. Her eyes became glassy reflections of sheer horror, masked almost immediately by an angry, rebellious refusal to believe. "Get away from me! You're lying! No! No! My girl is all right! My girl is all right!"

Her cries followed me out into the quiet darkness. Collapsing on the lawn, I remember digging my fingers into the damp, cool soil, tearing up great clumps of earth and flinging them wildly in all directions while someone screamed in the distance. Later, as I lay listening to the silence, I realized that the someone was me.

Coping with pain of that magnitude is a very personal thing. You have to somehow surface out of that ocean of disbelief and numbness before you can take the first breath of acceptance and begin receiving comfort and support from others. It is during those first nightmarish hours that the Holy Spirit, the Comforter, is so precious and real. He breaks through the emotional holocaust to breathe life and hope directly into one's spirit.

The immediate responsibilities of Sharon's sudden death fell on me, for Mama could not possibly make all the arrangements and Daddy was away once again. Toward the end of the previous summer, he had flown to Basel, Switzerland, for an exhaustive series of tests at the famed University Hospital. They discovered that the very core of his nervous system was completely exhausted, and the process of rebuilding it would be lengthy and complicated.

September 20, 1968

Darling Wife,

Tomorrow I will have been in the hospital for four weeks. Two I was kept asleep and the last two I have so many pills and insulin injections so that I cannot remember things from hour to hour. . . . Yesterday and today they are giving me a short respite from insulin, so I hired a car just for today, drove 90 miles or so here to Berne just to remember the happy times we had here. It is lonely but nice because of you.

The doctors now give positive diagnosis of severe exhaustion of my vegetative nervous system. I must remain in hospital for these shots of daily insulin, and have to stay under observation for side effects. . . . Then, now that the purely physical impairment is clearly identified and under treatment, I will begin psychiatric treatment for two hours regularly each week. . . . Since they have found something they can physically treat, I do not object to psychiatric treatment. Somehow I believe you would feel the same way. . . .

Cheerful is the news that I can be better than anytime in the past ten years with completion of this treatment.

Not so cheerful is the news that all this is caused by *over*exhaustion emotionally the past 21 years. The doctors expect me to keep disengaged from emotional tension for twelve months after the strong medical treatment.

I can only survive by living from day to day and by praying and trusting God to generously meet all needs of yours, Robin, Marilee, Sharon, and Lisa.

Meantime I cling to Romans 8:28. I love you!

Yours,

Bob

THROUGH THE LOOKING GLASS

The doctors' desire to keep Daddy emotionally disengaged almost kept them from telling him about Sharon's death altogether. As it was, he was allowed to come home for only one day, the day of the funeral. That night Mother, Daddy, Robin, and I huddled together in front of the den fireplace.

"I want you to pack up and come to Switzerland," Daddy said. "I may have to stay in Basel for as long as a year for treatments as an outpatient. I'll rent a chalet and we'll all be together. Come soon. I need you!" His voice broke with tearful emotion despite the heavy medication the doctors had prescribed to insure that he would not become overly distressed. Mama nodded, and we all moved closer together as plans were discussed.

The next day we watched Daddy board the plane for Switzerland, comforted by the fact that it was only a temporary separation. Soon we'd all be together, with time to share our mutual sorrow, to encourage and strengthen one another, and with God's help to discover the new direction we were to go as a family.

The unavoidable business of getting through the holidays and preparing to leave left us little time to mourn. It was as if subconsciously we had tucked our sorrow away until that time when as an entire family we could take it out and give it proper expression, after which healing could begin. Oh, the tears came frequently and that sudden stab like a hot poker in the heart left us breathless and shaken many times as we'd think of Christmas without Sharon or, worse yet, forget for a moment only to have the agonizing truth crash in on us as if for the first time. But most of the time we operated out of a God-given reserve that promised to hold us together until we could afford to let go.

But something happened between that night in December when Daddy entreated us to join him and the day we stepped off the plane in Basel the following February. While we applied for passports, got shots, packed, and arranged to close the house up for a year, Daddy continued to receive insulin treatments and other mind-controlling, personality-changing drugs aimed at counteracting the "definite setback in the vegetative system" he had experienced due to the "past few weeks of shock and sorrow," as he put it in one of his letters.

Whatever effect the drugs had on Daddy's mind, the man who picked us up at the Basel airport was a stranger we neither knew nor understood. For him, much of the past had been blocked out medically, and with it went certain natural feelings and responses.

From the beginning he was uncomfortable with us, finding us painful intruders into the safety of the little world into which he had escaped . . . a world totally isolated from pain, disappointment, guilt, the responsibility of yesterday, and the frightening uncertainty of tomorrow. In this world there was only today and, as Daddy repeated several times in his letters, "I can only survive by living from day to day."

The daily log Mother kept of our trip expresses her painfully honest impressions as we all stepped through the looking glass into a world where down was up and up was down, and absolutely nothing made sense.

> February 14, 1969
>
> Bob was waiting for us at the airport. He had a Mercedes car to take us to an apartment he had obtained for us in his apartment building. It was very nice—immaculately clean. He had some flowers in a vase and a few groceries in the kitchen. We freshened up, and then went to a nice restaurant for dinner. It was on the Rhine. We came back and went to bed. We slept fairly well. Robin slept with Bob in his little apartment.

The first sign that things were out of kilter was our peculiar living arrangement. Daddy didn't rent a chalet, as he had promised. Instead, he put Mother and me in an apartment downstairs from the small bachelor one in which he was living. His cramped quarters made it appear more practical for Robin to room with him, and the floor that separated him from

THROUGH THE LOOKING GLASS

Mother and me became a convenient line of demarcation across which we were free to visit but not to stay.

Sunday, February 15

Sunday we unpacked and had a quiet day. Robin was very happy and loves the snow. Marilee seems interested in the prospect of meeting people, and Bob is kindly and seems glad we are here, although time and circumstances have built an indecipherable wall. I am still numb most of the time. When I think of Sharon, and I do almost constantly, it still is not real that she is gone. I get such a large pang inside, I wonder how I will manage. But I am trying. I miss her—I do so miss her—I cannot even write my feelings.

Wednesday, February 19

I slept fairly well through the night, and awakened around 5:00 A.M. Marilee came in around 7:00 and we had tea. I thought I would try getting up, which I did before eight, and then I saw Bob leaving in his car. . . .

Bob said every morning he stops by and sees different people when I questioned him where he goes each A.M. from 8–11. He was a bit irritated that I asked him, but I feel he has things he is not open about. Maybe I'm wrong. Hope so. He is fatter and looks drawn. We have come such a long way, I hope I find an answer for something—anything. . . .

It didn't take long for it to become painfully obvious that our coming had been a mistake. Daddy just didn't know what to do with us, and his relationship with Mother deteriorated from day to day. What had begun as a hopeful attempt to unify the family quickly became an emotional endurance test.

Friday, February 21

Bob's hatred of me shows up so much more here and it is hard to bear. But I must, and I also must shift gears somehow. There

MAN OF VISION, WOMAN OF PRAYER

is a direction for me. Robin is happy, and I must be careful with Marilee. I cannot talk to her. I should not. It is wrong. I say silly and stupid things, looking for pity, understanding, or something. . . .

Why am I here? What chance is there of anything? When was it too late? Dear Sharon, even your death seems to be no rebuke to us. Shame on us. How selfish we are. I must not let my girls be hurt.

Wednesday

. . . I took a cup of coffee up to Bob's apartment. He said "Come in" and seemed cordial. I sat on the sofa and we had the only conversation thus far of significance. He discussed his belief and lack of belief—his feelings that "I expected God to take care of my children and I cared for others. He didn't," etc. . . . He seemed to leave me out of his vehemence. I listened. He then said, "I haven't talked like this for a long time." I said, "It's O.K." and put my arms around him, but he was stiff. . . .

Wednesday—A Week Later

Marilee and I sat with the doctor for 45 minutes. . . . He feels Bob and I should come in together next week, but he will see Bob tomorrow first. . . . He did say that Bob had no mental problem. It was just a matter of emotional fatigue, which he has had before and could be treated anywhere. Also, he said, when we resume living together (if) we should return to the States. . . .

Marilee and I joined Bob and Robin for lunch, but Bob was very depressed. He looked bad and very distant. We tried to chat and be friendly, but he would not. He did tell us that we would have to give up our apartment, as the landlord had called, but that we could take a few days. I know he wants us to leave, but if I go, I will say good-bye forever. I cannot work miracles. I hardly believe in them anymore . . . but if they do ever happen, this is the hour.

THROUGH THE LOOKING GLASS

Friday

I talked to the doctor today and he said Bob was bad, but we needed to resolve some things and he hoped we would come in together, but he didn't know if Bob would agree. I told him I would do anything I could to help the situation.

Sunday

Bob and I talked at length about our being here. He is not happy we are here and feels we should leave because of expenses. He is irritated that I can feel free to stay. He says I should go home and sell the house. He has provided for me well, and now I must start being careful, etc. His considerable expenditures are his concern. . . . And yet *we* should leave now because it costs to be here. I told him I thought we were going to stay with him, that Marilee and I would move to one room, etc. He just is not happy we are here. That's all. . . .

Monday

I went to American Express travel bureau and got our tickets for Florence, Italy . . . including Bob's. . . . After midnight Bob came in and said he wouldn't be going with us. I knew then I would not come back to Basel. I packed everything and went to bed at 1:00.

During those days Daddy was as changeable as the seasons, often going through winter, spring, summer, and fall all in one day. So it came as only a mild surprise that the next day he was packed and ready to go to Italy with us. Robin was overjoyed, but I, recognizing how unnatural everything was, battled confused feelings of hurt and disillusionment. And although I tried not to show it, Mother read me like a book.

Tuesday

Marilee needs direction. . . . So often I look at her and she looks so sad, deeply hurt—a look that says, "I can hardly bear it"—and then I ache, for I feel this so much of the time. I can't bear it, and I don't think I will ever get over this feeling. I think of Sharon's little girl, our darling Lisa, and wonder how she is, this precious girl of ours—and a stranger is raising her. Oh, Sharon, what were you thinking? Our whole world upside down and inside out, aching, hurting, in such a quandary. No answers for anything. I've thought of Sharon so much—always—always, even though I don't write it constantly. I just can't seem to find any answer for her taking her life. . . . Oh, God, please, *please, please*!

Returning from Italy, Robin and I decided to spend a couple of days in Vienna, while Mama waited in Basel and Daddy checked into the hospital for more tests. He had again made it clear that he thought we should leave.

Monday

I called the doctor. . . . He had little to say, mainly that their business was to heal the body and if I made conditions worse, it was wiser that I leave. I told him it would just be temporary, that until the core of the problem was dealt with, Bob would not get better. He said he understood, but there was nothing he could do. I hung up with a thank you and good-bye.

I took a bath and got dressed and suddenly felt very dizzy. I tried to reach Bob Evans in Paris. In order to do this I had to call the Bill Yoders in Geneva. . . . As a result of the call, Mrs. Yoder invited us to visit her in Geneva. I will consider it.

I can now look back on that frightening, chaotic time and see God's hand quietly at work through it all. It seems utterly impossible that the man who wept as he told us he needed us and wanted us with him and who wrote to Mother just weeks before we arrived—"We shall soon be together again. And with all my heart I pray that I may know how to be a greater joy to you"—was the same person who announced in a fit of

THROUGH THE LOOKING GLASS

rage, "These are my people, my friends. You are visiting. If you don't want to fit in with my life, get out!"

The only answer is that he was not the same man. Through the years my father had been battered and bruised, and each fresh wound required a little longer to heal. In the latter years the wounds were particularly deep and painful. One would barely begin to form a scab before another would be inflicted, and then another, until emotionally he became a mass of bloody, open wounds. The final blow was Sharon. When she died, it was as if he threw his hands up in unconscious surrender, turning his back on the past and on anything and anybody even remotely connected with it.

He was unwilling to talk about Sharon, and he pronounced any display of grief on our parts morbid and unhealthy. Any mention of home or old friends was likely to inflame his temper or leave him depressed and moody. We soon found ourselves guarding each word in an attempt to avoid unpleasantness, but it was impossible. Our very presence was like salt in his wounds. Daddy's desperate attempt to deny the agony of his own soul could never succeed with us there as constant reminders of everything he was running from.

At the end of May, Mama decided to accept the Yoders' loving invitation to visit them, and we left Basel for Geneva. It was there that we first heard of Dr. Francis Schaeffer. Mrs. Yoder felt that we should counsel with him; she had even talked to him on the phone about our coming to L'Abri. But Mother wasn't certain she wanted to go, and eventually we went on to Paris where Bob and Jeanette Evans made us welcome. Robin and I found Paris enchanting, but for Mother its beauty and romance elicited a very different response.

Thursday, April 3

To think I am in Paris under these strange and different circumstances. I came feeling fairly strong, because it seemed the next place in line for Robin. . . . Of course, I never thought I would come alone without Bob. Who would think I could manage alone? The city is particularly lovely. Early spring, flowers in bloom. The city seems cleaner. The buildings are washed. I feel a certain sense of familiarity about it all. Yet everything is empty—and very lonely. . . .

How could Bob not love me? I've never done anything to him—betrayed him, forsaken him. I bore his children, waited over twenty years for him, and when he could finally be with me, he doesn't want me. And he has nothing left.

It is now the 4th of April. Sharon would be 28. Oh, Father, please Father! Read my cries and help. . . .

God heard those cries, for a few days later Mother and I found ourselves standing on a little patch of heaven high on the side of an alp near the resort town of Villars, Switzerland. Neither of us had ever heard of Francis Schaeffer or L'Abri until our friends, the Yoders, suggested we go there. I felt a positive stirring immediately. Losing Sharon had been the first major hurt of my life and that, coupled with Daddy's peculiar behavior, had left me in desperate need of some answers. Other friends urged us to go. Willing to accept their urgings as more than a coincidence, but uncertain what help a total stranger might be, Mama arrived at L'Abri too cautious to be hopeful, but open to whatever God might have.

My first impression of L'Abri was an overwhelming sense of peace. Looking out over the lush green valley to the snow-capped mountains beyond, the air itself seemed laced with a healing balm that soothed our frazzled nerves and eased the tension from our faces. The love and joy of the Lord was unmistakably apparent in the smiles that greeted us, and we knew God had brought us to someplace very special.

While I settled my things in the dormitory-style bedroom where I was to stay for the next five days, Mrs. Schaeffer led Mother upstairs to her husband's study. He was out hiking, but was due back momentarily. Mother's few minutes alone gave her a chance to acquaint herself with the man by study-

THROUGH THE LOOKING GLASS

ing his small office. The walls were lined with books from floor to ceiling, and Mother couldn't help wondering if he had really read them all. At that time she wasn't aware that he had written several of them.

Hearing footsteps coming up the stairs, Mama put on her official "Mrs. Bob Pierce" face and prepared to greet Dr. Schaeffer. But the man who entered the room caught her off guard and immediately disarmed her. Dressed in hiking boots and knickers, his rugged features framed by a mane of fine, silvery hair, and his eyes brilliantly alive and interested, he took Mother's hand in a warm, solid grasp and said, "Hello, Lorraine."

The significance of those two words is still being revealed to Mother today, for in that simple greeting was the whole crux of what God wanted Mother to understand. All her life she had lived in someone else's shadow. First she was Floyd Johnson's daughter, then Bob Pierce's wife. Now, at the very time she felt the greatest failure, when it appeared that all she had stood for was meaningless and vain, God sent someone to call her by name and say, "My dear Lorraine, do you have any idea who you are? How wonderful and special and unique you are? You have been created in the image of God, for His glory and pleasure. Don't let anyone rob you of the unique specialness of being you!"

Dr. Schaeffer's words cut through Mother's insecurity and pain, stirring embers of hope and anticipation that through the years she had allowed to cool in the sad assumption that she simply wasn't "one of the gifted ones." Although they didn't change the situation with Daddy or bring Sharon back, his words restored that which the past months had destroyed—her sense of self-worth.

When we left L'Abri, neither Mother nor I were the people we were when we arrived. God met us both on that mountain, providing us each with the special love and encouragement we needed. During the days of happy fellowship with the other young people staying there, and during the quiet hours of teaching and counseling with Dr. Schaeffer, I rediscovered the reality of life in Jesus. And I learned two very important things. One, that there are some things in this life for which there are no pat answers. And two, that it's all right if we don't have all the answers, because God's love and faithfulness are great enough to bridge all the gaps; as long as we keep sight of Jesus, it's not necessary to always understand.

The time with Dr. Schaeffer had helped Mother and me stand up spiritually once again. If for no other reason, the trip had been worth the price. But we certainly couldn't afford to wander around Europe indefinitely like a tribe of Eurail gypsies, and since Daddy couldn't keep us with him there was nothing left to do but go home.

Chapter 30

HOME AGAIN?
•

"I bruise you, you bruise me. We both bruise too easily . . . too easily to let it show. I love you, and that's all I know." Those Paul Simon lyrics run through my head as I think of my parents—two hurting people in desperate need of love and comfort and understanding, unable to make contact with the very ones who could fulfill those needs—each other.

But despite all the angry protests to the contrary, their love never died. During the next nine years, Satan would do his best to destroy it, pervert it, and finally deny that it ever existed at all. But the bond God had ordained and established thirty years before could not be so easily broken, not only because this miracle of God is far stronger than the wiles of the enemy, but because deep in their hearts neither of my folks wanted it to be.

Coming home from Europe was a curiously empty experience. We all needed time to recover from the emotional beating we had taken. Robin's youth and naturally sunny disposition allowed her almost immediately to push the unpleasantness of the past months into a corner of her consciousness and get on with the joyous adventure of living. I used to watch her laughing and playing and think, "How does she do it? Doesn't she see what's happened? Doesn't she understand?" I see now that Robin's laughter and unquenchable enthusiasm was a gift from the Lord to us all. She was a consistent spark of normalcy that kept us in touch with the realities of the day.

MAN OF VISION, WOMAN OF PRAYER

Holding on to that reality became one of my most difficult battles. God had gifted me with an unusually active imagination that had provided me with worlds of adventure throughout my childhood. Then, in junior-high school I did my first one-act play, and after that I ate, drank, and slept theater. I had the lead in every high-school production, and I did summer stock with a director from the Pasadena Playhouse the summer after my graduation. The emotional outlet on stage seemed to lessen my need to fantasize offstage, but during the months following Europe I found myself escaping more and more into that make-believe world where Sharon still lived, where everybody loved one another, and where I felt safe and accepted.

But I was constantly being jerked back to reality. Everywhere I looked there were reminders of Sharon, and the realization that she was gone would send me into terrible bouts of depression and uncontrollable weeping. I realize now that those hours of groaning and crying expressed far more than my grief over Sharon's death; they were expressions of all the hurt, confusion, and frustration that had built up inside me over the past years.

As for Mama—well, she went on being Mama, holding the fabric of our lives together, trying to be strong because she knew Robin and I needed her to be. Only in the night hours, after Robin and I were asleep, would she allow herself to examine her thoughts and feelings, writing everything down just as Sharon had.

Laguna Beach, July 23, 1969

I am here with my two girls for a week. It seems I am not gaining any strength, knowing any direction, at all. The weeks and months go by. I really want to feel sensitivity God-ward. I don't beseech God. Perhaps, until I do, I'll go on day after day—dry, alone—in this "away world" where only I can be with all that has happened to smack my being within so totally. Tonight as I look out the bedroom window the sea is silver with moonlight and quiet. I have just finished reading July 23 of

HOME AGAIN?

> Mary Tileston's *Joy and Strength*. The reading was especially good. My head agrees and says "Yes, this is truth," but my heart is without response. I have asked God to help my heart, soul, and spirit to soon be alive to "truth." What else can I do? You see, Sharon is still so real.

As is often the case, distance and time began to put things back into proper perspective. Mother had been through too much with Daddy, she had seen God miraculously intervene too many times in their relationship to feel that things would not eventually work out. Although she didn't understand all the medical implications (no one ever took time to explain to Mother either the treatments or their probable aftereffects) or fully comprehend the extreme dimensions of the spiritual warfare being waged, she knew Daddy had not been himself much of the time we had been together.

And despite her emotional lows, she never doubted that when Daddy was healed physically and emotionally, their relationship would be restored as God once again led them out of a troubled time of testing to a new plateau of ministry and blessing.

Her confidence was bolstered by Daddy's renewed correspondence. The same day that Mother wrote those words at Laguna, Daddy wrote the following letter. He was still confused and seeking direction for his life, but wherever he was going he obviously intended to take Mother with him.

Basel, Switzerland, July 23, 1969

My Darling Wife,

I am homesick for you. And Robin and Marilee. The medical treatment ending, my thoughts are overwhelmingly of home and you. My nerves are steady now. Only my mind is still unclear. It is unclear to me how to go about finding a new meaning in the business of doing God's will.

John Haggai has offered me the job of being chancellor of the

MAN OF VISION, WOMAN OF PRAYER

Arosa International Training Institute starting September 15 and meantime has asked me to go with him to India for two conferences in Delhi and Bangalore starting August 7. . . .

I know with certainty that there is no meaning to life without Christ at its center, and I am torn between the desire to come home—with nothing in view to work at—or taking this apparently open door with John. To regain sanity it is necessary to be employed for the Lord.

Please let me receive your thoughts at this time and any ideas you have.

I love you,

Bob

Shortly after that letter arrived, Mother received a call from the board of Food for the World, a small organization under the auspices of World Literature Crusade. They were looking for someone to take over the work, and they wanted to know if Daddy would be interested.

A small organization Daddy could take in any direction he felt led—the package seemed to have Daddy's name written all over it! Mother could hardly wait to contact him. His immediate response was understandably subdued, but Mother encouraged him to see the possibilities. At least it was a start. So on his way home Daddy stopped in Los Angeles to sign the papers, making him president of an organization with a net worth of about eighteen dollars. Eventually he would change the name to "Samaritan's Purse" and broaden the concept of the ministry from supplying food to aiding all types of needs on an individual or small scale.

In early fall of 1969, Daddy moved home from Basel. For my father, coming home meant far more than searching out a new life; it meant facing up to the old one. While Mother, Robin, and I had gone through the stages of mourning Sharon's loss together, gradually finding the constant reminders of her more sweet than bitter, Daddy had succeeded in avoid-

HOME AGAIN?

ing such confrontations almost entirely. And while the three of us had grown accustomed to our dissociation from World Vision, Daddy hadn't even begun to tackle that psychological mountain. For over a year he had been carefully sheltered and protected, relieved of the responsibility of thinking or feeling. If something had hurt him, he had been given emotional painkillers. If something had upset him, the doctors had prescribed it away.

Now he came back to a house in which Sharon's voice still seemed to echo, to a city where all roads seemed to lead to World Vision, to a world which seemed to have stood still, waiting to taunt him by its very changelessness.

I was in New York the first few months Daddy was home. Dick Ross was producing the film version of *The Cross and the Switchblade* and had generously offered me the opportunity of learning about film-making firsthand. So at nineteen I found myself with an apartment on 56th Street in Manhattan, working with Pat Boone, Don Murray, and an unknown named Erik Estrada (currently star of television's *CHIPs*)—doing everything from typing scripts to laundry.

Daddy came to New York for a couple of days, and we took in a Broadway show and ate at the Four Seasons. He was cheerful and loving, the proud, doting father I remembered; it was good to be together.

After he left, New York seemed bigger and lonelier than ever before, and I began to think longingly of home. Finally, I could stand it no longer and asked Dick if I could leave early.

But I soon discovered that the idealized picture of family life I had envisioned while in New York was far from reality. The atmosphere at home was charged with tension, as if an uneasy truce had been called but everyone knew the war was far from over. Mother was overly solicitous, like an insecure child trying too hard to please. And Daddy was immaculately polite, his stiffly proper responses putting up a wall more impenetrable than his anger ever had.

None of us knew how to break through that wall. I suppose we all felt that in time Daddy would just snap out of it and gradually things would get back to normal. But "normal" didn't really exist for Daddy any more, and that realization must have filled him with fear and desperation.

One day he announced he was going to paint the house . . . all by himself. He bought brushes, ladders, buckets, and gallons of paint, attacking the project as if his life depended on it. For two weeks he sanded and scraped and painted, working up to fourteen hours a day, setting up big spotlights so he could paint after dark. Having no understanding of the need that birthed his obsession, we all watched Daddy with raised eyebrows, laughing at his extraordinary behavior. My heart still breaks as I envision the man, spotlighted high on a ladder, a painter's cap pulled over his greying curls, his face and arms spattered with paint, dripping with perspiration despite the chilly night air, feverishly painting a call for help no one had the ears to hear.

I enrolled in a drama workshop in Hollywood, determined to become the first Christian Sarah Bernhardt. Daddy had been angry that I didn't go back to college; he felt that a good education came next to being saved. Today I wish I had listened, but then I had stars in my eyes, insisting with the cocky assurance of inexperience that I knew what I was doing. I loved the Lord, and someday when I had really "made it" as an actress, God would use me as he did Pat Boone and Anita Bryant.

Mother and Daddy never felt good about the direction I was going, and I knew it. But in my own way I had begun to rebel. I didn't smoke, drink, or swear. I was a virgin and would remain one until I married. And I truly desired to serve the Lord—but my way, not His. And therein lay the seeds of my destruction, the weak link that left me vulnerable to deception.

The first day of drama class I met a young man who was ten years older than I, who had been married before, and who didn't know how to say "good morning" without using a four-letter word. But he was also tall, dark, handsome, re-

HOME AGAIN?

markably talented, and utterly charming. He both frightened and fascinated me, and before I knew it we were going out after class and I had invited him home for dinner.

Mother and Daddy immediately saw why I was attracted to Scott. He was funny and bright, and had a vulnerable quality that made Mother want to "mother" him. He began coming to the house often, and we would have long discussions about the Bible and Jesus. He seemed sincerely interested and open, so my folks let him keep coming. But they also kept an anxious eye on our relationship, constantly cautioning me not to get too involved.

My response was always the same. "Don't worry. Scott's only a friend. I want him to meet Jesus. I'm not going to fall in love. I can handle it."

And so, as I struggled to stay emotionally unattached, Mother and Dad sought to somehow reconnect the lines of communication that years of separation and heartbreak had severed.

It was February, 1970, one of those bright, clear winter days when the air is clean, the sky is blue, and the mountains appear so close you could touch them. Robin was out playing with a friend and I was reading when I heard loud voices. It seemed Daddy had taken all of Mother's credit cards out of her wallet without her knowledge, and Mother wanted them back. The argument was hot and heavy, with Daddy roaring that Mother spent too much money and Mother strongly denying the accusations, pointing out that he had no idea what it cost to feed and clothe two growing girls.

Every married couple in history has had a similar argument at one time or another, and it certainly wasn't a new tune around our house. But this particular day things got out of hand. The credit cards were the spark that lit the fuse on a whole keg of dynamite, and as the smoke cleared Mother and I watched Daddy walk out the door, suitcase in hand.

The next few weeks were a collage of emotional crises—one overlapping another in a crazy patchwork of hurt and anger and fear. We all expected Daddy to move home at any moment. Then one day we were informed that all our credit had been cut off, including the market and the drug store, and the next day the phone company called to say they'd been instructed to disconnect our telephone. Gradually it began to sink in that Daddy was serious; he had made the break.

And yet he didn't disappear from our lives. He moved into a motel only five minutes away and called or came over whenever he felt like it. Two weeks after he left he sent Mother a beautiful valentine, signing it with love. In April, he wrote several letters from overseas, addressing them to "My Beloved Family" and making statements like, "I am thinking of you constantly, praying for you and loving you, each one, with all my heart."

It was his inconsistency, his constant contradictions that wore Mother down emotionally and physically. For weeks she carried that valentine around with her, looking for someone Daddy respected to step in and help rectify the situation. The card was evidence that Daddy still loved her and that their relationship was salvageable, but it was a flimsy defense against Daddy's adamant insistence that she see a lawyer.

Day after day, Robin and I watched Mother agonize over the situation. She was unable to conceal the total devastation of her soul. At times it would be so bad that Robin would run to me for reassurance that Mama was going to be all right, her little face pinched with worry and her eyes filled with pain and questions I couldn't answer.

At times like that I felt as if I had the whole world on my shoulders. I would have done anything to ease Mama's pain and stop the snowball effect of the past few tragic years. I wanted to grab Daddy and scream, "Why are you doing this? We love you! We need you! You're killing her. Stop it! Stop. Just stop!"

But of course, I never did. During this time Scott became an increasingly important person in my life. He was always there to encourage me and hold me, his presence providing strength and security. While concerned friends and loved

HOME AGAIN?

ones did their best to make me see the danger, I continued to deny that there was anything serious between us—right up until the day in July, 1970, when Scott and I eloped.

The following September Daddy took Mother to court, where they were legally separated.

Chapter 31

SEPARATION
•

Mother never recovered from Daddy's taking her to court. Like Sharon's death, it was something that just couldn't happen, one of those things God wouldn't *allow* to happen. She accepted Sharon's death because she had no choice. She accepted my marriage because she didn't want to lose me. But the legal separation was something Mama never accepted.

Some people said they had seen it coming for years. Certainly the relationship had had its ups and downs from the very beginning, and the pressures of the last ten years had been particularly damaging.

Back in May of 1966, Mama had written Daddy a letter she never intended to send. It read, in part:

Dearest Bob,

I've just finished reading some of the letters you wrote to me, dated from 1947 to 1958. What ever happened to those people, you and me, who wrote such letters? How could those years (lonely, trying, testing, tiring, yet victorious) be ignored, tossed aside as if they counted for so little, when in truth they were the most valuable, perhaps, we will have ever lived? Anyway, I was glad to be reminded of the past, realizing the tremendous investment of lives and faith and love. It's too bad we lost out somewhere, and the words on paper, from us both, couldn't have continued. What a wonderful inheritance for our children. What a story they tell. . . .

Lovingly,

Lorraine

SEPARATION

And yet, it was in November of that same year, on their thirtieth wedding anniversary, that Daddy presented Mother with a beautiful pearl ring, writing, "You are a 'pearl of great price.' I wanted to give you at least one good pearl with the lustre and glow I pray we may have in the rest of life together."

Recognizing that their problem was a lack of communication, not a lack of love, Mother sought counseling during the mid-sixties. It was hard for her to admit they needed this kind of help, and even harder to break free of the thought that truly spiritual people sought help only from God, not men. But she was determined to find some answers for their problems.

Unfortunately, the verdict was always the same: "We can do no more until your husband comes in with you." This Daddy never would do.

Now the long hard years of holding on seemed to mean nothing. Over thirty years of marriage had been dismissed with the bang of a gavel. Alimony . . . child support . . . the house—the home God had given her seventeen years before—to be sold . . . Robin cut up and passed out evenly. (You get her Christmas. I get her Thanksgiving.) It was a nightmare from which, for the next eight years, Mother would stubbornly insist she would one day wake up.

For Daddy, on the other hand, the separation seemed to take some enormous burden off his shoulders. Now he had only to provide those things prescribed by law, and he was free to pop in and out of our lives as he saw fit. For the next few years that's what he did, calling at the last moment one or two nights a week when he was home to invite us to dinner, knowing that even if we had dinner on the stove we'd turn it off and rush to be with him. I very seldom remember turning down an opportunity to be with my dad, even though occasionally I resented his last-minute appearance.

Robin and I never stopped loving Daddy with a fierce, protective love that forced us to respond whenever he reached out. No matter how angry we became over some of the things he did, no matter how we resented his treatment of Mother, we never stopped worrying and caring about him. We sensed that he was terribly lonely, and that he needed us. And we needed him. Daddy always joined us on holidays or special occasions, even moving home for the week between Christmas and New Year's for the first few years. (Mother had decided not to sell our house, as the court had ordered.)

You would have thought we were expecting royalty the way Mama would fuss—rearranging the furniture in his room, stocking the cupboards with his favorite foods, doing everything she could think of to make the house comfortable and appealing, and constantly beseeching God for the one gift her heart desired—her husband home again. Every Christmas her heart would swell with hope as she watched him pull into the drive and take his suitcase out of the car. And every New Year's Day that heart would break as she watched him walk out the door once again.

As the months passed and Daddy showed no sign of changing his mind, Mother vacillated between feelings of hopeless despair and indignant anger. In March of 1971, she wrote:

> Difficult, painful days are these. I was able to unload my heavy heart a bit but there's so much that pains and hurts that where a place is made empty by talk and tears, it just fills up with more of the same. It is like all the tears and crying washed nothing at all away. . . .
>
> [I have always believed that] God is our partner, and at work and that things will work out in God's way, that no matter how things appear to be, nothing can keep my marriage from healing. Now, I'm asked "Why?" Why should I expect this miracle any more than the times when God just doesn't intervene in situations? All I know is I couldn't, just couldn't let go. I know I've offered love, thoughtfulness, kindness, etc., and then at times (valentines, dinner invitations, and etc.) Bob seemed to want to be friends. But suddenly today HE SET ME STRAIGHT. HE SAID, "I WILL NOT BE JOCKEYED BY YOU. I WILL NOT

SEPARATION

COME TO THE HOUSE FOR DINNER. I WILL NOT SET A PRECEDENT OF THIS KIND. *WE ARE* LEGALLY SEPARATED. IT IS DONE."

NO!

How humilitating, how painful. PAINFUL!

I don't know what to do. Nothing eases the pain. The children hurt. Robin has stomachaches.

Later that year Daddy returned to Switzerland for more treatments. Mother wrote to his doctor, hoping he might offer a glimmer of hope.

> It is with deep concern and a sense of real urgency, that I write to you concerning my husband, Robert Pierce.
>
> I know that he once again is suffering from emotional fatigue, and I trust he is resting and healing there in Basel. However, I know too that his problems are complex, and there is no easy solution. But I love him, and want very much to help him. I know he is very angry. It would seem that for these past months most of his anger is unleashed at me, but I discern something *greater* than my causing him such displeasure. It runs so much deeper.
>
> Whatever his anguish is about, and no matter how impossible some situations may seem, there must be an answer.
>
> It is very difficult to turn off thirty-five years of your life, belonging, and sharing, children, and work and life as it's lived when two people belong together. Obviously I'm unable to accept Bob's legal separation, as I care so much. . . .

The letter went on to describe our previous trip to Switzerland and Daddy's unnatural behavior, then concluded:

> Thank you for so patiently wading through this lengthy letter. Hopefully it will help you in your treatment of Bob. There is much for Bob to come home to—children, love, and work that two people can share. But somehow we must be able to *talk*,

freely and honestly, without anger and fear. Resentments, cruelty, bitterness, too, must be faced and somehow, with God's help, we must benefit by our mistakes, and finish our course together.

The doctor never responded to Mother's letter, probably because he had nothing to say, no hope to offer, no answers to give. Even close friends and family, including Robin and me, began intimating that Mother should give up for the sake of her own sanity and health. Although our advice was motivated by loving concern, it reeked of faithlessness, and as tempting as it was to walk away from the whole mess, Mother could never bring herself to turn her back on God's Word. She continued to stand on His promises, even though as time passed it became an increasingly lonely place to stand.

> It seems that I am standing alone in my resistance against this breakup of my marriage, in that my arguments never have anyone pointing with me to God's Word. He is so specific about this and I have taken a total stand not only because I love Bob, but mostly because God's Word backs me up. But the few I have sought counsel from have not pointed to the Word, just to our human circumstances. Where are God's people who will stand with me in resistance against this evil?

In the meantime, Daddy determined to get on with his life, like a person trying to put a puzzle together with half the pieces missing. He started working again, producing a film for Lillian Dickson and taking the first steps to get Samaritan's Purse off the ground. His name still carried weight, and the world was full of people who loved him and considered it an honor to help him.

He found great release in travel, and accepted many invitations to go overseas. But he never moved his home base to the Orient, as he often had said he was going to do. Instead, he kept an apartment close to home. And while he was away he wrote beautiful letters, as if the physical distance freed him

SEPARATION

to draw near to us without fear and to feel the great sense of loss we all suffered. One of those letters, written from Hong Kong in 1972, closed with these words: "We are all 'shipwrecked on God,' as Hudson Taylor once said. He will deliver us. I love you, each of you, Mama, Marilee, and my Robin. Daddy."

"We are all 'shipwrecked on God.'" Although most of the time I was not there to see his tears or hear his cries, I know that no one suffered more than my father during those years. Doctors can make their physical diagnoses. Psychiatrists can make their psychological observations. Theologians can expound on spiritual implications. But only God sees the whole picture. Only He knows why Daddy was driven to cut himself off from the ones who loved and needed him the most, and whom he so desperately needed in return.

The world would say he just "fell out of love." But I sat many times with Daddy trying to make some sense out of things, and I heard him say over and over, "I love your mother. I've always loved her. She's the only woman I ever have loved or ever will love. But I just can't come back." He'd look so lost and alone, nothing like the strong, assured, man-of-the-world image he presented most of the time, and I would ache for him.

At other times, the mere mention of Mother's name would send him into venomous rages that would soon spread to others who had hurt him—World Vision, Sharon, and any other painful area in his life. He had made Mother a symbol of all the failures and disappointments he could not face up to; leaving her was his way of exorcising the ghosts of the past.

Chapter 32

REALITY VS. CIRCUMSTANCE

So far I have written only the human facts, not the spiritual reality of our situation. For when you know God and are living within the realm of His power, authority, and abundant mercy, reality has little to do with circumstances.

Reality during those years was God's unfailing provision, His tender watchfulness, His continuous displays of faithfulness and concern, and His constant reassurance that although He had not seen fit to spare us this walk through the valley, He would stay close beside us every step of the way. Ultimately, the victory would be ours.

Reality was God's unwavering compassion for His servant, a man He had called to the front lines of the heaviest warfare, and who now bore the scars of that warfare. Understanding as none of us could the toll the many battles had taken, God never removed His blessing from my father's ministry. On the day he died, Daddy's bags were packed and ready to go as God continued to use him to touch others in His name. But Daddy had failed to heed the Word's injunction not to forsake the wife of his youth, and it seemed God attempted to "yank" Daddy back into line by allowing Satan to continue to plague his body and mind.

In 1972, the muscles in one of Daddy's eyes stopped functioning. The doctor said this was caused by the high blood sugar Daddy had many years before, and the muscle failure was usually irreversible in one his age. For months he wore a patch to cover the useless eye.

Scott and I had spent the past two years on the road doing

REALITY VS. CIRCUMSTANCE

theater and learning how wrong we were for each other. I also had discovered how empty and meaningless life is without Christ at the center. A few months before, I had come home to stay with Mother, as I always did between engagements, and God had touched me in a very special way. Some friends took me to The Church On The Way, where the truth of God's Word was being revealed to me as never before. Of course, the truths were old, but my understanding was new and my faith unlimited.

One day Daddy came to the house, as he often did. Looking at him that day, I just knew God wanted to heal his eye. I asked him if I could pray for him. A little self-consciously, I laid hands on him as I had seen others do, and I prayed a simple but sincere prayer, honestly believing that when I was finished Daddy would remove his patch to find the eye restored. When I finished the eye was unchanged, but Daddy took me in his arms and through tears he said, "None of my children has ever prayed for me like that. It means so much to me. I love you, Sweetheart, and I thank you with all my heart."

Two weeks later, Daddy was sitting at his desk working on correspondence when his secretary walked in and stopped suddenly. "Your eye! Dr. Bob, your eye!"

Unconsciously, Daddy had pushed his patch up to make reading easier, too deep in thought to notice that both eyes were functioning normally. Miraculous healing in the midst of infirmity was the reality of our situation.

Reality was God's hand on Robin and me, holding us steady and directing us through years that would influence the rest of our lives. The separation was harder on Robin than on me, for while I escaped into marriage she was left to walk a daily tightrope between the two most important people in her life. It fell to her to help pick up the pieces and to do everything in her power to encourage Mother and keep her constantly aware that she was not alone. Night after night Robin would awake to the sound of muffled weeping in the other room, slipping out of bed to offer what comfort she could.

MAN OF VISION, WOMAN OF PRAYER

Robin was twelve when Daddy left—a dangerous time for a child of this generation to suddenly be left without a father's influence. Yet Robin never lost her sweetness or innocence; she never used her family situation as an excuse to rebel or to reject the principles by which she was reared. Instead, it was frequently her childlike expressions of faith that would stoke the dwindling flame of belief within Mother's heart at a particularly dark hour. As she watched Robin grow from a young girl to a beautiful, godly young woman, Mother never ceased to be conscious of the special gift God had given her in this child of her autumn years.

Reality was God's unfailing encouragement and provision for Mother throughout those long, lonely years. Dr. Schaeffer's admonition to allow God to show her who she was and to step out as a person with something to offer spurred Mother into action. Coming home from Europe, she volunteered to work with the young people in her church, starting with junior high and then high school.

To her amazement, the young people responded to her in an unusually open manner, sensing that she really cared. She discovered she had a special gift of communicating the truth of God's Word in a way they could accept and relate to. Many began coming to her with their questions and problems, calling her "Mom" and bringing their unsaved friends to meet her. A number of young men and women came to know Jesus as a result of Mother's love and interest.

As Mother gained confidence in her own abilities, God broadened her ministry. In 1972 and 1973 she organized and oversaw a large portion of the Southern California Women's Great Commission Prayer Crusade, a vision God gave Vonette Bright to organize women to pray for their country. Many of those groups continue to this day.

Soon after Daddy left, Mother decided to attend an art class with a friend. She had always enjoyed sketching but had never considered her talent important enough to develop. Now, at fifty, she didn't care if people laughed or found her efforts unworthy. She needed something to keep her mind

REALITY VS. CIRCUMSTANCE

off her problems. To her surprise, she found that when she sat down in front of a canvas all else was forgotten. She could sit for hours, lost in the patient blending of color and form. And she was good. Not just "it's-nice-for-a-hobby" good, but genuinely, naturally talented. The sense of special accomplishment was an unexpected bonus as friends began requesting their own paintings by "Lorraine," hanging them in homes across America and beyond.

Yes, the reality of our lives had little to do with the sticky web of confusion and pain in which the enemy had caught us. And through it all, the most unbelievable miracle of all was the gift of faith God gave Mother—to believe that the whole structure of lies and misunderstandings and bitterness and unforgiveness would one day collapse as easily and totally as a house of cards, without foundation or support. Year after year, her confession never changed.

"I don't understand why God has allowed this to happen, but I know as surely as I live that He will not let it end this way. The longer we go and the more hopeless the situation, the greater the victory will be. And when that day comes we'll climb to the highest mountaintop together, and shout, 'God has healed our family!' "

Of course, faith like that doesn't go unchallenged. Satan was always there with a discouraging word, especially in the night hours when sleep wouldn't come and when Mother had nothing to do but think and hurt. Sometimes the mental anguish would build to such an intensity that it would demand physical release, like a volcano on the verge of erupting. At times like that Mother would escape to the soundproof privacy of her car, driving around aimlessly in the dead of night with the windows closed tight, confident her screams would go unheard by the sleeping neighborhood.

And that faith was almost impossible to find when she would collapse on her face before the Lord, so weary of soul and body that thoughts of "going home" as Sharon did would flash through her mind. But Mother never turned her anger or despair on God. Instead, she would pour her heart out to Him, engaging Him in a running dialogue during the day and writing her thoughts in the evenings. On November 18, 1972, Mama wrote this prayer:

> Dear God, my Father, my Lord, my Savior:
>
> Please, please help me to know what to do right now. . . . I don't want to do *anything* to grieve You or to lose ground I believe You've helped me to hold. But, oh dear God, there's so much unfinished business, so many needs to deal with. . . . I need wisdom and guidance for Robin. I'm so weary. Sleep doesn't rest me. And she is so vital and yet restless. Please, dear Lord, help us. The house is too much to keep and yet in the midst of all the unsure and unknown, it is an earthly sanctuary. Where can we go? What do I do? . . .
>
> I need grace and wisdom in Marilee's situation. Don't let me fail her. I love her so much. But, Lord, she needs You to guide her, correct her, and give her direction. I pray for her, and give her to You. I will never turn from You. *Never!* It is You who have borne me through these years and I love You, but I need You to help my unbelief and strengthen my faith. Help me to "do all, and stand." My heart hurts, and my soul and whole being are feeling overwhelmed, but You said when the enemy comes in like a flood, then the Spirit of God would lift up a standard against him. Thank you.
>
> Oh, Jesus, I love you and the greatest wonder of it all is that You love me. YOU CARE. Oh, to care and be cared for. And You said, "I care for you."
>
> Thank you for hearing my plea in this needful hour.
>
> Your child, Lorraine.

And God gave this answer to Mother's heart, which she recorded at the time.

> The truth is this, Lorraine. Remember as you view the scene that you "battle not against flesh and blood," but against principalities, powers, rulers, darkness of this world (Satan and his angels). I say the battle is mine. I will repay, so I'll take care of

REALITY VS. CIRCUMSTANCE

earthly battles. Your warfare is not with carnal weapons, but mighty through Me "to the pulling down of strongholds." Put on the armor I give you. Do all to stand.

Fight the good fight of faith. Believe. Endure hardness as a good soldier of Jesus Christ. Yes, you are a soldier. There is a battle. You are in it as long as you are on this earth, but it is so very important to remember that you are held in complete and total love . . . armed by My Spirit and by My might. Be aware of Satan's devices. He is out to devour and destroy you, but don't fear what men shall do unto you, for you've already won the battle because of My Son. You see, your enemy has already been tried and sentenced.

Look to your General. Trust in your Captain. Don't give up. When you fall, My everlasting arms are there! Get up, tighten your armor, and go back into battle strengthened by your own failures. Learn the lessons. The strategy I have already devised will be made known to you as you need it. You are more than conqueror. Best of all, you are loved completely, totally, tenderly—with compassion and understanding that cannot be described.

But while God's Word and His Spirit kept reassuring us that even though the battle was bloody the war was already won, Satan continued to wreak havoc with our relationship with Daddy, breaking down communications and twisting the simplest events into devastating experiences.

Daddy's memory remained badly crippled from the treatments he received in Switzerland, and the medication he continued to take left his mind frequently unclear about more current happenings. Mother, Robin, and I frequently found ourselves being rebuked for things we had never said or done, or being chided for not doing something we had done. Even simple conversation became difficult; our words became twisted or perverted between the speaker's mouth and the listener's ears. We were all victims of spiritual sabotage, as over and over again our best intentions ended in anger and tears. It was indescribably frustrating for all of us.

MAN OF VISION, WOMAN OF PRAYER

One day Mother answered the phone to hear Daddy's voice greeting her warmly and with great excitement. "Something wonderful has happened. I'm in Canada, and God has met me in a tremendous way up here. I can't even begin to describe what's happened, except that I have such joy and peace, and feel such love for everybody. I'm going to call everyone I've been bitter toward and ask them to forgive me for my unforgiveness. But I wanted you to be the first to know. As soon as I get home, I'll come over and tell you all about it!"

Speechless with joy, Mother dropped to her knees by the phone, crying and laughing, unable to do anything but praise the Lord. God had heard her endless prayers, and His Spirit had touched Daddy's heart. It was a miracle. As soon as he could, Daddy was going to come home and share it with her.

But the days passed and Daddy didn't come. While he followed through on everything else he said he was going to do, the love and forgiveness flowed in every direction but Mother's.

After her hopes had soared so high, the disappointment of Daddy's unaltered attitude toward her was almost more than Mother could bear. She entered a period of growing depression and listlessness, often remaining in bed for days at a time.

In September of 1973, Daddy invited Mother and me to a large banquet where the film he had produced for Lillian Dickson was premiering.

Two months before, Scott and I had officially separated, and it was an especially emotional and needy time for me. Although I was keenly aware of God's hand on my life, I was not eager to face a large crowd of old friends and Christian leaders who would ask questions I was not yet comfortable with nor confident enough to answer. And it would be a hundred times more awkward for Mother than for me, since so many people were unaware of the separation. And those who were aware would wonder why she was there.

Yet Daddy continued to insist that we come, and it seemed to mean so much to him that we finally agreed. He said he

REALITY VS. CIRCUMSTANCE

would meet us in the lobby and personally escort us to the table he would reserve for us.

We arrived at the hotel a few minutes late, expecting Daddy to be waiting. But he was nowhere in sight, and it soon became obvious that he wasn't going to meet us. Perhaps we had missed him, or an emergency had kept him involved. We entered the crowded banquet room to discover that not only was no table reserved for us, but the only empty seats were in the back by the door. Confused and self-conscious, we sat down, catching an occasional glimpse of Daddy as he went from table to table greeting his guests. Perhaps he didn't see us, or maybe he was angry that we were late, but he didn't stop at our table or acknowledge us in any way the entire evening.

Looking around at the roomful of people, so many of whom represented warm memories of the past; looking at Daddy, so handsome in his tuxedo, talking and laughing and hugging people just as he always had; looking at Mother, her head held high, graciously conversing with a woman across the table who had no idea who she was; I was overwhelmed by a sense of longing for a time and place that no longer existed. I wanted the world to turn right side up once again, and for Daddy to come put his arms around us and take us with him back into that warm, secure circle of acceptance and belonging. But we didn't belong any more, and my body ached with the pain of loss.

I began to cry. I cried through the opening prayer and the three-course dinner. Twice I went to the ladies' room to try to pull myself together, but I would no sooner return to the table than the silent flow of tears would begin again. Finally Mother asked if I wanted to leave. We gathered our things but I could not leave without saying good-bye to Daddy. Perhaps he really hadn't seen us, and I didn't want him to be hurt, thinking we hadn't come.

Later, he told friends that I had timed my good-bye minutes before he was to get up and speak in order to purposely upset him.

MAN OF VISION, WOMAN OF PRAYER

In recent months our times together represented a chain of similar mini-disasters, and it was obvious that none of us could stand the strain much longer. I suggested that Mother, Robin, and I write Daddy a letter, and since it was my idea it was left to me to do the honors.

September 20, 1973

Dear Daddy,

After much talk and prayer over the present family situation, Robin, Mother, and I have decided the wisest thing to do is to write this letter. . . .

The first important thing which needs to be stated is that we all love you, and our need of your love and participation in our lives as husband and father has never been greater. We pray constantly for the day the Lord, in His great mercy and wisdom, will miraculously unite us in His perfect bond of love, and make us what we need to be to one another, to make us a family in the most beautiful sense of the word.

But as the time goes by and the distance between us grows greater, we are filled with an overpowering feeling of despair and frustration, as our best intentions are turned time and again into something hurting and ugly. . . .

Obviously, we cannot go on this way. You and Mother are slowly dying before Robin's and my eyes. Robin is frightened and confused, and filled with feelings she can't cope with. And I, at this particular time of great need and searching, find the whole situation unbearable. . . .

We all believe in and look forward to the day that the Lord will heal the wounds and wash away all the bitterness, resentment, and pain, and help us to so totally forgive and love each other that the old things will become new! He can and will do this for us, Daddy, but only as we allow Him to. We three are most willing to kneel right now and submit all the "old" things to the Lord. All we need to start this new life is you and your honest desire to do the same. But until the time when you feel this is what you want, too, let's not hurt each other any more

REALITY VS. CIRCUMSTANCE

by pretending things are right when they aren't. It hurts too much to have you pop into our lives for a dinner or a holiday and then pop out again. We know you feel the confusion and pain of not having your rightful place and authority in our lives when we are together. But surely you can understand that a man must take his place and accept his authority on a full-time basis, as husband and father, in the way the Lord ordained.

The result of my well-intentioned meddling was a year of silence. That had not been the result we'd hoped for, but I am not at all sure it wasn't the result God wanted. We all had received an emotional thrashing over the past years, and Mother and Daddy were showing signs of physical weakening from the constant friction. It was almost as if God gave us a year of "R and R," removing us from the combat zone so that even though the war still raged around us, we were out of the direct line of fire.

For months we neither saw Daddy nor spoke to him, but we were still a family. And nothing that had happened could break that bond. Robin was the first to break the silence.

July 9, 1974

Dear Daddy,

I have been thinking of you so much lately. Mainly just realizing how much I do love you and miss you! I feel badly about the way things have been between us. The situation seems to be pretty painful. And to reach out is a lot harder than I think you know. Not that I don't want to; I'm just not sure how to go about it. It seems if I tell you I love you or need you, it's taken a different way—usually that I want something. That has never been my intention. The only thing I've wanted was my father's love. I am trying *so hard* to understand this situation and the way you feel. One thing I do realize is that in a case like this no one can really win and a lot is sacrificed.

Please love me, Daddy. Don't be against me and my feelings.

MAN OF VISION, WOMAN OF PRAYER

> This letter is sent with all my love. I need you and wish things could be different.

Daddy responded immediately, calling Robin to say he loved her more than his own life, and that he would take her to lunch so they could have time to talk. He also said he felt things would be better for us all. Two days later he called to say he was leaving the country, and the lunch never happened. But the ice had been broken, and during the next few months we took the first shaky steps toward reestablishing relations.

I found out that Daddy was speaking at a church in North Hollywood, close to my apartment in Van Nuys, and I called and asked him if I could come and bring someone special I wanted him to meet. The previous July I had met a young Bible college student named Robert John Dunker. The second time I saw him the Lord told me we would marry (although it took Bob considerably longer to get the message!). And so on a Sunday evening in early November, the two Bobs in my life met for the first time. I hadn't seen Daddy in over a year.

That Thanksgiving the Pierce family gathered together to praise God for all His blessings and mercies. With Daddy at one end of the table and Mama at the other, we held hands and sang before tackling the traditional feast of roast turkey, Mama's special dressing, and sweet potatoes crusted with melted marshmallows. Framed in the large dining room window with Mama's china and crystal sparkling in the candlelight, we must have presented the perfect portrait of a happy, unified family. But at the end of the evening Daddy drove off in the cold, dark night to return to his own apartment.

The following May, Daddy walked me down the aisle and sat next to Mother as Bob and I became one in Jesus. It was the last time they would really be together until the miracle.

Chapter 33

LEUKEMIA!
•

"Well, Baby, Daddy's got leukemia. Looks like I'll be going home soon."

Leukemia! Although I didn't understand exactly what it meant, I knew it was a type of cancer, and the very word sent a chill down my spine. And yet Daddy said it so casually that I began to wonder if I was overreacting. Perhaps it wasn't as serious as it sounded.

Bob and I had returned from our honeymoon to find Daddy admitted to Scripps Clinic for tests. We drove to La Jolla, planning to rescue him from the hospital for a couple of hours to have a nice dinner and tell him about our idyllic sojourn from Carmel to San Francisco to Tahoe. But while he had sounded gung-ho on the telephone, Daddy barely had enough strength to glance through our wedding pictures, and when he tried to get out of bed the color drained from his face and his legs wouldn't hold him. His doctor stepped in to say they should have some definite results in a day or two, and Daddy promised to call as soon as he heard.

When that call came, the tone of his voice seemed to indicate good news, and I remember feeling like he wanted me to congratulate him rather than commiserate with him.

It was my father's total lack of self-pity or fear of dying that allowed those around him to accept his impending death without discomfort or self-consciousness. To be absent from the body was to be present with the Lord—perfected, whole, and healthy. It was a transformation Daddy looked forward to with real peace and anticipation. He was still a relatively young man, only sixty years of age, but he was tempted at first not to prolong his stay on earth by refusing any medical treatment designed to slow down the explosion of red blood cells that would eventually take his life.

But my father was too vital to simply lay down and die. In fact, the news of his illness seemed to recharge him, filling him with the determination to pack every second of life God gave him with ministry. He continued to travel extensively, coming home for several weeks of radiation or chemotherapy, then taking off again for the wilds of Borneo or some equally primitive part of the world. At no time did Daddy permit his illness to dictate the boundaries of his world. January, 1976, found him in Saigon helping thousands of refugees, taking time to run down a troubled young soldier for his worried parents back home, and helping friends get out of the country. During that time he sent Mother this telegram.

January 5, 1976

Mrs. Bob Pierce,

I love you. Aware your prayers as we spent dangerous week in North. Huge refugee program developing. Keep praying.

Love, Bob

Perhaps his words of love sparked a new flicker of hope in Mother's heart. Certainly nothing else offered any encouragement. They hadn't seen one another since the week of my wedding, at which time Daddy had invited Mother and Robin to dinner. But the plans were postponed until after he got out of the hospital, and then they were forgotten altogether. It was as if the news of cancer slammed the book shut, as far as Daddy was concerned. He refused to see Mother from that day forward, except for one brief interlude.

The complete severing of all contact with Daddy except through legal channels was very difficult for Mother. She desperately needed someone in whom she could confide, and

LEUKEMIA!

she had no one except Robin and me—with whom she knew she shouldn't talk—and a few close friends she felt she couldn't be totally honest with. So she began seeing a Christian psychologist, a compassionate, intelligent woman who quickly became more friend than doctor.

One day they were talking and Mother expressed again how much she wanted Daddy to move home. "He shouldn't be alone through these days. He should be surrounded by his family and loved ones. He doesn't have to take me back as a wife. He doesn't even have to talk to me if he doesn't want to. I'll move into the back bedroom and he can have our room. If only he'd let me take care of him, nurse him, be close to him. That's all I want. I'd settle for that."

To Mother's total shock, the psychologist picked up her phone and said, "Send Dr. Pierce in, please."

Mother watched with open mouth as Daddy entered the room, greeted her and the doctor with equal warmth, and seated himself tensely in a chair. Fortunately, the doctor did most of the talking, repeating Mother's invitation almost word for word. When she was through, Daddy firmly declined, saying that under no circumstances would he consider such an arrangement.

As if in a bad dream, Mother watched him walk out the door, unable to believe what had just happened.

The effects of this complete breakoff between Mother and Daddy were manifold. Since all communication now took place through their lawyers, things became more and more impersonal. The courts had allotted Mother what they considered a fair share of Daddy's income, an amount that barely covered essentials. Soon it shrank to less than enough, as the cost of living soared out of sight.

In the first few years of their separation, Daddy was quick to cover any emergencies or extra expenses. Mother found that with him as insurance against the unexpected, she could make it. But as time went on Daddy became less inclined to help. He was increasingly perturbed at Mother's refusal to sell the house, as the court had ordered.

MAN OF VISION, WOMAN OF PRAYER

While Robin was still in high school, Daddy agreed that it would be unnecessarily cruel to force her to leave her friends, her school, and the only home she had ever known. But after she graduated Daddy started pressuring Mother to sell, an idea she found increasingly unsettling. She had nowhere to go and no money to go with, so she scraped and pinched and managed to hold on, despite Daddy's growing displeasure.

The resultant financial disputes led to a series of letters containing various demands, threats, counteroffers, and compromises, all effectively camouflaged in the profundity of the law. But neither Mother nor Daddy could bring themselves to actually carry their grievances back into court.

It's hard to explain what happened to Robin and me during Daddy's last three years. It is human nature to adapt to even the most unnatural and painful circumstances, and after a while we simply began accepting what we were helpless to change. The past few years had taught us to be strangers from Daddy, and the sands of time had gradually buried our common ground as we were remolded and shaped by daily events, which no longer touched often enough to interweave.

Perhaps if we had had a better father-daughter foundation to begin with, we wouldn't have lost touch so easily. But there never had been time for cultivating the kind of soul-level relationship some fathers have with their children. My image of my father had always been more heavily influenced by who he was and what he did than by his personal involvement in my life, simply because he wasn't there most of the time. And, as Sharon expressed, when he was there we felt inhibited about sharing our inner feelings and needs, fearing he would find them shallow or, worse yet, a burden. So even in the best of times there were parts of each of us that Daddy never saw. And of course, there was much about him that we never understood.

As time passed it became increasingly hard for Robin and me to figure out where we fit in Daddy's life. His illness had made him dependent upon a few close associates who seemed to form a kind of adoptive family in which we had no

LEUKEMIA!

part. Our times together became more and more formalized, and we had absolutely no involvement in the practicalities of his life. In the first few months of his illness, Bob and I offered to be of service in any way we could, but we were always told, "Oh, don't bother. So-and-so will do it." Finally we got out of the habit of offering, an unfortunate mistake that Daddy interpreted as rejection and lack of concern on our parts.

A chief cause of our confusion and worry was Daddy's order that his doctor release no information to any member of the family. The doctor strictly obeyed, refusing to answer either written or telephoned inquiries about Daddy's condition. Since we could get no official word as to how he was doing, we were vulnerable to any rumor or bit of misinformation to drift down the grapevine.

On one particularly traumatic day in the fall of 1976, Mother received a call from an old friend saying he'd just heard that Daddy had passed away while overseas and he wanted to express his sympathies. Well, Daddy *was* away, and none of us had heard from him or about him for weeks, so there was a possibility that the story was true. Calls were placed all over the Orient until Daddy was located, very much alive. Needless to say, the incident left Mother shaken for weeks, and Robin and I determined to protect her from any future unnecessary anguish.

Daddy himself was our main source of information. Although my relationship with him was about as stable as a vial of nitroglycerin, I was determined to keep the door open, and I would call or write every few weeks to see how he was. At times the news would be good. The treatments seemed to be working and he would feel relatively strong and well. But frequently the report was totally negative. His blood count was up, the treatments were having little effect, and the doctors gave him only weeks to live.

At first such news would send us all into an emotional tailspin, Robin and I jumping each time the phone rang, Mother grappling with the realization that Daddy might die, leaving her to live with the pain and failure of the past eight years. But as the months passed, it became apparent to all of us that something extraordinary was happening.

The doctor's original prognosis had been six months to a year. But Daddy passed the one-year mark and then the two- and three-year anniversary of the discovery of his illness, surviving several crises that should have killed him. The doctors began to take note. One young specialist told Daddy shortly before he died, "You may not be aware of it, Dr. Pierce, but every doctor on the floor is keeping daily tabs on your progress. Around here you're considered something of a miracle."

Yes, Daddy was a walking miracle. Just as his life had been ordered and directed by God Almighty, so would be his death. The cancer could continue to eat away at his body, but God would choose the hour of his homegoing. The realization of this truth became deeply rooted within all of us, bringing comfort and a sense of security in the assurance that God was in control.

Daddy believed God continued to sustain him because He had more work for him to do. And indeed He did. He continued to bless Daddy's ministry all over the world through his work with Samaritan's Purse.

During the last year of his life, Daddy was definitely weakened not only by the ravages of the disease, but by the painful effects of the experimental treatments he offered to take. At times he was so weak he was unable to walk, but even this didn't deter him; he simply added a collapsible wheelchair to his traveling gear.

Another addition was a box carefully packed with vials of medication and assorted pills. The doctors had explained that when the end came, it could be excruciatingly painful without sophisticated medication, which Daddy would find unavailable in many parts of the world. So he talked them into giving him his own supply, since it was his wholehearted desire and intent to be overseas on the battlefield when the Lord took him home.

But the Spirit of God ministered something quite different

LEUKEMIA!

to our hearts. We believed that God would not release Daddy to go home until somehow, some way the family situation had been redeemed.

The story of greatness is not the story of a man or a woman or a family who runs and never stumbles or falls; rather, it is the story of those who dare to run *and* stumble *and* fall, and who by the grace of God pick themselves up to run again and again and again. The story of victory is not one without pain or sacrifice or disappointment, but one of holding on, of standing fast on the promises of God's Word, of knowing that while we may never understand the "whys," someday we shall see Him face to face, and it will be worth it all!

It is essential to understand that while God's heart is broken over the millions of lost, starving, homeless people in the world, He is no less moved by the desperate cries of a torn and bleeding family, the discarded waste of countless attacks and battles. God cares about the brokenhearted, and He is intimately involved in individual suffering. To have taken Daddy home without first reaching out a healing hand to touch the gaping wounds inflicted upon this family would have been totally contrary to God's nature and character.

Although our hearts had received the promise, it became increasingly difficult for our heads to comprehend just how this restoration would take place. Daddy absolutely refused to even speak to Mother, much less see her. "I never expect to see your Mother on this earth again," he would say. "We'll just wait until we get to heaven. We'll have our glorified bodies, there will be no more unforgiveness or pain, and we'll be able to love and accept one another in perfect love."

Robin's relationship with Daddy had taken a definite turn for the worse. In December of 1977, she had married Victor Ruesga, a Christian boy who was studying to be a landscape contractor. Daddy had been seriously ill and was hospitalized at the time of the wedding, so he missed the opportunity to walk his youngest down the aisle. But this was one of those times when Jesus miraculously touched his body, and he was home again two days after the wedding.

Eager to make it up to Robin, he stopped by the newly-

MAN OF VISION, WOMAN OF PRAYER

weds' apartment on New Year's Day, intending to discuss an appropriate wedding gift. Somehow Mother's name came up, eliciting from Daddy an unexpected and uncalled for recounting of all her weak points. The outburst was probably inspired by Daddy's sensitivity to the fact that she had been at the wedding and he had not. Robin responded by asking Daddy to please not talk about Mother like that in her home. Taking her request as a rebuke, he stormed out of the apartment.

Later that day I called Daddy to wish him a Happy New Year. Unaware that he was still seething from the earlier confrontation, I spent thirty minutes trying everything in my power to avoid an argument. However, it became clear that I was fighting a losing battle, and I hung up—totally perplexed as to how my New Year's greeting had ended in such disaster.

So 1978 arrived to find Daddy pretty much alienated from all three of us; certainly none of us was among his top ten favorite people. Mother and Robin were at a loss as to how to approach him, but I had an advantage they didn't have—his granddaughter.

Michelle Lorraine Dunker arrived on November 5, 1976. A few weeks before, Daddy and I had argued and, as a result, Michelle was nearly eight months old before Daddy came to see her.

I'll never forget watching him get out of his car and walk up our front drive. His steps were slow and unsteady, like those of a very old man. I hadn't seen him for months, and I was unprepared for the change. He looked so fragile, his face unnaturally flushed from the chemotherapy he'd been receiving.

I had prayed all morning that Michelle would respond well. Babies are very unpredictable at eight months of age, and Daddy was a total stranger to her. But an angel must have whispered in her ear, for at her first sight of him she broke into a big, gurgling grin, flashing all eight "toofers" and raising a pair of chubby, dimpled arms in his direction. His

LEUKEMIA!

eyes filled with tears, as did mine, and he announced with grandfatherly pride, "I have a picture of this baby taken sixty-two years ago. She looks just like me!"

I probably wouldn't have had the courage to keep knocking on the door of Daddy's life if I hadn't had Michelle. But she was the one person in our family who represented pure joy and love with no painful associations, and I was determined that he was going to have at least this grandchild in the loneliness of what might be his last year.

Confusion and misunderstanding continued to be the enemy's major weapon in those final months. In the spring of 1978, Daddy suffered another major crisis, lying inches from death for several days. Several weeks before, he, Bob, and I had had dinner together. It had been a congenial, happy time just before he left for overseas. I had asked him to call as soon as he got back so we could have him over, and he had promised he would.

When I hadn't heard from him in several weeks, I called his apartment and was greeted by the familiar sound of his answering tape. I called every few days, assuming that the tape meant he was still away. Finally I called his office to see when they expected him home, only to be informed that he'd been in the hospital for well over a week. Dumbfounded, I asked why I hadn't been called. I was told that Daddy had left strict instructions that none of the family was to be informed unless we first called to inquire after him.

So, while Mother and Robin purposely left him alone because they thought that's what he wanted, and while I waited to hear that he was home, Daddy lay in a hospital bed, willing to die alone because he was convinced nobody cared about him.

Chapter 34

THE MIRACLE
•
"Never doubt in the dark what God told you in the light." The words are not dated. I have no idea when Mother wrote them in the small, tattered copy of *Daily Light*, but they are a reminder of one of the countless times God met Mother in the privacy of her prayer chamber.

Although our heavenly Father proves His faithfulness many times in our lives, few of us are strong enough to live on past experiences or remembered victories. Mother had always found it imperative to hear God's current word for today. It was the only way she could survive. As she expressed recently, anyone who thinks they can make it on experience or hope or knowing Jesus alone is in for some difficult times. We must put it all together, and allow Him to speak fresh grace and wisdom and encouragement every day.

Between the covers of that little book is the continuing account of God's "fresh grace" for Mother through the past twenty years. So often the daily reading seemed more like a personal letter, written to address her particular battle or need of the moment, and she would underline and date the promise, claiming it for Daddy or for herself or for all of us. No matter how often she read through this book, the Scriptures in it never lost their freshness or potency. They offered the handle of hope she needed to make it through the day.

Daily Light, September, 1972

Now for a season, if need be, ye are in heaviness through

THE MIRACLE

manifold temptations: That the trial of your faith, being much more precious than of gold that perisheth, though it be tried with fire, might be found unto praise and honor and glory at the appearing of Jesus Christ. . . . We glory in tribulations also: knowing that tribulation worketh patience; And patience, experience; and experience, hope (1 Pet. 1:6, 7; Rom. 5:3, 4).

Daily Light, April, 1973

The Lord is a God of judgment: blessed are all they that wait for him. . . . And it shall be said in that day, Lo, this is our God; we have waited for him, and he will save us: this is the LORD; we have waited for him, we will be glad and rejoice in his salvation. . . . If we hope for that we see not, then do we with patience wait for it (Is. 30:18; 25:9, Rom. 8:25).

Daily Light, May, 1974

I will seek that which was lost, and bring again that which was driven away, and will bind up that which was broken, and will strengthen that which was sick (Ezek. 34:16).

Daily Light, January, 1975

I am but a little child: I know not how to go out or come in. . . . If any of you lack wisdom, let him ask of God . . . and it shall be given him. . . . Daughter, be of good comfort (1 Kin. 3:7; James 1:5; Matt. 9:22).

One day in early 1978, Mother answered the phone and was surprised to hear the gentle, broken English of Dr. Han, now pastor emeritus of the great Yung Nak Church in Seoul, Korea. He was in town and wanted to see her that very afternoon. Mama knew his desire to see her was more than purely social, but she was totally unprepared for what he had to say.

According to Dr. Han, Daddy had expressed his intention to settle his affairs in the States and then go overseas to spend his remaining days among the people he had given his life to. Dr. Han had come to personally inform Mother of the plans being made to cremate and bury Daddy's remains in a special place on the grounds of Yung Nak Church. He spoke softly and carefully; in his culture family ties are very strong, and he sensed that his words were most painful for Mother to hear.

Mama thought of the green rolling hillside overlooking the "Wee Kirk of the Heather" at Forest Lawn, where both Papa Johnson and Sharon lay, and where one day she and Daddy had always planned to rest side by side. Now, it seemed, even this privilege was to be denied her.

Mother's distress over this latest blow caused her to open her heart to Dr. Han, telling him of her continuing love for Daddy and her deep desire to see their marriage reconciled.

Dr. Han was so moved that he left the house promising to talk to Daddy. For the next couple of days Mother lived with hope, unwilling to disregard even the smallest possibility that the outcome might be different this time. But days passed and Dr. Han didn't call.

Finally Mother called him, and he settled the matter once and for all with his sorrowful declaration, "I'm sorry, Mrs. Pierce. There's nothing I can do."

In July and August of 1978, Bob and I had the opportunity to be with Daddy on several occasions. The leukemia, the radiation, the chemotherapy, and the experimental nuclear treatments he had received had taken their toll. His complexion would vary from sunburned pink to chalky grey, most of his hair had fallen out, and although his face and stomach were bloated his arms and legs were pathetically thin. And yet he never gave up. Every time we saw him he was nattily dressed, his shoes were shined, and a silver-grey hairpiece made up for what he had lost. All things considered, he was still a fine-looking man, ending his days with dignity and pride.

During one visit in late August, Daddy talked openly about his life and death, saying how sorry he was for any pain he had caused Robin and me, and that he loved us and wished things had been different.

"I only wish you both had had a chance to really know your Daddy," he said in a broken, husky voice.

THE MIRACLE

When we parted that night I knew there was little time left. I thought about calling Mother, but Daddy seldom mentioned her name anymore, and I had seen nothing in his attitude to indicate that his feelings about her had changed. I knew if I told her he was really fading she would try to contact him, and I feared it would lead to one more nasty, painful confrontation. I didn't want it to end that way, for both of their sakes, so I didn't say anything to her.

But Robin was a different matter. I knew how much she loved Daddy, and he obviously wanted to see her, so I called to tell her the situation, encouraging her to contact him immediately.

No sooner had we hung up than Robin called Mother to tell her about Daddy. That phone call set off a chain of events that some may call coincidence or luck. But as far as we're concerned, it was pure miracle.

Mother's first inclination was to call Daddy's doctor. She had been through too many false alarms to accept this report without checking with a medical authority. In the past, the doctor had never agreed to talk with her, but it happened that Daddy's regular doctor was on vacation. A young doctor was in charge, and as he was unaware of the family conflicts, he was more than happy to talk to Dr. Pierce's wife. From him Mother learned that Daddy's most recent treatments had been totally ineffectual, and his life expectancy was less than two weeks.

The news shot through Mother's being like an electric current. Daddy was dying. She had known that someday the disease must kill him, but she had never really believed it. Now it was real—horribly, terrifyingly real—and its reality drove her to action. Picking up the phone, she attempted to reach Daddy. Learning he was out of town, she had to content herself with leaving a message for him to call her back.

The top of the page in Mother's *Daily Light* for September 1, 1978, reads, "Bob called me today!" The fact that Daddy responded to her call is the second major link in our chain of miraculous events.

MAN OF VISION, WOMAN OF PRAYER

They talked for an hour and a half, and although the first half of their conversation came uncomfortably close to being the disaster I had feared, the fact that they talked so long is significant in itself.

For years, at the least sign of conflict or disagreement Daddy had tuned out, finding the discussion of certain problems and issues too upsetting to handle in his physical and emotional condition. Although we all understood his need to avoid any extreme emotional stress, it did leave us—particularly Mother—in a frustrating and helpless position as we saw the years confuse and exaggerate so many problems that open, honest interaction could have resolved.

Mother and Dad's phone conversation could easily have dissolved into one more unsatisfying "non-communication" where both talk and neither listen, if God had not decided that this was the moment to blow away some of the fog and begin clarifying issues that for years had been wrapped in layers of self-pity, unforgiveness, disappointment, and confusion. Oh, voices rose and angry feelings were expressed, but instead of throwing out accusations and complaints like hand grenades and then running for cover, my parents stood their ground, facing one another with an openness they hadn't experienced for many years.

Mother found that Daddy's overpowering volume and verbal dexterity no longer intimidated her. The knowledge that she might never have another opportunity to speak her heart and mind gave her a calmness and an authority she had been incapable of in the past. And Daddy responded with equal honesty, taking time to really listen and think about what she was saying. More than once he conceded that the medication he had taken through the years had left him fuzzy and unsure about many things.

Of course, that conversation didn't resolve the problems thirty-five years had created. But it did open a door that had been slammed shut and bolted tight. And it gave Mother the opportunity to express a truth that all the forces and schemes of hell couldn't change. "I love you. The girls love you. We

THE MIRACLE

are your family and always will be. We represent you and belong to you, and *nothing* will ever change that."

At the end of the conversation Daddy asked, "What is it you want, Lorraine?"

Mama answered, "Before you go home, I want you to call your children and grandchildren and me to come be with you and let the family be together one last time. Don't give me an answer now. I want you to have time to think and pray about it. Call me when you have an answer."

A few hours later Daddy called back. "Mama, will you and the girls have dinner with me tomorrow night at six? Sheraton Universal."

Daily Light, September 2, Morning

Cast not away therefore your confidence, which hath great recompence of reward. For ye have need of patience, that, after ye have done the will of God, ye might receive the promise (Heb. 10:35, 36).

Before six the next evening we pulled into the parking lot. This was one appointment for which none of us wanted to be late. We were all excited and a little nervous with that kind of tingly anticipation one feels before something wonderfully uncertain is about to happen.

But while our stomachs fluttered with butterflies, our spirits rested in calm assurance. We had enlisted the prayer support of many friends. Bob and I had asked the entire elder body at The Church On The Way to get on their knees on our behalf, and we were wonderfully conscious of God's covering and presence. Walking into the hotel lobby, we felt like we were being escorted by a guard of heavenly beings, the very splendor and magnificence of which would be enough to send satanic forces scurrying back into their pit.

Stopping for a moment, we formed a circle and agreed together in prayer. Then we hurried up to the suite Daddy had reserved for us.

MAN OF VISION, WOMAN OF PRAYER

We heard him before we saw him. Walking down the corridor toward the open door of the suite, we could hear his strained voice complaining to the management over the phone that things were not as he had requested. He had gone to the trouble of sending one of his secretaries earlier in the day to insure that everything would be right, but the room had not been set up correctly. As we entered we could see his hand shake as he set the receiver back in place, and we wondered if this was a preview of things to come. But as soon as he saw us the tension eased from his face, and he gestured to us with a smile. "Come in, come in!"

Walking into that room was like coming into the warmth out of a cold, stormy night. It was as if a blanket of peace had settled over the entire evening. We could sense it immediately as each of us went to embrace Daddy. His eyes were bright with love and excitement, his pain and discomfort temporarily forgotten. Mother stood hesitantly by the door, drinking in the display of affection but too uncertain to automatically include herself in the happy goings-on.

"Mama, if I could get out of this chair I'd come over there and kiss you," Daddy said, sensing her hesitation.

That was all she needed. Mama stepped across the room, bridging nine years of separation and pain, and we all watched with aching throats and tear-glazed eyes as Mama and Daddy embraced.

After that the evening flew by, each moment slipping through our fingers like grains of sand, yet each leaving an indelible impression on our hearts and minds. We talked and laughed, without the tension or uneasiness we had come to associate with our times with Daddy. It was like the past ten years hadn't happened at all. There were no apologies or attempted explanations; they weren't necessary. We loved one another. We loved being together. We were a family.

Our dining room overlooked the hills of the San Fernando valley, and we sat at a large round table feasting on shrimp cocktail, prime rib, and good conversation. Daddy sat next to Mother, pouring her coffee and fixing it the way she liked

THE MIRACLE

it—with much cream and little sugar. They looked so natural together, talking, laughing, enjoying their children and grandchildren, and taking special delight in the antics of little Michelle, who at twenty-two months had no idea of the significance of this momentous occasion.

Robin and I were both pregnant, and as we sat around the table discussing whose baby was going to be named what, Daddy commented a bit wistfully, "My, we certainly are going to have a brood, aren't we?" We knew he was thinking that he wouldn't be there to see those new grandbabies, and as the sun slipped behind the mountain ridge the dying light took on a sad yet somehow appropriate significance.

After dinner we got out the trusty old Instamatic, wanting to capture in pictures as much of the evening's joy as possible. Daddy was a good sport, smiling gamely as we grouped and regrouped around him. But the energy and effort the evening had demanded of him began to show. The effects of his medication began to wear off, and Mama was the first to recognize that for Daddy's sake our visit must come to an end.

"Bob, we know you're getting tired and we don't want to keep you any longer than you should stay. I just want to tell you how much this evening means to the children and me. We'll remember and cherish it as long as we live, and we thank you with all our hearts." Then, after a slight hesitation she added, "Would you mind if we prayed together?"

"Not at all, Mama."

So Mother began to pray, praising God for the miracle of that night, for His faithfulness through all the years, and particularly asking His blessing and loving mercy on Daddy. As her prayer came to an end Daddy picked it up, thanking the Lord for a lifetime of usefulness in His service and then praying for each of us by name. At one point he laid his hands on Robin's and my stomachs, weaving into the design of those yet unborn that scarlet thread of faith and service through his powerful prayers of blessing and commitment. It was a precious, holy time, and while Michelle toddled from one knee to the next offering words of comfort and handfuls of Kleenex, we all wept openly, united in the sweet healing of tears and praise.

Daddy's prayer ended. A hush fell over the room as we all sat quietly, unwilling to disturb the sweetness of that special moment. Then Mother began singing softly, "Jesus, we just want to thank you, thank you for being so good," and we all joined in, raising our hands and voices to heaven. As that song ended, Daddy's thin but still mellow tones rang out with "Alleluia," and once again the room was filled with perfect harmony.

And so ended our evening, September 2, 1978 . . . a night of miracles.

Chapter 35

AN AFFAIR OF STATE
•

Daily Light, September 2, Evening

He brought me to the banqueting house, and his banner over me was love (Song 2:4).

Mother's note: "Praise our God, for He is! Pierce family reconciliation, reunion [after] eight years apart!"

Lying in bed that night, I couldn't sleep. I was filled with the wonder and incredible joy of what God had done. It is easy, when you've prayed and waited for a miracle for a long time, to be caught totally off guard when God answers. It wasn't that I had stopped *believing* God could do something, but somewhere along the line I had stopped *expecting* Him to do something. Now that He had, I was awed and excited and overwhelmed with a fresh awareness of God's power.

I felt very close to Daddy. I wanted to keep touching him somehow, to continue the intimacy of the evening. So at two in the morning I slipped out of bed and wrote him a letter to thank him and to tell him how much I loved him. I mailed it the next day, a Saturday, and since the following Monday was a holiday the letter wasn't delivered until Tuesday. I'll always be sorry I didn't telephone my "thank you," for Daddy never received my note.

The Saturday following our evening together, Daddy videotaped a missionary endorsement. Recently, we all had the opportunity of viewing those few minutes of tape. We wept as we saw my father's familiar figure, slightly bent and a little frail, perhaps, but clothed in the power and authority of the

MAN OF VISION, WOMAN OF PRAYER

One he served, proclaiming with a fire that only the Holy Spirit instills in the heart of a man the message of need and missionary challenge Satan has been helpless to silence.

> My single greatest concern is the growing inertia I see, inertia born out of our luxury and materialism. People are fooling themselves when they say the job is done. . . . The vast body of people in the world today have never been given enough information to know if they accept or reject Jesus. . . . Jesus commanded us to go to the uttermost parts of the earth. This has not been done yet in full. . . . It cannot be said that all men or even half of all men have been reached for Jesus, despite all the tools and affluence we have to work with—more than any other people in history. . . . Most people think what the gospel needs is more clever, skilled people, when what it needs is more people who are willing to bleed, suffer, and die in a passion to see people come to Christ!

The small room was full of family and close friends, those who had known Daddy best and loved him most. As the screen went blank and the room fell silent, someone softly commented, *"That* was what the man was all about."

Early Wednesday afternoon, September 6, 1978, with all unfinished business taken care of, Jesus took my daddy.

The following Monday, a memorial service was held in the great Hall of the Crucifixion-Resurrection at Forest Lawn Cemetery in Glendale. Nearly a thousand people came from all over the world to attend what one person described as "an affair of state in the kingdom of God."

It was there that God gave me words to relate the final and perhaps the greatest miracle of my father's life.

"Robin and I wanted to have this moment to speak to all of you on behalf of my mother and my sister, Sharon, who I know is seeing and hearing all that is happening here and holding Daddy's hand, rejoicing with him. I'm going to talk to you out of my heart. I'm going to talk to you as family

AN AFFAIR OF STATE

because I know you all loved my daddy, and that makes you family.

"Separation and distance were not foreign to the Pierce family. All my life I experienced going to the airport and watching my father get on a plane and fly thousands of miles and hours away from me. But you know, that kind of distance and separation wasn't hard, because we understood. Even as a small child I can remember weeping as I pictured the children, the hurting ones, the hungry ones my daddy was touching and helping. He made them real to us. He made that calling, that ministry, real to us.

"When Mother would say to me at the dinner table, 'You clean your plate. Remember all the starving orphans,' it wasn't just an empty phrase to me. That plate got cleaned. And when I'd be lonely for my daddy, I'd just think about all the little orphans that would run to him saying, 'Abaji,' 'Abaji' . . . Daddy! I didn't mind sharing him with them one bit.

"But many of you who have served Jesus know that there is a price to be paid. For us that price was a distance created by an enemy who hates us, who is out to destroy us, who wants to hurt us any way he can, and who was so angry at all the things that God had done through my father's life; a distance that couldn't be solved by getting on an airplane. A separation that was painful beyond words, which none of us wanted or even understood. Sometimes people love each other so much and try so hard, and all they can do is make it worse and hurt one another.

"And there came a time, not too long ago, when I talked to my father, who was in great pain (not only the anguish of body, but of spirit and soul), and he said to me, 'We'll be united in heaven, Honey. Our family will be together in heaven, all of us, perfectly. But I don't ever think it will happen here on earth.' At that time it had been nearly four years since we had been together as a family.

"But as you listen to what these wonderful men have said about my father, his ministry, and the work God did through him, I think you have to know that God wasn't going to let it end like that. You see, all aspects of life are important to God. And I just thank these men for helping me to remember, to see again in my heart and in my spirit, what it was all about and who my father really was, because that's how I'll always remember him and what he will always be to me . . . a great man, a loving man, a compassionate man.

"But God was concerned with that little part of him that belonged to us, too. And four days before Jesus took him home, my family was together again in a miraculous way that I won't even attempt to explain.

"My father arranged for a beautiful hotel suite and, even though he was in great pain and very weak, he dressed himself up in his finest, and he called all of us and said, 'Come be with me.' And we had an evening of such simplicity and joy. Oh, it was a holy evening. It was a miracle of God, but it was family. We came together, and we laughed and joked and were just people with one another. And for the first time in over four years, probably longer, we saw my parents embrace. For us to see that, the reconciliation, the restoration, the victory over the vicious attempt of the enemy to leave us today in anything but a place of rejoicing and victory, is a miracle.

"I'm proud of my father. I'm proud of everything about him. I said to my parents that evening, and I'll say to you and to them once again because I know Daddy's listening, 'Thank you for being our parents. More than that, thank you for being willing to be so wounded, to be so hurt, to give so much for the kingdom of God.'

"You see, everybody gets hurt. Everybody suffers in this world. But so many people suffer for no reason, for nothing of lasting significance or consequence. I'm proud that what we gave was for this cause, that Jesus might be glorified. And I praise Him for His faithfulness.

"It is worth it all!"